CONTENTS

Introduction	iii
How to use this book	iv
Maths Version 9·0 Curriculum Code Content Descriptions	v
Marking Grid	1
UNITS 1–8	**2**
TERM 1 REVIEW	34
UNITS 9–16	**38**
TERM 2 REVIEW	70
UNITS 17–24	**74**
TERM 3 REVIEW	106
UNITS 25–32	**110**
TERM 4 REVIEW	142
QUICK MATHS FACTS	146
ANSWERS	147

Targeting Maths Homework Year 6

Copyright © 2024 Pascal Press
ISBN: 978 1 925726 59 6

Published by Pascal Press
PO Box 250
Glebe NSW 2037
www.pascalpress.com.au
contact@pascalpress.com.au

Author: Ann & Johnny Baker
Publisher: Lynn Dickinson
Editor: Ruth Schultz
Cover and Text Designer: Janice Bowles

Typesetter: Ruth Schultz
Images & Illustrations: Dreamstime (unless otherwise indicated)

Printed by Wai Man Bookbinding (China) Ltd

Reproduction and communication for educational purposes
The Australian *Copyright Act 1968* (the Act) allows a maximum of one chapter or 10% of the pages of this work, whichever is the greater, to be reproduced and/or communicated by any educational institution for its educational purposes provided that the educational institution (or that body that administers it) has given a remuneration notice to the Copyright Agency under the Act.
For details of the Copyright Agency licence for educational institutions contact:
Copyright Agency
Level 12, 66 Goulburn Street
Sydney, NSW 2000

Reproduction and communication for other purposes
Except as permitted under the Act (for example a fair dealing for the purpose of study, research, criticism or review) no part of this book may be reproduced, stored in a retrieval system, communicated or transmitted in any form or by any means without prior written permission. All inquiries should be made to the publisher at the address above.

All material identified by AC | Australian CURRICULUM is material subject to copyright under the *Australian Copyright Act 1968* (Cth) and is owned by the Australian Curriculum, Assessment and Reporting Authority 2023. For all Australian Curriculum material, this is an extract from the Australian Curriculum.

Disclaimer: ACARA neither endorses nor verifies the accuracy of the information provided and accepts no responsibility for incomplete or inaccurate information. In particular, ACARA does not endorse or verify that:
- The content descriptions are solely for a particular year and subject;
- All the content descriptions for that year and subject have been used; and
- The author's material aligns with the Australian Curriculum content descriptions for the relevant year and subject.

You can find the unaltered and most up-to-date version of the material at http://www.australiancurriculum.edu.au.
This material is reproduced with the permission of ACARA.

NAPLAN*-style questions
* This is not an officially endorsed publication of the NAPLAN program and is produced by Pascal Press independently of Australian Governments.

Introduction

Targeting Maths Homework aims to build and reinforce Maths skills. This book supports the ACARA Australian Version 9·0 Curriculum for Year 6 and helps children to revise and consolidate what has been taught in the classroom. ACARA codes are shown on each unit and a chart explaining their content descriptions is on pages v and vi. The inside cover shows the topics in each unit.

The structure of this book
This book has 32 carefully graded four-page units. The units are divided between:
- ★ Number and Algebra
- ★ Measurement and Space
- ★ Statistics & Probability
- ★ Problem Solving.

Assessment
Term Reviews follow Units 1–8, 9–16, 17–24 and 25–32 to test work covered during the term, and allow parents and carers to monitor their child's progress. Children are encouraged to mark each unit as it is completed and to colour in the traffic lights at the end of each segment. These results are then transferred to the Marking Grid. Parents and carers can see at a glance if their child is excelling or struggling!

NAPLAN*-style questions
Each unit has a set of three NAPLAN*-style questions that directly match the learning in the unit and mirror question styles that frequently occur in NAPLAN. This is to ensure that children's familiarity and confidence with NAPLAN*-style questions is consistently developed.

- 🟢 **Green** = Excellent — 2 or fewer questions incorrect
- 🟠 **Orange** = Passing — 50% or more questions answered correctly
- 🔴 **Red** = Struggling — fewer than 50% correct and needs help

SCORE: /10   0-4   5-8   9-10

How to Use This Book

The activities in this book are specifically designed to be used at home with minimal resources and support. Helpful explanations of key concepts and skills are provided throughout the book to help understand the tasks. Useful examples of how to do the activities are provided.

Regular practice of key concepts and skills will support the work your child does in school and will enable you to monitor their progress throughout the year. It is recommended that children complete 8 units per school term (one a week) and then the Term Review. Every unit has a Traffic Light scoreboard at the end of each section.

SCORE /10 0–4 5–8 9–10

You or your child should mark each completed unit and then colour the traffic light that corresponds to the number of correct questions. This process will enable you to see at a glance how your child is progressing and to identify weak spots. The results should be recorded at the end of each term on the Marking Grid on page 1.

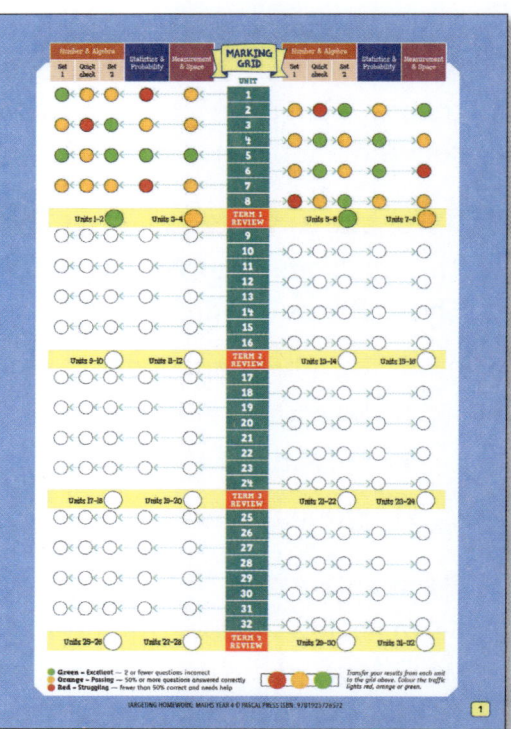

NOTE: The Problem of the Week sections do not appear on the Marking Grid as they often have multiple or subjective answers that cannot be easily scored.

The Term Review results are important for tracking progress and identifying any improvements in performance. If you find that certain questions are repeatedly causing difficulties and errors, then there is a good reason to discuss this with your child's teacher and arrange for extra instruction in that problem area.

Quick Maths Facts

The Quick Maths Facts on page 146 include multiplication tables up to 12 times, measurement equivalents, simple decimal–fraction–percentage conversions, a visual reminder of place value into the millions and the 'Days of the Month' rhyme. An accurate ruler has also been provided. Copy and laminate this page so that it is always available as a handy reference for your child.

Answers

The answer section on pages 147–164 can be removed, stapled together and kept somewhere safe. Use it to check answers when your child has completed each unit. Encourage your child to colour in the Traffic Light boxes when the answers have been calculated.

Australian Curriculum Correlations V9

Year 6 Maths		Number & Algebra	Statistics & Probability	Measurement & Space
ACARA CODE	CONTENT DESCRIPTION	UNITS	UNITS	UNITS
NUMBER				
AC9M6N01	Recognise situations, including financial contexts, that use integers; locate and represent integers on a number line and as coordinates on the Cartesian plane	1 2, 9, 16, 17, 25		
AC9M6N02	Identify and describe the properties of prime, composite and square numbers and use these properties to solve problems and simplify calculations	2, 7, 9, 16, 17, 23, 24		
AC9M6N03	Apply knowledge of equivalence to compare, order and represent common fractions including halves, thirds and quarters on the same number line and justify their order	3, 10, 18, 26		
AC9M6N04	Apply knowledge of place value to add and subtract decimals, using digital tools where appropriate; use estimation and rounding to check the reasonableness of answers	3, 10, 18, 25, 31		
AC9M6N05	Solve problems involving addition and subtraction of fractions using knowledge of equivalent fractions	3, 11, 15, 19, 26, 31		
AC9M6N06	Multiply and divide decimals by multiples of powers of 10 without a calculator, applying knowledge of place value and proficiency with multiplication facts; using estimation and rounding to check the reasonableness of answers	4, 12, 20, 22, 27, 28, 29		28
AC9M6N07	Solve problems that require finding a familiar fraction, decimal or percentage of a quantity, including percentage discounts, choosing efficient calculation strategies and using digital tools where appropriate	4, 5, 6, 20, 23, 29, 30, 31		20
AC9M6N08	Approximate numerical solutions to problems involving rational numbers and percentages, including financial contexts, using appropriate estimation strategies	5, 13, 20, 21, 30, 31		
AC9M6N09	Use mathematical modelling to solve practical problems, involving rational numbers and percentages, including in financial contexts; formulate the problems, choosing operations and efficient calculation strategies, and using digital tools where appropriate; interpret and communicate solutions in terms of the situation, justifying the choices made	8, 13, 14, 20		
ALGEBRA				
AC9M6A01	Recognise and use rules that generate visually growing patterns and number patterns involving rational numbers	1, 11, 15, 21		
AC9M6A02	Find unknown values in numerical equations involving brackets and combinations of arithmetic operations, using the properties of numbers and operations	6, 14, 24, 27, 32		
AC9M6A03	Create and use algorithms involving a sequence of steps and decisions that use rules to generate sets of numbers; identify, interpret and explain emerging patterns	7, 15, 21, 32		

TARGETING MATHS HOMEWORK: YEAR 6 © PASCAL PRESS ISBN: 9781925726596

Year 6 Maths

ACARA CODE	CONTENT DESCRIPTION	Number & Algebra UNITS	Statistics & Probability UNITS	Measurement & Space UNITS
MEASUREMENT				
AC9M6M01	Convert between common metric units of length, mass and capacity; choose and use decimal representations of metric measurements relevant to the context of a problem	27		1, 11, 12, 18, 20, 25, 29
AC9M6M02	Establish the formula for the area of a rectangle and use it to solve practical problems			3, 15, 22, 28, 32
AC9M6M03	Interpret and use timetables and itineraries to plan activities and determine the duration of events and journeys			4, 17, 24, 30
AC9M6M04	Identify the relationships between angles on a straight line, angles at a point and vertically opposite angles; use these to determine unknown angles, communicating reasoning			7, 14, 16, 23, 31
SPACE				
AC9M6SP01	Compare the parallel cross-sections of objects and recognise their relationships to right prisms			5, 10, 26
AC9M6SP02	Locate points in the 4 quadrants of a Cartesian plane; describe changes to the coordinates when a point is moved to a different position in the plane			2, 8, 9, 13, 16, 27
AC9M6SP03	Recognise and use combinations of transformations to create tessellations and other geometric patterns, using dynamic geometric software where appropriate			6, 8, 13, 19, 21
STATISTICS				
AC9M6ST01	Interpret and compare data sets for ordinal and nominal categorical, discrete and continuous numerical variables using comparative displays or visualisations and digital tools; compare distributions in terms of mode, range and shape		1, 3, 24, 25, 26, 29, 32	
AC9M6ST02	Identify statistically informed arguments presented in traditional and digital media; discuss and critique methods, data representations and conclusions		4, 12, 18, 23, 30	
AC9M6ST03	Plan and conduct statistical investigations by posing and refining questions or identifying a problem and collecting relevant data; analyse and interpret the data and communicate findings within the context of the investigation		5, 9, 10, 13, 15, 17, 20, 27, 28	
PROBABILITY				
AC9M6P01	Recognise that probabilities lie on numerical scales of 0 – 1 or 0% – 100% and use estimation to assign probabilities that events occur in a given context, using common fractions, percentages and decimals		2, 8, 11, 14, 16, 19, 21	
AC9M6P02	Conduct repeated chance experiments and run simulations with an increasing number of trials using digital tools; compare observations with expected results and discuss the effect on variation of increasing the number of trials		6, 7, 19, 22, 31	

MARKING GRID

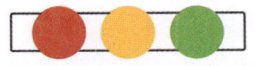

Number & Algebra			Statistics & Probability	Measurement & Space	UNIT	Number & Algebra			Statistics & Probability	Measurement & Space
Set 1	Quick check	Set 2				Set 1	Quick check	Set 2		
○	○	○	○	○	1					
					2	○	○	○	○	○
○	○	○	○	○	3					
					4	○	○	○	○	○
○	○	○	○	○	5					
					6	○	○	○	○	○
○	○	○	○	○	7					
					8	○	○	○	○	○

Units 1-2 ○   Units 3-4 ○   **TERM 1 REVIEW**   Units 5-6 ○   Units 7-8 ○

					9	○	○	○	○	○
○	○	○	○	○	10					
					11	○	○	○	○	○
○	○	○	○	○	12					
					13	○	○	○	○	○
○	○	○	○	○	14					
					15	○	○	○	○	○
○	○	○	○	○	16					

Units 9-10 ○   Units 11-12 ○   **TERM 2 REVIEW**   Units 13-14 ○   Units 15-16 ○

○	○	○	○	○	17					
					18	○	○	○	○	○
○	○	○	○	○	19					
					20	○	○	○	○	○
○	○	○	○	○	21					
					22	○	○	○	○	○
○	○	○	○	○	23					
					24	○	○	○	○	○

Units 17-18 ○   Units 19-20 ○   **TERM 3 REVIEW**   Units 21-22 ○   Units 23-24 ○

○	○	○	○	○	25					
					26	○	○	○	○	○
○	○	○	○	○	27					
					28	○	○	○	○	○
○	○	○	○	○	29					
					30	○	○	○	○	○
○	○	○	○	○	31					
					32	○	○	○	○	○

Units 25-26 ○   Units 27-28 ○   **TERM 4 REVIEW**   Units 29-30 ○   Units 31-32 ○

- **Green** = Excellent — 2 or fewer questions incorrect
- **Orange** = Passing — 50% or more questions answered correctly
- **Red** = Struggling — fewer than 50% correct and needs help

Transfer your results from each unit to the grid above. Colour the traffic lights red, orange or green.

TARGETING MATHS HOMEWORK: YEAR 6 © PASCAL PRESS ISBN: 9781925726596

UNIT 1

Number & Algebra

AC9M6N01

Integers

You are used to working with numbers greater than zero. Numbers greater than zero are called **positive numbers**.

There are also numbers which are less than zero. These are called **negative numbers**. Negative numbers have a minus sign in front of them: –2, –3, –4 and so on.

Whole numbers, whether they are positive or negative, are called **integers**.

This number line shows how negative numbers are positioned to the left of zero and positive numbers are positioned to the right of zero:

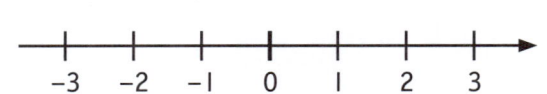

–3 –2 –1 0 1 2 3

You will also notice that the spaces between –1 and zero and zero and 1 are exactly the same.

Complete the number lines to find the numbers represented by the question marks.

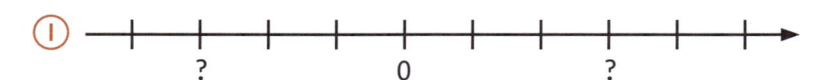

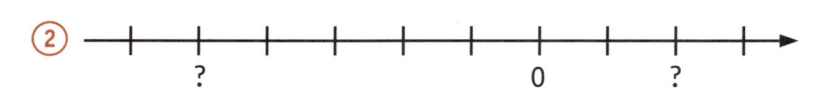

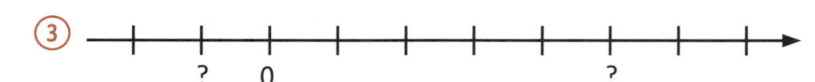

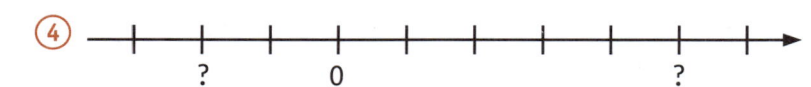

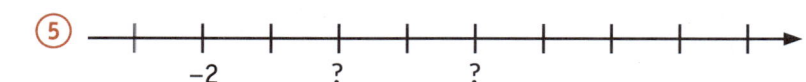

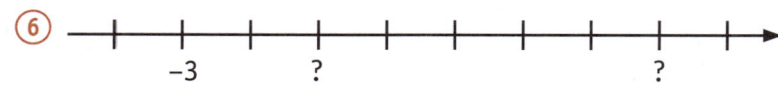

① ? 0 ?   ___ and ___

② ? 0 ?   ___ and ___

③ ? 0 ?   ___ and ___

④ ? 0 ?   ___ and ___

⑤ –2 ? ?   ___ and ___

⑥ –3 ? ?   ___ and ___

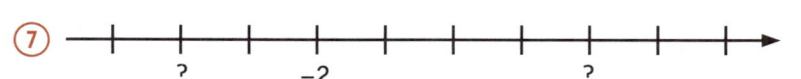

⑦ ? –2 ?   ___ and ___

SCORE /7   0-3   4-5   6-7

Quick Check

Fill in the missing integers in these sequences.

① –1, ___, ___, 2, 3
② ___, ___, ___, 0, 1
③ ___, ___, 0, ___, ___
④ ___, –1, ___, ___, ___
⑤ –6, ___, ___, ___, ___
⑥ ___, ___, ___, ___, 4
⑦ ___, ___, ___, –2, ___
⑧ ___, –2, ___, ___, ___
⑨ ___, ___, 1, ___, ___
⑩ ___, ___, ___, ___, 0

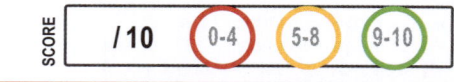

SCORE /10   0-4   5-8   9-10

Number & Algebra

UNIT 1
AC9M6A01

Growing Patterns

Hai and Liam have been making growing patterns with tiles.
This is the first pattern that they made:

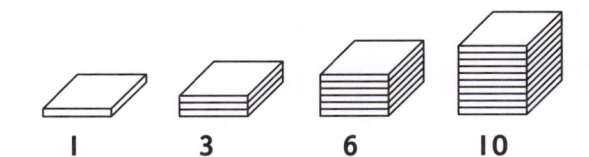

1   3   6   10

"Notice that we put out 1 tile for the first tower, then we added 2 more tiles to make the second tower, and then we added 3 more tiles to make the third tower, and so on.

"We made 10 towers altogether and would like to know how many tiles were in the 10th tower and how many tiles we used altogether."

Write the missing numbers.

① This is how the pattern started.
1, 3, 6, 10, ___, ___, ___, ___, ___, ___
The 10th tower will have ___ tiles and there will be _____ tiles used altogether.

② This is how the pattern started.
1, 2, 4, 7, ___, ___, ___, ___, ___, ___
The 10th tower will have ___ tiles and there will be _____ tiles used altogether.

③ This is how the pattern started.
1, 3, 2, 4, 3, ___, ___, ___, ___, ___
The 10th tower will have ___ tiles and there will be _____ tiles used altogether.

④ This is how the pattern started.
2, 4, 3, 6, 5, 10, 9, ___, ___, ___
The 10th tower will have ___ tiles and there will be _____ tiles used altogether.

⑤ This is how the pattern started.
1, 3, 5, 7, ___, ___, ___, ___, ___, ___
The 10th tower will have ___ tiles and there will be _____ tiles used altogether.

SCORE /5   0-2   3-4   5

Statistics & Probability

AC9M6ST01

Speed Trials Results

This graph shows the number of swimmers in the speed trials every 5 minutes between 3:30 pm and 4:00 pm.

① What was the **range** of the number of swimmers in each time trial? _____

② What was the **mode** of the number of swimmers during each time trial? _____

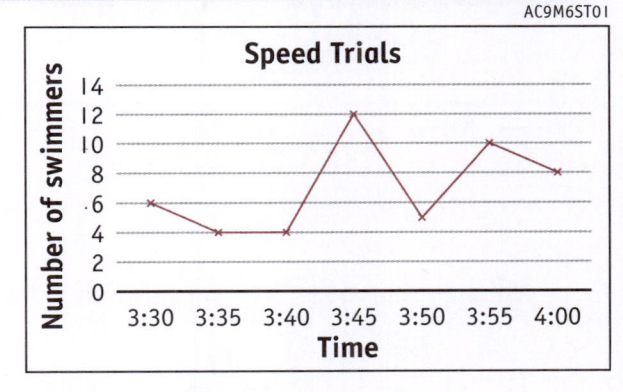

③ The graph shows a peak in the number of swimmers in the pool at what time? How many were in the pool at that time?

At _____ with ____ people in the pool

④ What was the difference in the number of swimmers between peak time and the quietest time?
____ people

⑤ How many swimmers participated in the time trials altogether?
____ people

SCORE /5   0-2   3-4   5

UNIT 1

Measurement & Space

AC9M6M01

Metric Conversions

There are 10 millimetres in 1 centimetre and 100 centimetres in 1 metre and 1000 metres in 1 kilometre.
We can use this information to convert between units of measurement.
To work out how many metres are in 6 kilometres,
we multiply the kilometres by 1000, which gives 6000 metres.
To work out how many centimetres are in 6000 metres,
we multiply the metres by 100, which gives 600 000 centimetres.
Finally, to find out how many millimetres that is
we multiply the centimetres by 10, which gives 6 000 000 millimetres.
To convert from millimetres to kilometres, reverse the process and use division.

Complete this conversion table by multiplying to get from kilometres to millimetres.

	Kilometres	km × 1000 to get metres	m × 100 to get centimetres	cm × 10 to get millimetres
①	4			
②	15			
③	$1\frac{1}{2}$			

Complete this conversion table by dividing to get from millimetres to kilometres.

	m ÷ by 1000 to get kilometres	cm ÷ by 100 to get metres	mm ÷ by 10 to get centimetres	Millimetres
④				5 000 000
⑤				1 800 000
⑥				7 500 000

SCORE /6   0-2   3-4   5-6

NAPLAN*-style Questions

①

Which integer does the ? on this line represent?

②

This is a growing triangle pattern.
How many dots will be in the tenth triangle?

③ How many millimetres are in 4·35 metres?

SCORE /3   0-1   2   3

4   TARGETING MATHS HOMEWORK: YEAR 6 © PASCAL PRESS ISBN: 9781925726596

Problem of the Week

UNIT 1

Number Patterns

Ruby, Sara and Min were exploring shape patterns made with matchsticks. Then they had an idea for an investigation.

"If we each grow our pattern ten times, how often will we use the same number of matchsticks as someone else?"

Ruby: I started with a triangle and then grew another triangle onto one side.

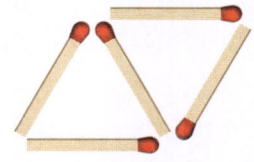

3 matches   5 matches

Sara: I started with a square and then grew another square onto one side.

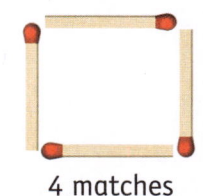

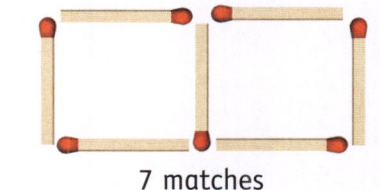

4 matches   7 matches

Min: I started with a pentagon and then grew another pentagon onto one side.

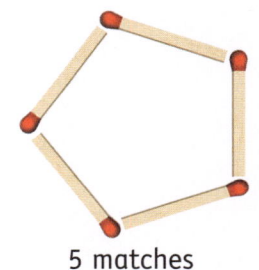

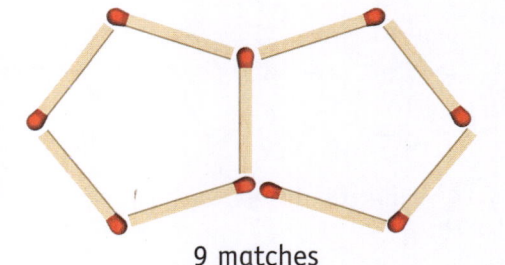

5 matches   9 matches

The Challenge: Use the table to show how many matches all three children had as they grew their patterns ten times.

	1	2	3	4	5	6	7	8	9	10
Ruby	3	5								
Sara	4	7								
Min	5	9								

① What is the smallest number that all three patterns use? ___

Extend the patterns to grow twenty times.

	11	12	13	14	15	16	17	18	19	20
Ruby										
Sara										
Min										

② What are the numbers that all the patterns use this time? _____

UNIT 2

Number & Algebra

Negative Numbers

We can count on or count back in positive or negative numbers on a number line.

For instance, start at −2 and count on or jump along the number line 5 times like this, and you finish on 3.

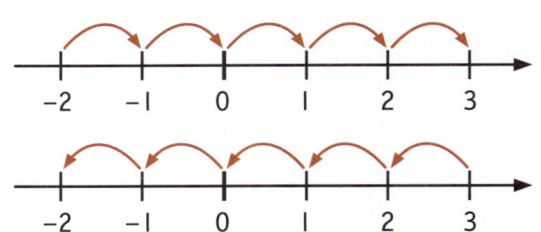

We can also count back 5 spaces on the number line, starting at 3 like this:

In both examples, we have just found the difference or the space between the numbers.

Follow the instructions for each number line.

① Start at −4 and count on 6 spaces.

−4 + ____ = ____

② Start at 3 and count back 8 spaces.

____ − ____ = ____

③ Start at −5 and count on 10 spaces.

____ + ____ = ____

④ Find the difference between −2 and 2.

____ − ____ = ____

The difference is ____.

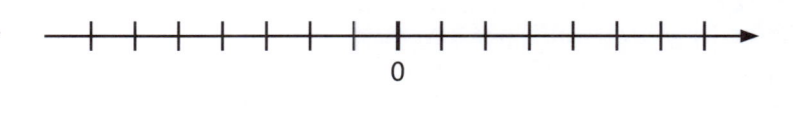

⑤ Find the difference between −6 and 3.

____ − ____ = ____

The difference is ____.

SCORE /5   0-2   3-4   5

Quick Check

Count on and back.

① Count on 6 from −4. ____
② Count back 3 from −1. ____
③ Count back 7 from 6. ____
④ Count on 7 from −5. ____
⑤ Count on 6 from −6. ____

Find the difference between the numbers.

⑥ −3 and 3 ____
⑦ 5 and −1 ____
⑧ −2 and 2 ____
⑨ −6 and 1 ____
⑩ 7 and −1 ____

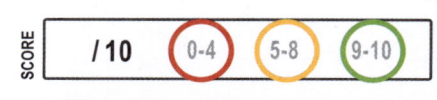

SCORE /10   0-4   5-8   9-10

Number & Algebra

UNIT 2

AC9M6N02

Finding Prime Numbers

A prime number is a number that has only 1 and itself as factors.
2 is a prime number because it has only 1 and 2 as factors.
4 is not a prime number because it has 1, 2 and 4 as factors.
Numbers with more than 2 factors are called **composite numbers**.

1	2	3	4	5	6	7	8	9	10
11	12	13	14	15	16	17	18	19	20
21	22	23	24	25	26	27	28	29	30
31	32	33	34	35	36	37	38	39	40
41	42	43	44	45	46	47	48	49	50
51	52	53	54	55	56	57	58	59	60
61	62	63	64	65	66	67	68	69	70
71	72	73	74	75	76	77	78	79	80
81	82	83	84	85	86	87	88	89	90
91	92	93	94	95	96	97	98	99	100

Follow the instructions to find all the prime numbers on the 100 grid.

1. Circle 2 then cross off all multiples of 2.
2. Circle 3 then cross off all multiples of 3.
3. Circle 5 then cross off all multiples of 5.
4. Circle 7 then cross off all multiples of 7.
5. The numbers in the circles and the numbers that have not been crossed off are all prime numbers less than 100. List them here.

_____

_____

_____

SCORE /5

Statistics & Probability

AC9M6P01

Probability

Probability can be expressed on a number line using a scale of 0 to 1, where 0 is impossible and 1 is certain. Probability can also be expressed as a percentage on a number line, from 0% to 100%. 0% is impossible, 100% is certain and 50% is a half chance and likely.

0% Impossible — 50% Likely — 100% Certain

Mark percentages on the number lines to show the likelihood of these events happening.

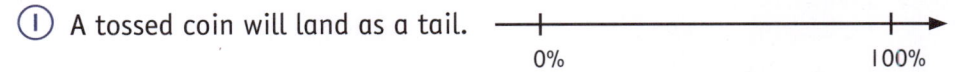

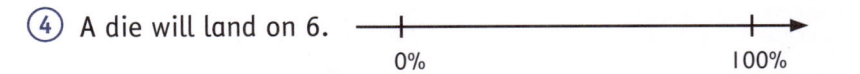

1. A tossed coin will land as a tail.   0% —— 100%
2. Saturday will be the next day after Sunday.   0% —— 100%
3. Your pencil lead will break as you complete this page.   0% —— 100%
4. A die will land on 6.   0% —— 100%
5. The local football team will win their next game.   0% —— 100%

SCORE /5

UNIT 2 — Measurement & Space

AC9M6P02

The Cartesian Plane

TERM 1

The diagram shows the key features of the Cartesian Plane.

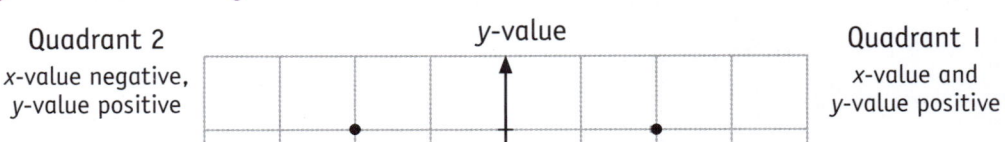

Quadrant 2
x-value negative,
y-value positive

Quadrant 1
x-value and
y-value positive

(−2, 3)   (2, 3)

y-value

x-value

(−2, −3)   (3, −3)

Quadrant 3
x-value and *y*-value negative

Quadrant 4
x-value positive,
y-value negative

The **Cartesian plane** is used for locating places on a map, for graphing points and for showing movements precisely.

It is named after the famous French mathematician, René Descartes.

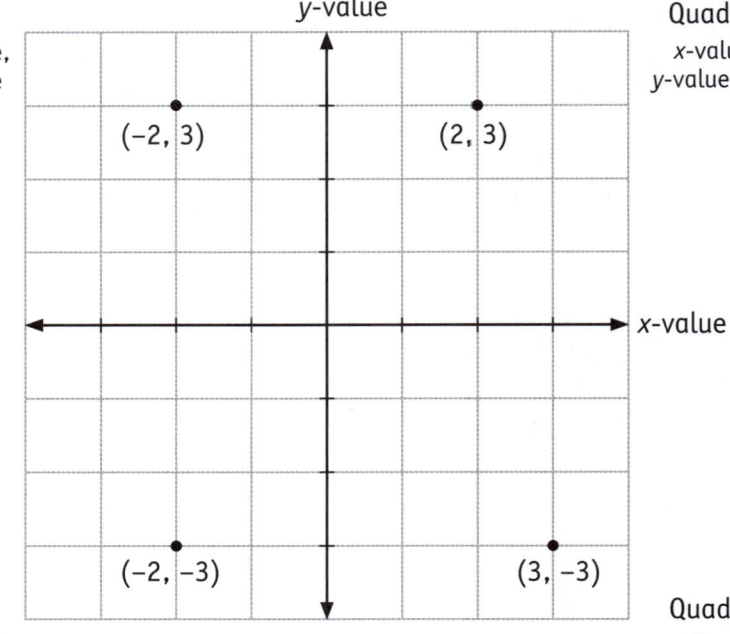

① In Quadrant 1, the point (2, 3) has *x*-value = 2 and *y*-value = 3.
List three more points in Quadrant 1 and show them on the plane. (__, __) (__, __) (__, __)

② In Quadrant 2, the point (−2, 3) has *x*-value = −2 and *y*-value = 3.
List three more points in Quadrant 2 and show them on the plane. (__, __) (__, __) (__, __)

③ In Quadrant 3, the point (−2, −3) has *x*-value = −2 and *y*-value = −3.
List three more points in Quadrant 3 and show them on the plane. (__, __) (__, __) (__, __)

④ In Quadrant 4, the point (3, −3) has *x*-value = 3 and *y*-value = −3.
List three more points in Quadrant 4 and show them on the plane. (__, __) (__, __) (__, __)

SCORE /12   0-5   6-10   11-12

NAPLAN*-style Questions

① Look at the spinner. Which of these events has about a 40% chance of happening?
○ You will spin an even number.
○ You will spin a prime number.
○ You will spin an odd number.
○ You will spin a multiple of 3.

② Mark the prime numbers.
○ 3   ○ 2   ○ 6   ○ 9   ○ 11

③ What is the difference between −6 and 9? ☐

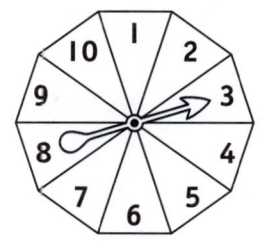

SCORE /3   0-1   2   3

8   TARGETING MATHS HOMEWORK: YEAR 6 © PASCAL PRESS ISBN: 9781925726596

Problem of the Week

UNIT 2 — TERM 1

Closest to Zero

To play this game that Ruby and Elsa invented, you need to sort out the numbers 1–5 from a deck of cards, shuffle them and deal five cards to each player.
- The black cards are for count-on and the red cards for count-back.
- Each player has a number line to mark their count-on moves and their count-back moves, starting from 0.
- After five rounds, the person who is closest to zero is the winner.

These are the cards in sequence that were played by Elsa, Tau, Ruby and Sara.

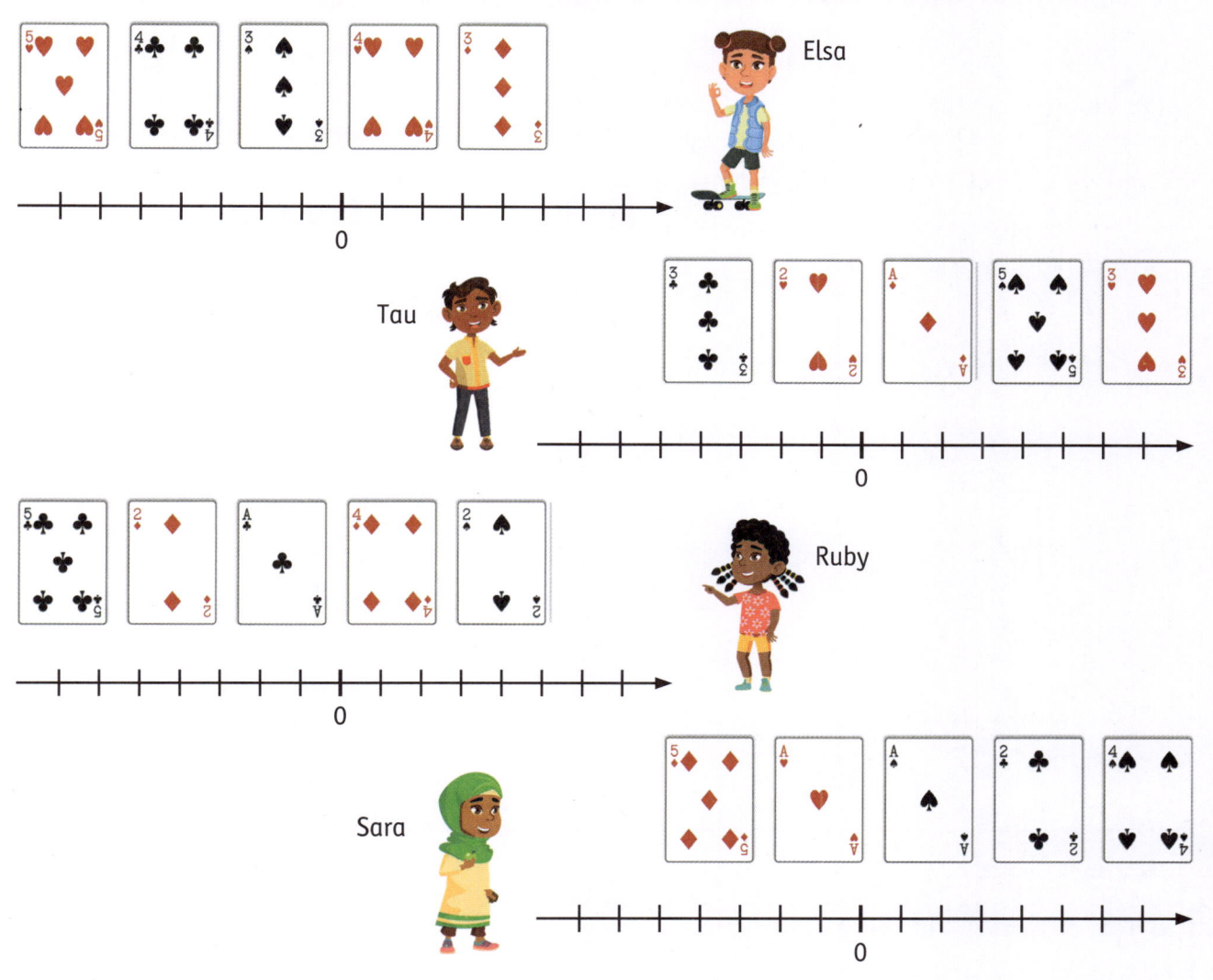

Elsa: 5♥, 4♣, 3♠, 4♥, 3♦

Tau: 3♣, 2♥, A♦, 5♠, 3♥

Ruby: 5♣, 2♦, A♣, 4♦, 2♠

Sara: 5♦, A♥, A♠, 2♣, 4♠

Challenges

1. Who is closest to zero? _____
2. Who is furthest from zero? _____
3. What is the difference between the score closest to zero and the score furthest from zero? _____
4. Draw 5 cards that would leave you as far away from zero as possible.
5. Draw 5 cards that would end you on zero exactly.

UNIT 3 — Number & Algebra

AC9M6N03, AC9M6N05

Fractions

To order or add fractions, it is important to first convert the fractions so that they have the same denominator.

To place $\frac{3}{8}$, $\frac{3}{4}$ and $\frac{7}{16}$ in order from smallest to largest, convert the first two fractions into 16ths because 16 is the highest denominator of the fractions in the list.

To convert $\frac{3}{8}$ into 16ths, multiply both the numerator and the denominator by 2:

$$\frac{2}{2} \times \frac{3}{8} = \frac{2 \times 3}{2 \times 8} = \frac{6}{16}$$

To convert $\frac{3}{4}$ to 16ths, multiply both the numerator and the denominator by 4:

$$\frac{4}{4} \times \frac{3}{4} = \frac{4 \times 3}{4 \times 4} = \frac{12}{16}$$

Now we can order the fractions from smallest to largest: $\frac{6}{16}$, $\frac{7}{16}$, $\frac{12}{16}$.

Convert these fraction strings and order them from smallest to largest.

	Fractions	Converted Fractions	Fractions in Order
①	$\frac{3}{5}$, $\frac{2}{10}$, $\frac{1}{2}$	$\frac{3}{5} = —$ $\frac{2}{10} = —$ $\frac{1}{2} = —$	—, —, —
②	$\frac{7}{12}$, $\frac{5}{6}$, $\frac{1}{3}$	$\frac{7}{12} = —$ $\frac{5}{6} = —$ $\frac{1}{3} = —$	—, —, —
③	$\frac{5}{8}$, $\frac{1}{2}$, $\frac{9}{16}$	$\frac{5}{8} = —$ $\frac{1}{2} = —$ $\frac{9}{16} = —$	—, —, —
④	$\frac{9}{14}$, $\frac{3}{7}$, $\frac{1}{2}$	$\frac{9}{14} = —$ $\frac{3}{7} = —$ $\frac{1}{2} = —$	—, —, —
⑤	$\frac{2}{3}$, $\frac{3}{4}$, $\frac{7}{12}$	$\frac{2}{3} = —$ $\frac{3}{4} = —$ $\frac{7}{12} = —$	—, —, —

SCORE /5   0-2   3-4   5

Quick Check

Convert these fractions into 12ths.

① $\frac{3}{4} = —$

② $\frac{2}{6} = —$

③ $\frac{8}{24} = —$

④ $\frac{1}{3} = —$

⑤ $\frac{2}{3} = —$

Convert these fractions into 18ths.

⑥ $\frac{1}{2} = —$

⑦ $\frac{2}{3} = —$

⑧ $\frac{5}{6} = —$

⑨ $\frac{5}{3} = —$

⑩ $\frac{4}{9} = —$

SCORE /10   0-4   5-8   9-10

Number & Algebra

Decimal Addition

Write these number strings correctly in column form. Then add them to find the total. The first one has been set up for you.

① 36·5 + 104·35 + 27·35

```
   36·5
  104·35
+  27·35
_____
```

③ 18·75 + 206·05 + 3·37

+ _____
_____

⑤ 6·5 + 13·005 + 27·63

+ _____
_____

② 180·6 + 39·75 + 2·05

+ _____
_____

④ 19·007 + 2·38 + 20·06

+ _____
_____

⑥ 12·37 + 6·008 + 3·96

+ _____
_____

SCORE /6   0-2   3-4   5-6

Statistics & Probability

Comparing Data Displays

North Street Primary School have conducted a survey of the favourite sports of their Under 8s and Over 8s. They have shown the data in a two-way table and on a side-by-side column graph.

Sport	Under 8s	Over 8s
Cricket	12	21
Soccer	20	22
Tennis	18	23

Sports Survey — side-by-side column graph showing Cricket, Soccer, Tennis on the Sport axis and Number of votes (0–25) on the horizontal axis.

Key: Under 8s   Over 8s

① How many Under 8s were surveyed? _____

② How many fewer Under 8s preferred cricket than Over 8s preferred tennis? _____

③ In which category are Under 8s and Over 8s closest?

_____

④ Which diagram makes it easier to see the shape of the data collected?   Table / Graph

⑤ Which diagram makes it easier to find the range of the data?
Table / Graph

SCORE /5   0-2   3-4   5

UNIT 3

Measurement & Space

AC9M6M02

Area of a Rectangle

The formula for finding the area of a rectangle is:
multiply the **width** of the rectangle **by** the **height** of the rectangle.

This rectangle is 4 cm wide and 3 cm high.
It is a 4 by 3 rectangle.

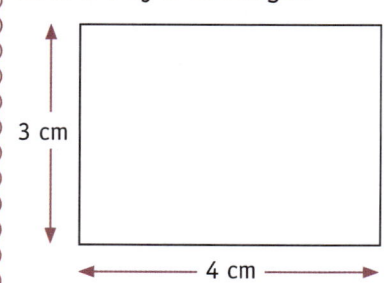

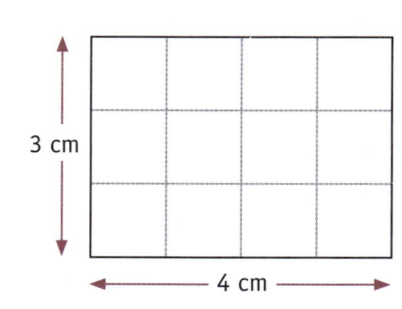

3 cm | 4 cm

This diagram shows the squares within the rectangle.
You could count them all but it is faster to use multiplication:
4 cm × 3 cm = 12 cm².

Use the multiplication formula to find the area of a rectangle with these dimensions.

① 4 by 8 centimetre rectangle ____ × ____ = ____ cm²

② 7 by 9 centimetre rectangle ____ × ____ = ____ cm²

③ 13 by 5 centimetre rectangle ____ × ____ = ____ cm²

④ 4 by 7 metre rectangle ____ × ____ = ____ m²

⑤ 9 by 8 metre rectangle ____ × ____ = ____ m²

⑥ 12 by 13 metre rectangle ____ × ____ = ____ m²

⑦ 3 by 4 kilometre rectangle ____ × ____ = ____ km²

⑧ 15 by 20 kilometre sheep station ____ × ____ = ____ km²

SCORE /8   0-3   4-6   7-8

NAPLAN*-style Questions

① One-metre-square carpet tiles are on special for $31 a tile at the moment.
How much will it cost to tile an area of 9 metres by 7 metres?

②
Which fraction is represented by ? on this number line?

○ $\frac{1}{4}$ ○ $\frac{1}{3}$ ○ $\frac{3}{8}$ ○ $\frac{5}{16}$

③ What is 3·75 + 14·075?

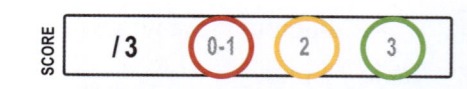

SCORE /3   0-1   2   3

Problem of the Week

UNIT 3

Investigating Shapes with the Same Perimeter

Elsa and Liam have been investigating rectangles that have the same perimeter. Their side lengths are always a whole number of centimetres.

I think I have found all the rectangles that have a perimeter of 20 cm.

- 7 cm × 3 cm
- 5 cm × 5 cm
- 6 cm × 4 cm

My rectangles all have a perimeter of 16 cm, but I don't think I have found all of them ... yet!

- 6 cm × 2 cm
- 5 cm × 3 cm
- 4 cm × 4 cm

The Challenge

Use this grid to show Elsa and Liam what rectangles they missed. Remember, the perimeters must be either 20 cm or 16 cm with side lengths in whole centimetres.

Then add the rectangles you find to the tables below.

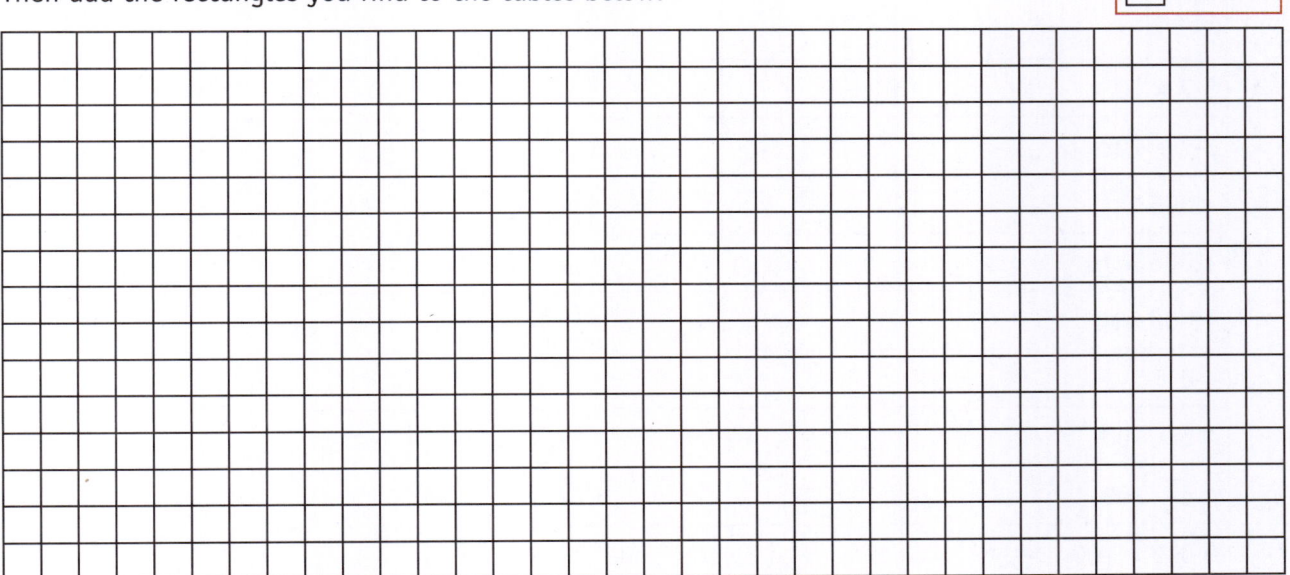

☐ = 1 cm²

Use this table for rectangles with a perimeter of 20 cm. Find their areas.

Height (cm)			3	4	5			
Width (cm)			7	6	5			
Perimeter (cm)			20	20	20			
Area (cm²)			21	24	25			

Use this table for rectangles with a perimeter of 16 cm. Find their areas.

Height (cm)		2	3	4			
Width (cm)		6	5	4			
Perimeter (cm)		16	16	16			
Area (cm²)		12	15	16			

What did you discover about the area and perimeter of rectangles?

UNIT 4 — Number & Algebra

AC9M6N06

Multiplying and Dividing Decimals

	Hundreds	Tens	Ones	.	Tenths	Hundredths	Thousandths
36·2		3	6	.	2		
36·2 × 10	3	6	2	.			
36·2 ÷ 10			3	.	6	2	

The table above shows the effects of multiplying and dividing a decimal number by 10. Notice how the decimal point does not move each time but the numbers do move.

- Numbers move one space to **left** when multiplied by 10 because they are 10 times **larger**.
- Numbers move one space to the **right** when divided by 10 because they are 10 times **smaller**.

When multiplying or dividing by 100, the numbers move two spaces to the left or right.

Complete the table to show each multiplication or division.

		Hundreds	Tens	Ones	.	Tenths	Hundredths	Thousandths
①	3·7				.			
②	3·7 × 10				.			
③	3·7 ÷ 10				.			
④	13·06				.			
⑤	13·06 × 10				.			
⑥	13·06 ÷ 10				.			
⑦	4·6				.			
⑧	4·6 × 100				.			
⑨	4·6 ÷ 100				.			
⑩	0·012 × 100				.			

SCORE /10 0-4 5-8 9-10

Quick Check

Complete these multiplications and divisions.

① 6·5 × 10 = _____
② 17·5 ÷ 10 = _____
③ 27·5 × 10 = _____
④ 36·75 ÷ 10 = _____
⑤ 106·73 ÷ 10 = _____
⑥ 2·36 × 10 = _____
⑦ 3·75 × 100 = _____
⑧ 14·6 ÷ 100 = _____
⑨ 108·75 ÷ 10 = _____
⑩ 3·765 × 10 = _____

SCORE /10 0-4 5-8 9-10

TARGETING MATHS HOMEWORK: YEAR 6 © PASCAL PRESS ISBN: 9781925726596

Number & Algebra

UNIT 4

AC9M6N07

Fractions and Division

Finding a fraction of a quantity is the same as dividing a number or amount.

To find $\frac{1}{3}$ of 12, you divide 12 by 3: **12 ÷ 3 = 4**

To find $\frac{2}{3}$ of 12, you find $\frac{1}{3}$ of 12 and then multiply by 2: **12 ÷ 3 = 4 , 2 × 4 = 8**.

Complete these fraction of a quantity questions.

① What is $\frac{3}{4}$ of 12?   ___ ÷ ___ = ___ ,   ___ × ___ = ___

② What is $\frac{2}{3}$ of 30?   ___ ÷ ___ = ___ ,   ___ × ___ = ___

③ What is $\frac{3}{5}$ of 20?   ___ ÷ ___ = ___ ,   ___ × ___ = ___

④ What is $\frac{5}{8}$ of 40?   ___ ÷ ___ = ___ ,   ___ × ___ = ___

⑤ What is $\frac{4}{9}$ of 27?   ___ ÷ ___ = ___ ,   ___ × ___ = ___

⑥ What is $\frac{7}{10}$ of 50?   ___ ÷ ___ = ___ ,   ___ × ___ = ___

SCORE /6   0-2   3-4   5-6

Statistics & Probability

AC9M6ST02

After-school Activities Survey

Survey of After-school Activities

Student	Age	Activity
Olivia	11 y	swimming
Liam	8 y	tennis
Shin	10 y	swimming
Apollo	9 y	swimming
Ava	8 y	horseriding
Ash	10 y	tennis
Mai	9 y	horseriding

Student	Age	Activity
Sophia	9 y	horseriding
James	10 y	swimming
Han	8 y	swimming
Ezra	9 y	tennis
Nova	11 y	swimming
Jayden	11 y	horseriding
Riley	10 y	swimming

① Complete the side-by-side column chart of the survey data for under 10 students and 10 or over students.

② How many 10 or over students were surveyed? ___

③ Which two activities were equally popular with under 10 students?

_____ and _____

④ Which activity had the most students altogether, and how many students was that?

___ students did _____.

⑤ Which activity was most popular with under 10 students?

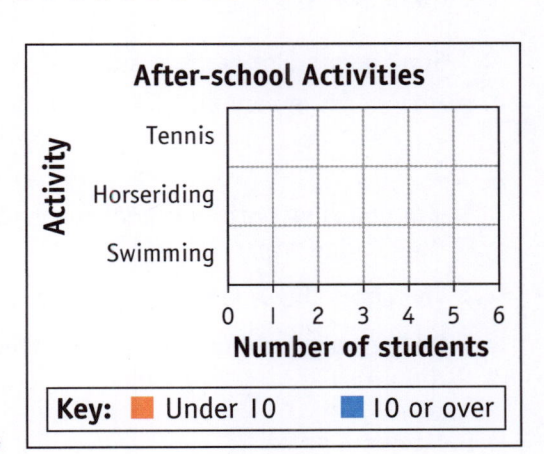

_____

After-school Activities

Activity: Tennis, Horseriding, Swimming
Number of students: 0 1 2 3 4 5 6

Key: ■ Under 10   ■ 10 or over

SCORE /5   0-3   4   5

TARGETING MATHS HOMEWORK: YEAR 6 © PASCAL PRESS ISBN: 9781925726596

UNIT 4 — Measurement & Space

AC9M6M03

Timetables

This is the Ideal TV Surfing Timetable.

4:00	4:30	5:00	5:30	6:00	6:30	7:00	7:30

Snow White	Donald Duck	The Little Mermaid
Ninja	Rainbow Fish	Ben 10	Wish Dragon
Captain Underpants	Small Foot	Wish Dragon	Home
Son of Bigfoot	Carmen San Diego	The Simpsons

① At what time does Carmen San Diego finish?
____

② How long does Small Foot last?
____

③ What can you watch between 5:00 and 6:00 and still see the whole show?
____

④ How long does the longest show last? ____

⑤ Plan a $3\frac{1}{2}$ hour Cartoon Marathon from this timetable.
____
____
____
____

You must watch complete shows. No channel surfing!

SCORE /5   0-2   3-4   5

NAPLAN*-style Questions

① 365.65 × 10 = ____

② Sara spent $\frac{5}{8}$ of her $40 savings. How much money did she have left?
$____

③ Min and Alex both had $50 to spend on their 3-day trip.

The chart shows when they spent their money.

On Tuesday, how much more did Min spend than Alex?

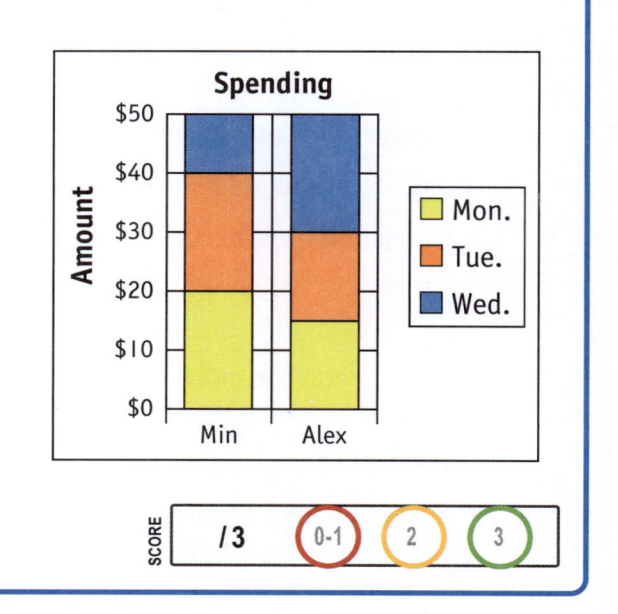

$____

Spending (bar chart: Mon. yellow, Tue. orange, Wed. blue; Min and Alex)

SCORE /3   0-1   2   3

16 TARGETING MATHS HOMEWORK: YEAR 6 © PASCAL PRESS ISBN: 9781925726596

Problem of the Week

UNIT 4

Holiday Savings

Hai, Liam and Elsa have been saving for the summer holiday. They each want to save $200.

At the end of the first week:

- Hai had saved five times as much as Liam. 
- Liam had saved two-fifths of what Elsa had saved. 
- Elsa had saved $30.

How much more money do they each need to save to reach their $200 target?

Show your working here.

① Hai needs to save another _____.

② Liam needs to save another _____.

③ Elsa needs to save another _____.

At the end of the second week:

- **Elsa:** I now have one-third more than Liam. 
- **Liam:** I now have four-fifths of what Hai has saved.
- **Hai:** I have saved $90.

How much more money do they each still need to save to reach their $200 target?

Show your working here.

④ Hai needs to save another _____.

⑤ Liam needs to save another _____.

⑥ Elsa needs to save another _____.

UNIT 5

Number & Algebra

AC9M6N07

Division by Decimals, Fractions and Percentages

0·6 of $50, $\frac{6}{10}$ of $50, 60% of $50

These amounts are all the same and each can be worked out using what you already know.

For 0·6 of $50, you know that 0·6 × 10 = 6, so
0·6 × 50 = 0·6 × 10 × 5 = 6 × 5 = 30.

For $\frac{6}{10}$ of 50, you know that $\frac{1}{10}$ of 50 = 5, so
$\frac{6}{10}$ × 50 = 6 × $\frac{1}{10}$ × 50 = 6 × 5 = 30.

For 60% of $50, you know that 60% of 100 = 60 and 50 is a half of 100, so 60% of $50 is half of $60 = $30.

**Show a smart strategy for finding these amounts and write the answers.
Tau has included some clues to get you started.**

	Problem	Strategy	Answer
①	20% of $60	10% is half of 20% 10% of $60 = $6	20% of $60 = 2 × $6 = _____
②	$\frac{4}{10}$ of $160	$\frac{1}{10}$ of $160 =	
③	40% of $150	10% of $150 = _____	
④	0·2 × $80	0·2 × _____ = _____	
⑤	75% of $60		
⑥	11% of $100		
⑦	$\frac{7}{10}$ of $140		

SCORE /7   0-3   4-5   6-7

Quick Check

① 10% of $50 = _____
② $\frac{3}{10}$ of $60 = _____
③ 0·5 of $60 = _____
④ 20% of $120 = _____
⑤ $\frac{2}{10}$ of $18 = _____
⑥ 11% of $100 = _____
⑦ 60% of $60 = _____
⑧ 0·2 of $36 = _____
⑨ $\frac{4}{10}$ of $100 = _____
⑩ 40% of $80 = _____

SCORE /10   0-4   5-8   9-10

Number & Algebra

UNIT 5

AC9M6N08

Making Approximations

$\frac{9}{10} + \frac{1}{2}$ is about $1\frac{1}{2}$ because $\frac{9}{10}$ is almost 1.
0·3 × $97 is about $30 because 0·3 × $100 is $30.
48% of $70 is about $35 because 48% is almost a half.

Suggest approximate answers to these questions and explain your reasoning.

Approximate Answer	My Reasoning
① 0·5 + 0·45 is about _____ because	
② 4% of $102 is about $____ because	
③ 0·21 × $70 is about $____ because	
④ 33% of $90 is about $____ because	
⑤ $\frac{7}{8}$ of $82 is about $ ____ because	
⑥ 0·25 × $81 is about $____ because	

SCORE /6   0-2   3-4   5-6

Statistics & Probability

AC9M6ST03

Interpreting Graphs

These charts show the number of pets owned by the students in Year 6 from three schools.

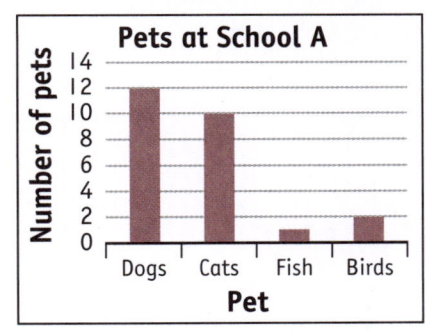

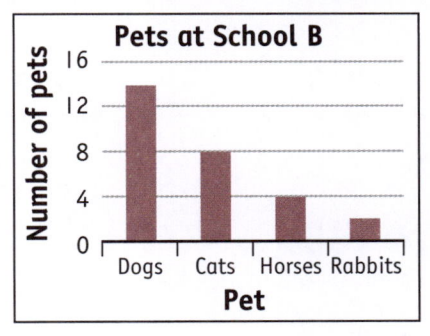

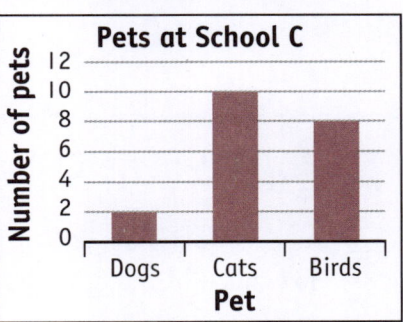

[Pets at School A bar chart: Dogs 12, Cats 10, Fish 1, Birds 2]
[Pets at School B bar chart: Dogs 14, Cats 8, Horses 4, Rabbits 2]
[Pets at School C bar chart: Dogs 2, Cats 10, Birds 8]

① At first glance, which school's Year 6 students appear to have the most pets? ___

② Which school's Year 6 students actually have the most pets? ___

③ What is different about the graphs?
_____

④ Why do you think School B's students have horses but the other schools' students don't?
_____

⑤ Why do you think that School C's students have fewer dogs than the other schools' students?
_____

SCORE /5   0-2   3-4   5

TARGETING MATHS HOMEWORK: YEAR 6 © PASCAL PRESS ISBN: 9781925726596

UNIT 5

Measurement & Space

AC9M6SP01

TERM 1

Cross-sections

These objects have been sliced at different angles.
The cross-sections show the shape of the sliced object.
Join each object to its cross-section.

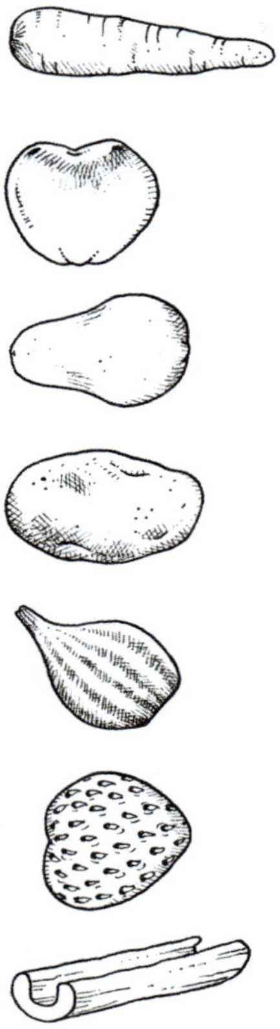

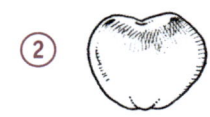

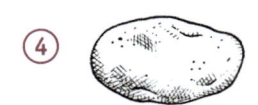

Objects	Cross-sections
① carrot	A
② apple	B
③ potato	C
④ potato	D
⑤ garlic	E
⑥ strawberry	F
⑦ celery	G

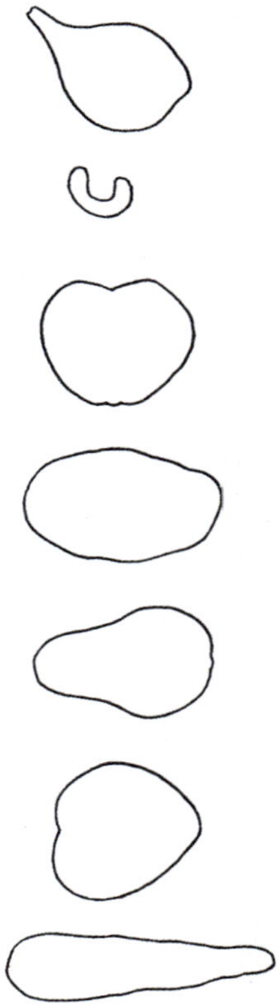

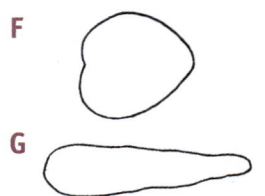

SCORE /7   0-3   4-5   6-7

NAPLAN*-style Questions

① Sara's iPhone had 12% of its battery left.
How much of the battery has been used? ____%

② Min had saved enough to buy a $200 bicycle.
When she went to buy it, the price had been reduced by 15%.
How much did Min have left from the $200 that she had saved? $____

③ Which of these shapes could be the cross-section of a cone?

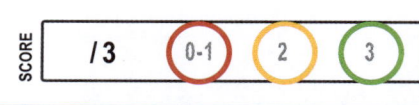

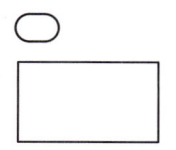

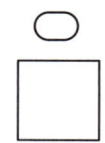

SCORE /3   0-1   2   3

Problem of the Week

UNIT 5

Drawing Cross-sections

"Good morning, class. Today our investigation will be to search for cross-sections.

"Find 3D objects that you can slice through. Then draw the original shape and the shape of the new face that you made by slicing through it. I am expecting you to find at least ten different objects for your investigation."

Alex called out, "I'm going to slice through my doughnut!" and everyone else in the class laughed.

TERM 1

Draw your 10 objects and the faces of the cross-sections that you make when you cut through them.

	The Object	The Cross-section		The Object	The Cross-section
①			⑥		
②			⑦		
③			⑧		
④			⑨		
⑤			⑩		

TARGETING MATHS HOMEWORK: YEAR 6 © PASCAL PRESS ISBN: 9781925726596

UNIT 6

Number & Algebra

AC9M6N07

Fractions of a Price

Often when shopping, you need to know how to estimate or work out fractions of a price.

For example, to buy 250 g of cherries which are $18 a kilogram, you need to know that 250 g is $\frac{1}{4}$ of a kilogram.

A quarter of $18 can be found by dividing by 4 or by repeated halving, as in half of $18 is $9 and half of $9 is $4·50.

Show how you would work out each of these shopping examples.

The Shopping Problem	How to Work It Out
① How much would it be for 250 mL of juice when one litre of juice is $12?	
② What change will there be from $20 after buying $\frac{3}{4}$ of a kilogram of apples priced at $6 per kilogram?	
③ Salami is $56 per kilogram. How much would it be for 100 g?	
④ If dress fabric was $12·80 per metre, how much would $2\frac{1}{4}$ metres cost?	
⑤ Saffron can be very expensive. It can cost $1000 per kilogram. How much would 20 g cost?	
⑥ Blue cheese was $3·50 for 200 g last week. This week it has gone up by 75c per 100 g. How much is one kilogram of blue cheese now?	

SCORE /6   0-2   3-4   5-6

Quick Check

① $\frac{1}{4}$ kilogram at $26 per kg = _____

② $\frac{3}{4}$ kilogram at $50 per kg = _____

③ 75 cm at $6 per metre = _____

④ $\frac{1}{10}$ kilogram at $26 per kg = _____

⑤ 200 g at $10 per kg = _____

⑥ 750 mL at $8 per litre = _____

⑦ $2\frac{1}{2}$ L at $3·70 per litre = _____

⑧ $\frac{3}{5}$ kilogram at $15 per kg = _____

⑨ 250 g at $50 per kilogram = _____

⑩ 150 cm at $16 per metre = _____

SCORE /10   0-4   5-8   9-10

UNIT 6

Number & Algebra

AC9M6A02

Order of Operations

When you see a number sentence like this: **40 ÷ 2 × (4 + 6)** you have to use **order of operations** to find out what the value is.
- First, you have to work out the part inside the **B**rackets.
- Then you work out any **D**ivisions or **M**ultiplications.
- That leaves the **A**dditions and **S**ubtractions to work out.

The letters **BODMAS** show the order in which you have to work out the values:

Brackets, **O**ver, **D**ivision, **M**ultiplication, **A**ddition and **S**ubtraction.

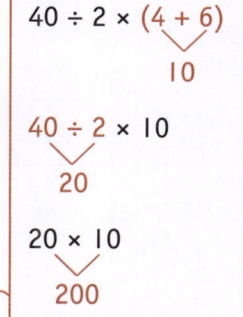

$$40 ÷ 2 × (4 + 6)$$
$$\downarrow$$
$$10$$
$$40 ÷ 2 × 10$$
$$\downarrow$$
$$20$$
$$20 × 10$$
$$\downarrow$$
$$200$$

Solve these number sentences using the BODMAS strategy.

① 3 × 8 ÷ (4 + 2)

= ___ ÷ ___

= ___

② 20 ÷ 5 × (3 + 5)

= ___ × ___

= ___

③ (5 + 7) ÷ (10 − 4)

= ___ ÷ ___

= ___

④ (30 − 12) ÷ (12 − 3)

= ___ ÷ ___

= ___

When you see a number sentence with no brackets like this: **3 × 8 + 16 ÷ 2**, the BODMAS strategy tells you to do the Division first, then the Multiplication. After that, do the Addition and Subtraction.

Solve these number sentences using the BODMAS strategy.

⑤ 5 × 6 + 16 ÷ 2

= ___ + ___

= ___

⑥ 18 ÷ 3 + 21 ÷ 7

= ___ + ___

= ___

SCORE /6   0-2   3-4   5-6

Statistics & Probability

AC9M6P02

Toss Two Coins

Toss two coins and record the result as 2H, HT or 2T.

① What was the result? ___

② Now toss the coins 8 times and count the number of times each outcome occurred.

Did you get the result that you expected? ___

③ Why was that? _____

Heads (H)   Tails (T)

No scores for these questions.

TARGETING MATHS HOMEWORK: YEAR 6 © PASCAL PRESS ISBN: 9781925726596

UNIT 6 — Measurement & Space

AC9M6SP03

Tessellation

Some shapes **tessellate** which means they fit together with no gaps or overlaps.

These triangles fit together with no gaps.

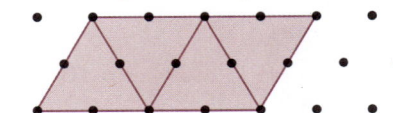

Triangles that tessellate.

These quadrilaterals leave a space when we fit them together.

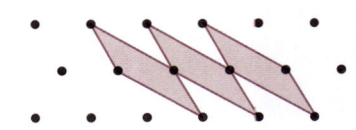

Quadrilaterals that do not tessellate.

Use the dot grid to investigate which of these shapes tessellate.

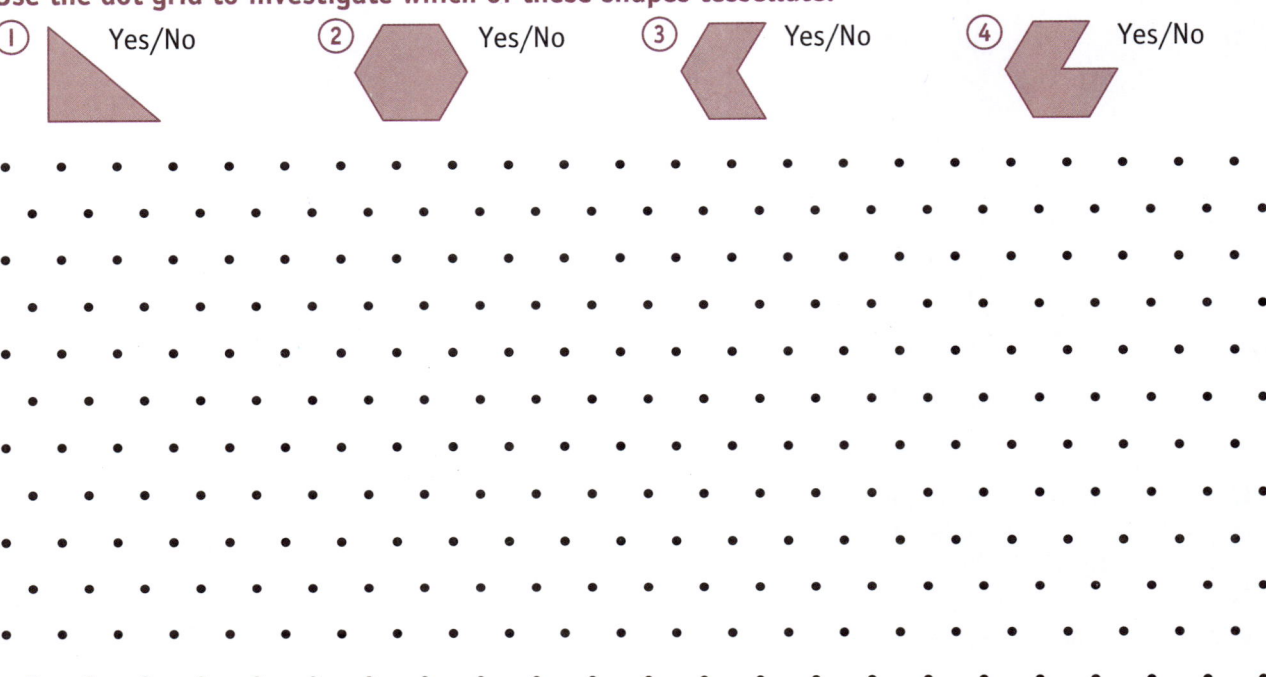

① Yes/No   ② Yes/No   ③ Yes/No   ④ Yes/No

SCORE /8   0–3   4–6   7–8

NAPLAN*-style Questions

① How much would 250 g of olives cost when olives are $18 per kilogram?

$ _____

② 3 × 6 + 21 ÷ (3 + 4) = ?

◯ 17   ◯ 21   ◯ 29   ◯ 31

③ Which of these shapes will tessellate?

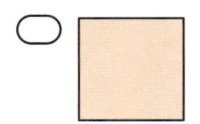

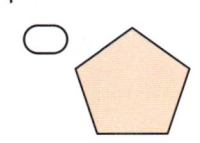

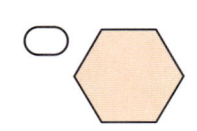

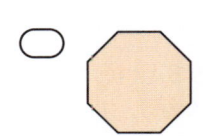

◯ square   ◯ pentagon   ◯ hexagon   ◯ octagon

SCORE /3   0–1   2   3

24 TARGETING MATHS HOMEWORK: YEAR 6 © PASCAL PRESS ISBN: 9781925726596

Problem of the Week

UNIT 6

AC9M6A01

Patterns with Two Shapes

"Good afternoon, class.

"On this page I have prepared special grids for you to use to make two tessellating patterns. And yes, you may colour in your pattern if you would like to.

"But each of your patterns must include two of these shapes, and you must not use the same shapes in both tessellating patterns.

"These are the shapes for you to use, and you can use them at any size you like:"

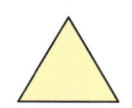

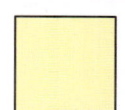

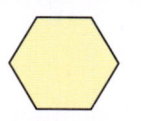

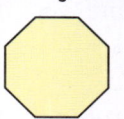

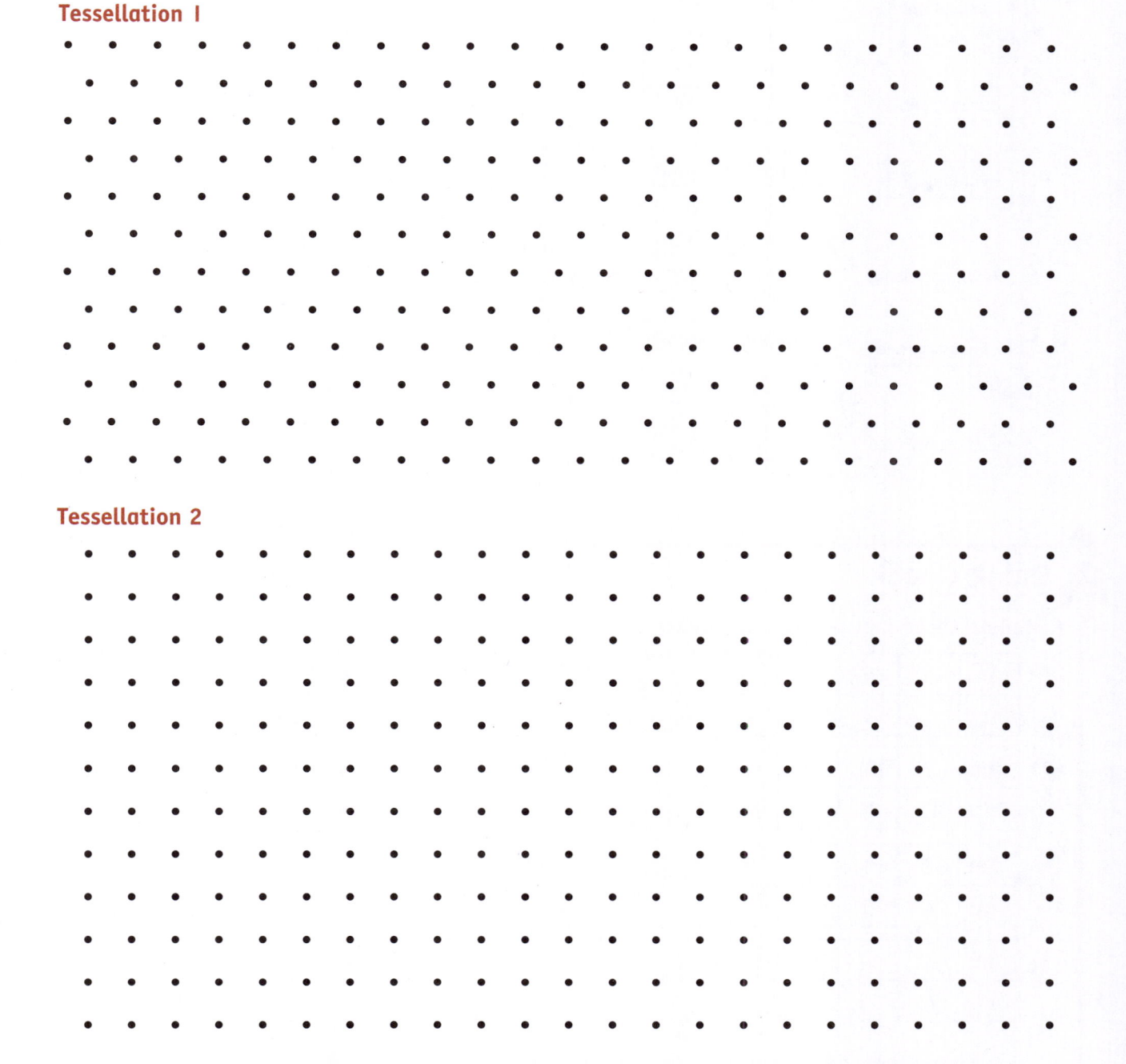

Tessellation 1

Tessellation 2

Thank you for taking the time to make these tessellations. We hope you like them!

UNIT 7

Number & Algebra

AC9M6A03

Patterns and Pattern Rules

"One of my favourite things in maths when I was your age," Mr Green told his class, "was the Function Machine."

"When a number was put in, the function rule was applied and an answer came out.

"For an input of 3, 4 and 6, a record was made of the output which was 6, 7, 9. You could then look at the sequences and work out the function rule. In this case, it was + 3."

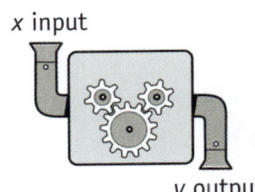

x input
y output

Input	Output
3	6
4	7
6	9

Write the function rules for these machines.

① 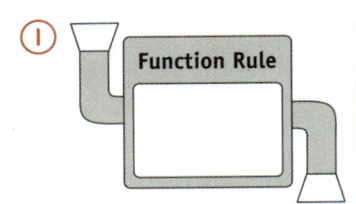 Function Rule

Input	Output
5	10
6	12
7	14

② 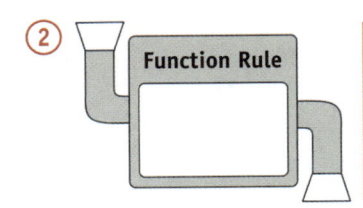 Function Rule

Input	Output
3	9
4	12
5	15

③ 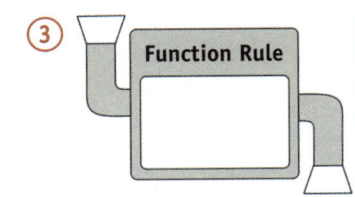 Function Rule

Input	Output
12	10
14	12
15	13

④ 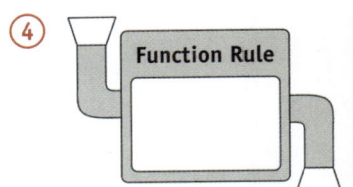 Function Rule

Input	Output
18	9
6	3
26	13

⑤  Function Rule

Input	Output
24	6
32	8
16	4

⑥ 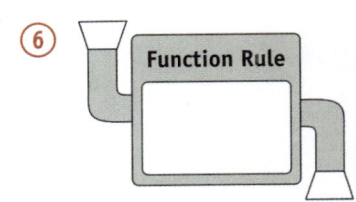 Function Rule

Input	Output
18	12
64	58
100	94

SCORE /6   0-2   3-4   5-6

Quick Check

Complete these input–output sequences.

①
In:	3	26	14	
Out:	5	28		36

②
In:	2	14	8	
Out:	12	84		36

③
In:	2	3		8
Out:	4	5	11	

④
In:	98	17		29
Out:	96	15	46	

⑤
In:	8	14		17
Out:	12	18	26	

⑥
In:	4	26	15	12
Out:	12	78		

⑦
In:	15	36	12	
Out:	5	12		11

⑧
In:	6	94	36	
Out:	26	114		107

SCORE /8   0-3   4-6   7-8

Number & Algebra

UNIT 7

AC9M6N02

Square Numbers

You can use tiles or grid paper to investigate which numbers can make a square. These numbers are called square numbers.

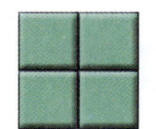

4 is a square number.

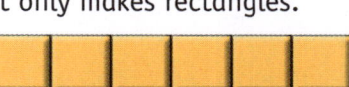

6 is not a square number. It only makes rectangles.

Find all the square numbers to 100.

Continue colouring the grid and writing the square numbers as multiplication facts.

| 2 × 2 = 4 |
| 3 × 3 = 9 |
| |
| |
| |
| |
| |
| |

Notice how the 2 by 2 square was coloured and then a different colour used to show the next square number, 3 by 3.

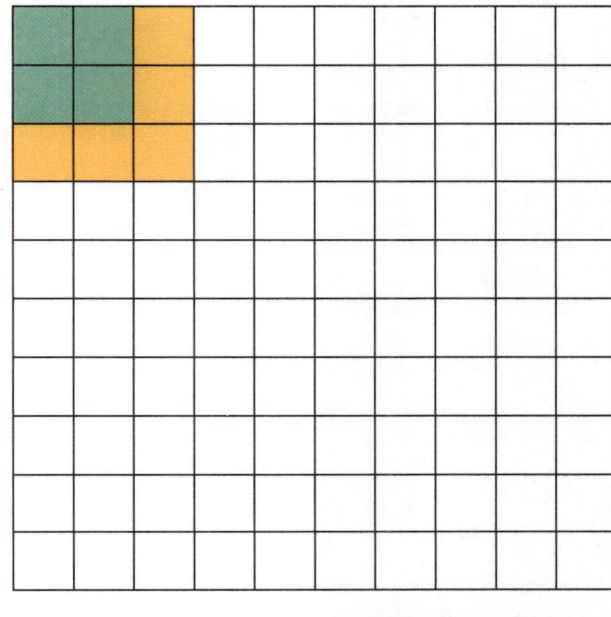

SCORE /7   0-3   4-5   6-7

TERM 1

Statistics & Probability

AC9M6P02

Total of 2 Dice

① Complete this table to show the ways of making the possible totals from 2 to 12 using two dice.

Dice 1

+	1	2	3	4	5	6
1						
2						
3						
4						
5						
6						

Dice 2

② Which total has the best chance of being thrown?

____

③ Which totals have the least chance of being thrown?

____ and ____

④ What is the chance of the total being 4, 5, 6, or 7?

____ in ____ or ____%

SCORE /4   0-1   2-3   4

TARGETING MATHS HOMEWORK: YEAR 6 © PASCAL PRESS ISBN: 9781925726596

27

UNIT 7 — Measurement & Space

AC9M6M04

Problem Solving with Angles

Angle Facts

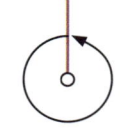

- There are 360° in a full rotation.
- There are 90° in a right angle. 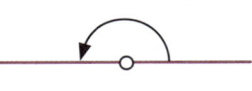
- There are 180° in a straight-line angle.
- Vertically opposite angles are equal to each other. (120°, 60°, 60°, 120°) 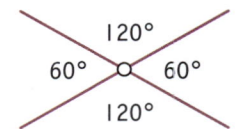

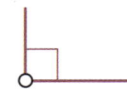

Use the angle facts to find the angles marked ?.

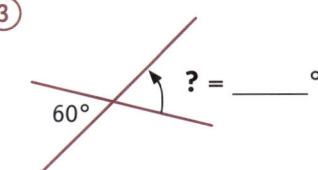

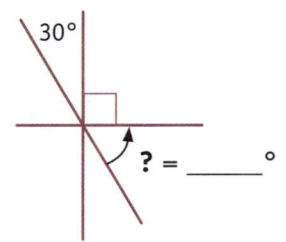

① ? = _____°

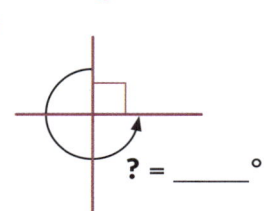

② 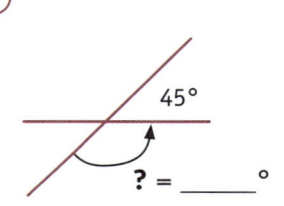 45°, ? = _____°

③ 60°, ? = _____°

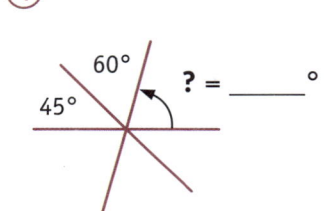

④ 60°, 45°, ? = _____°

⑤ 30°, ? = _____°

⑥ 57°, 57°, ? = _____°

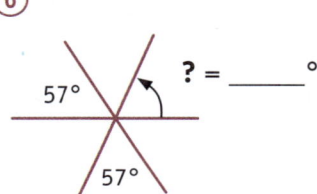

SCORE /6   0–2   3–4   5–6

NAPLAN*-style Questions

① What is the function rule for this sequence?

○ + 4   ○ + $\frac{4}{10}$ ○ + 0.04   ○ + 0.5

In:	3·6	7·2	9·7
Out:	4	7·6	10·1

② Which of these numbers is not a square number?

○ 1   ○ 6   ○ 9   ○ 16

③ How many degrees is angle C?

_____°

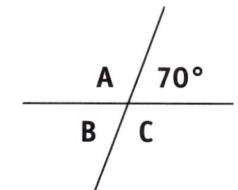

A / 70°
B / C

SCORE /3   0–1   2   3

28   TARGETING MATHS HOMEWORK: YEAR 6 © PASCAL PRESS ISBN: 9781925726596

Problem of the Week

UNIT 7

AC9M6A01

Pavers for my Patio

"I bought three identical packets of large garden pavers.

"I thought there would be at least 40 pavers, but the packets had fewer than I expected.

"I want a rectangular patio that is at least 3 pavers wide, and more would be better.

"The tiler has opened the packets and sent me a text to say that he can make:
- a square patio or
- a rectangular patio with an even number of pavers along one side and an odd number of pavers along the other side.

"He wants to know which of the patios I want him to make. I sent a text back to say I'll think about it and text him later."

TERM 1

The Challenges
- How many pavers might there have been in each of the three packets that Mr Green bought?
- What are the possible patio shapes that the tiler can make with the pavers that he has?

Note: The tiler must use all the pavers and not cut any of them into pieces.

① Use the grid to show the possible patio sizes.

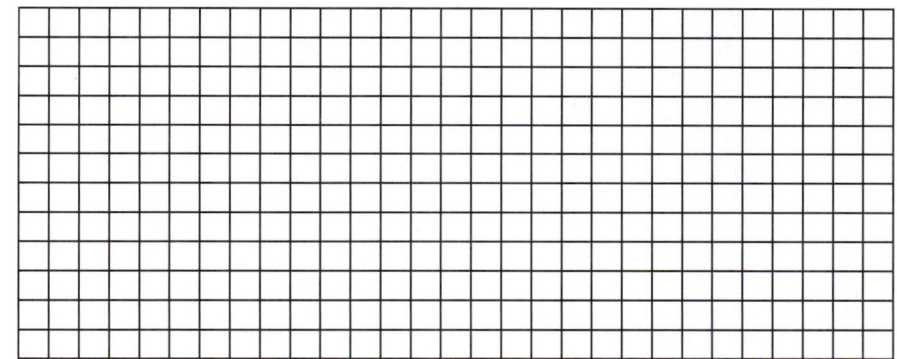

> One patio plan can be square, so a list of square numbers will help you find the possible packet sizes.

② The possible number of pavers could be ____, ____, ____.

Extra Challenge

Mr Green thinks he might buy one more packet of pavers.
What different sizes of rectangular patios could be made if one more packet of pavers was available?

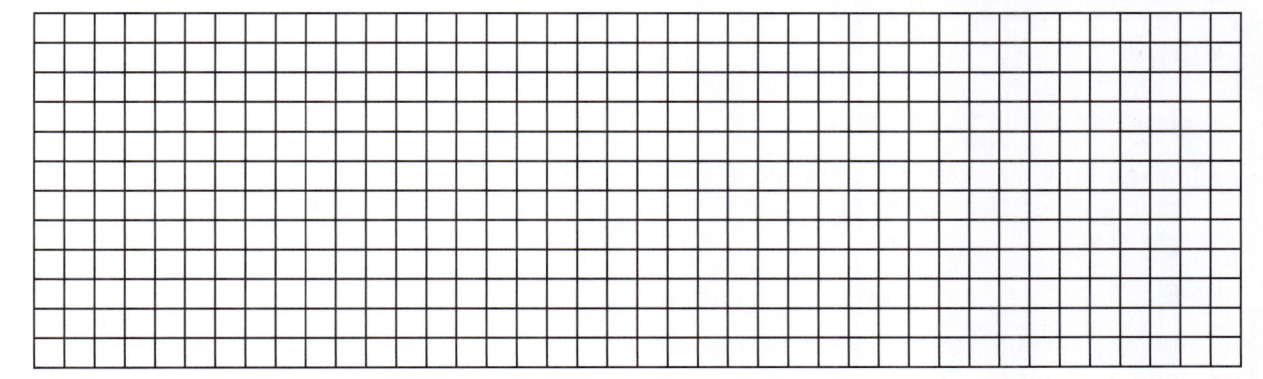

③ Which size patio would be best for Mr Green to ask for? _____

UNIT 8

Number & Algebra

AC9M6N09

On a Budget

I get paid $50 a week for the odd jobs that I do and I have saved $360 so far.
My goal is to have $500 saved in 5 weeks' time.

I have some expenses each week:
- $21 going to the movies,
- $6 on junk food (drink and lollies),
- $15 at the tuck shop,
- $5 on bus fares to footy training.

How can I reach my $500 target in just 5 weeks?

Show Min how she can reach her goal.

1. How much does Min need to save in the next 5 weeks? $_____

2. How much does Min spend each week? $_____

3. How far short of her target will Min be if she makes no spending changes? $_____

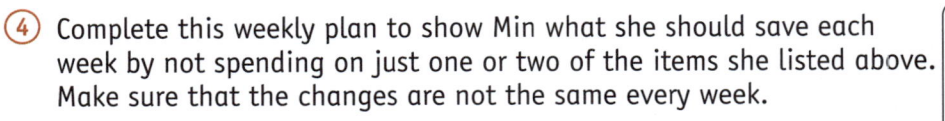

4. Complete this weekly plan to show Min what she should save each week by not spending on just one or two of the items she listed above. Make sure that the changes are not the same every week.

There are some ideas in the Quick Check questions that you will find very useful.

	Week 1	Week 2	Week 3	Week 4	Week 5
Expenses to save on					
$ saved					
$ spent					

5. What is the total amount saved by your plan? $_____

6. How much will Min have saved by the end of 5 weeks? $_____

Score 1 point for each week of savings.

SCORE /11   0-5   6-9   10-11

Quick Check

Some ways for Min to save money!

1. **Week 1:** If Min does not go to the movies and have junk food, how much will she save?

    $_____

2. **Week 2:** If Min misses football training and does not spend at the tuck shop, how much will she save?

    $_____

3. **Week 3:**
    What if Min chooses to miss out on the movies and junk food again? How much extra will she have saved so far?

    $_____

Over to you now to make sure that Min saves the exact amount to reach her goal.

SCORE /3   0-1   2   3

Number & Algebra

UNIT 8

AC9M6N09

Unit Cost Problems

When you are out shopping, you need to make choices about **best buys**.
For example, which is the better buy: 3 avocados for $4·50 or 5 avocados for $7?
To choose the best buy, you have to find the answer to two division sums.

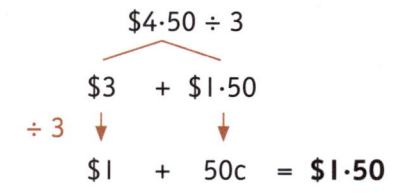

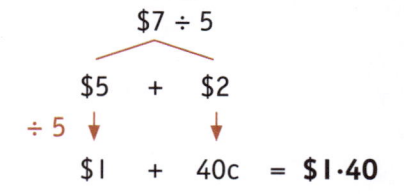

$$\$4·50 \div 3$$

÷ 3: $3 + $1·50 → $1 + 50c = **$1·50**

$$\$7 \div 5$$

÷ 5: $5 + $2 → $1 + 40c = **$1·40**

In this case, the larger $7 bag is the better buy, as each avocado is 10c cheaper than those in the $4·50 bag.

Work out these best buy examples.

① 5 oranges for $3·50 or 8 oranges for $5·20

_____ _____

② 50 tea bags for $5·50 or 75 teabags for $7·50

_____ _____

③ 6 protein bars for $7·20 or 8 protein bars for $9·20

_____ _____

④ 6 packs of sultanas for $5·40 or 10 packs of sultanas for $10·20

_____ _____

⑤ 4 packs of burger buns for $4·80 or 8 packs of burger buns for $7·20

_____ _____

SCORE /5   0-2   3-4   5

Statistics & Probability

AC9M6P01

Make a Spinner

Colour the probability spinner to show these chances.

① 25% chance of spinning red
② 0% chance of spinning black
③ 15% chance of spinning yellow
④ 30% chance of spinning green
⑤ Equal chance of spinning blue or white
⑥ What is the % chance of spinning white?

____% chance

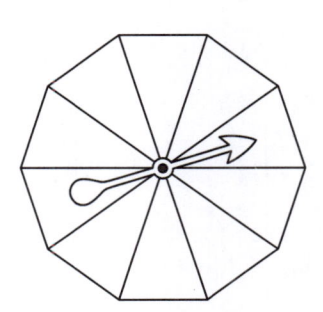

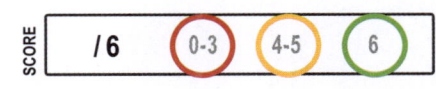

SCORE /6   0-3   4-5   6

TARGETING MATHS HOMEWORK: YEAR 6 © PASCAL PRESS ISBN: 9781925726596

UNIT 8 — Measurement & Space

AC9M6SP02, AC9M6SP03

Translation of a Shape

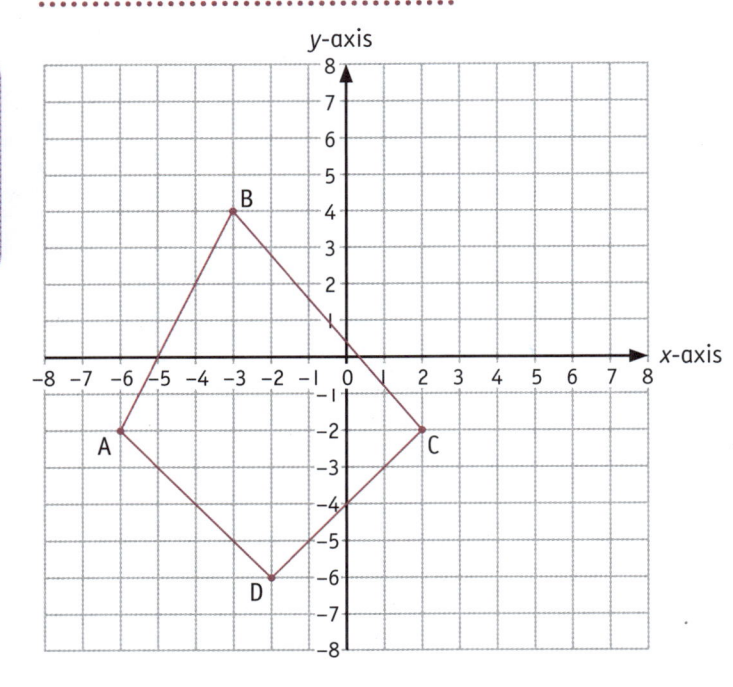

TERM 1

Give the coordinates for these points.

1. A (__, __)
2. B (__, __)
3. C (__, __)
4. D (__, __)

5. Translate the shape 4 units to the right and 3 units up and draw it in the new position.

Give the new coordinates for these points.

6. A (__, __)
7. B (__, __)
8. C (__, __)
9. D (__, __)

SCORE /9   0-4   5-7   8-9

NAPLAN*-style Questions

1. Hai bought a six-pack of small juice boxes for $7·80. How much did each juice box cost?

   $_____

2. Liam has $95. He saves $45 a week. How long until he saves enough for this $600 bicycle?

   ____ weeks

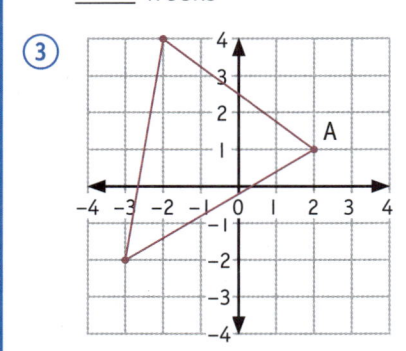

3. When this shape has been translated 3 units to the left and 4 units down, what will be the coordinates of point A?

   (___, ___)

SCORE /3   0-1   2   3

TARGETING MATHS HOMEWORK: YEAR 6 © PASCAL PRESS ISBN: 9781925726596

Problem of the Week

UNIT 8

Holiday Destination

Planning a holiday and budgeting for it is a major undertaking for many families. After Christmas every year, our family chooses a two-week interstate holiday destination. We then start planning. This means working out the costs for airfares, hotels and so on, and creating timelines for travel.

We always start our holiday on the last Saturday in July and return 14 days later.

The Challenge
This challenge is a research task that is similar to Elsa's family research.

1. Choose a destination in another state.

2. Find the cheapest return airfares for the holiday. Record the flight dates and times and total cost.

3. Find a hotel at your destination and work out the cost for your family for one night and then for two weeks.

4. Identify 4 special outings for the holiday and cost them for your family.

5. Allow $200 each day for the family spending allowance. How much will the holiday for your family cost altogether?

6. How much would your family need to set aside each month to make sure that you have enough money for the holiday?

Review: Unit 1 and Unit 2

AC9M6N01, AC9M6N02, AC9M6A01, AC9M6M01, AC9M6P02

Complete the number lines to find the numbers represented by the question marks.

① 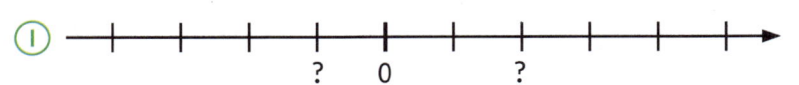 ___ and ___

② ___ and ___

What is the difference between the two numbers?

③ −4 and 5 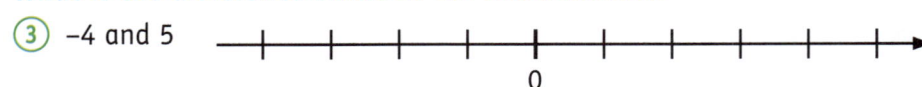   The difference is ____.

④ −7 and −3 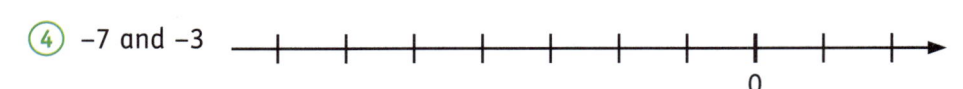   The difference is ____.

⑤ 6 and −1 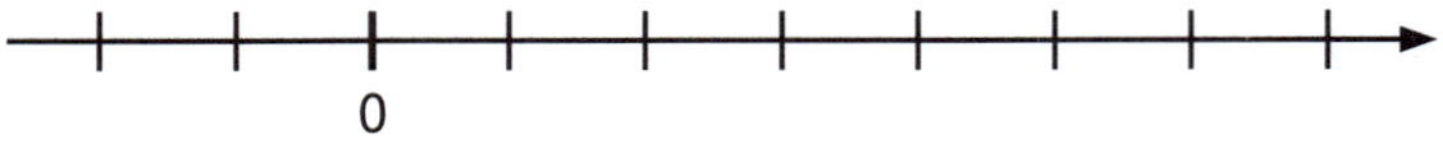   The difference is ____.

Continue these sequences.

⑥ 3, 9, 4, 12, 5, ___, ___, ___, ___, ___

⑦ 4, 7, 5, 8, 6, ___, ___, ___, ___, ___

⑧ How many millimetres are in 1·5 metres? _____

⑨ How many centimetres are in 5 kilometres? _____

⑩ Circle the prime numbers.
2, 5, 6, 7, 9, 13, 18, 25

Mark percentages on the number lines to show the likelihood of these events happening.

⑪ The news will be on television tonight.

0%   100%

⑫ This spinner will land on an even number.

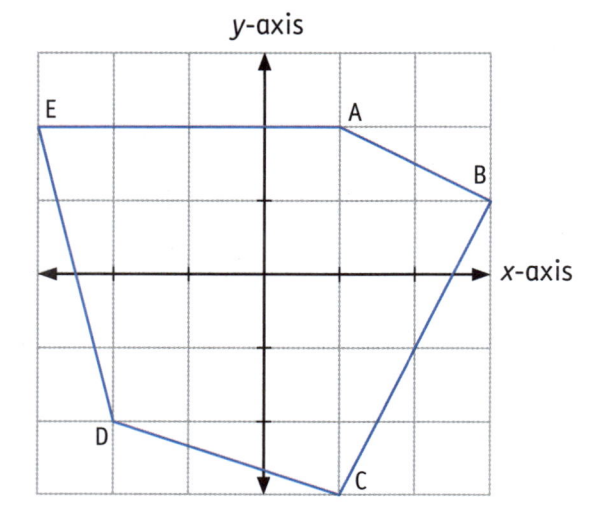

0%   100%

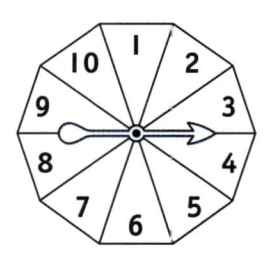

What are the coordinates of the corners of this shape?

⑬ A = (___, ___)

⑭ B = (___, ___)

⑮ C = (___, ___)

⑯ D = (___, ___)

⑰ E = (___, ___)

Review: Unit 3 and Unit 4

Convert these fractions into 16ths.

① $\frac{3}{4} = \frac{}{16}$ ② $\frac{5}{8} = \frac{}{16}$ ③ $\frac{16}{32} = \frac{}{16}$

Convert these fractions into 18ths.

④ $\frac{1}{3} = \frac{}{18}$ ⑤ $\frac{4}{9} = \frac{}{18}$ ⑥ $\frac{1}{2} = \frac{}{18}$

Write these numbers in column form and add them.

⑦ 27·05 + 36·007 + 8·01

⑧ 105·26 + 3·7 + 80·05

Find the areas of these rectangles.

⑨ 6 by 6 metre rectangle

___ × ____ = _____ m²

⑩ 3 by 12 centimetre rectangle

___ × ____ = _____ cm²

⑪ 7 by 8 kilometre rectangle

___ × ____ = _____ km²

⑫ 3·5 by 8 millimetre rectangle

___ × ____ = _____ mm²

Complete these multiplications and divisions.

⑬ 3·6 × 10 = _____

⑭ 47·05 × 100 = _____

⑮ 95·6 ÷ 10 = _____

⑯ 36·75 ÷ 100 = _____

Complete these money questions.

⑰ What is $\frac{3}{4}$ of $36? $_____

⑱ What is $\frac{2}{5}$ of $60? $_____

⑲ What is $\frac{5}{8}$ of $64? $_____

⑳ What is $\frac{5}{6}$ of $48? $_____

Use the side-by-side column graph to answer these questions.

㉑ How many students were surveyed altogether?

_____

㉒ How many more 10 or over students than under 10 students were in the survey?

_____

㉓ Which activity was the most popular overall?

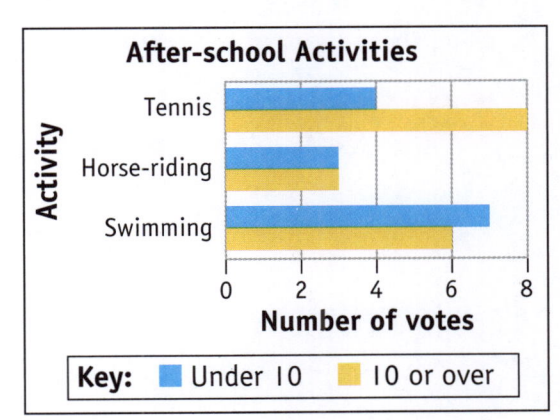

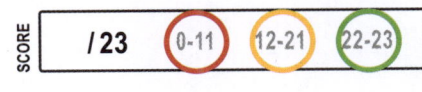

_____

After-school Activities

Key: ■ Under 10 ■ 10 or over

Review: Unit 5 and Unit 6

AC9M6N07, AC9M6N08, AC9M6A02, AC9M6SP01, AC9M6P03

Use smart strategies for these division questions.

		Strategy	Answer
①	20% of $60		
②	0·4 of $80		
③	$\frac{3}{10}$ of $72		
④	30% of $90		
⑤	0·25 of $50		
⑥	$\frac{5}{10}$ of $120		

Complete these questions with close approximations.

⑦ $\frac{3}{4} + \frac{3}{10}$ is about ___ because _____

⑧ 39% of $80 is about $_____ because _____

What would make these cross-sections? Choose from a pineapple, a tomato or a lemon.

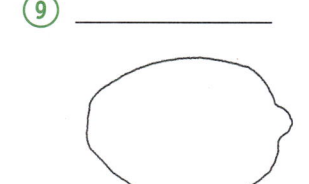

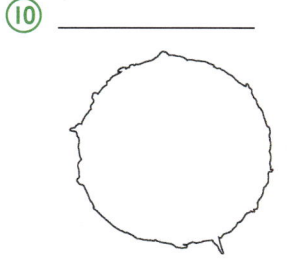

⑨ _____   ⑩ _____   ⑪ _____

Find the fractions of these prices.

⑫ 300 g of cheese at $36 per kilogram   = $ _____

⑬ $1\frac{3}{4}$ metres of fabric at $16 a metre   = $ _____

⑭ $\frac{1}{2}$ L of orange juice at $3·60 for 250 mL   = $ _____

⑮ Draw a tessellating pattern using these shapes.

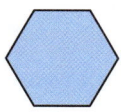

Solve these number sentences using BODMAS.

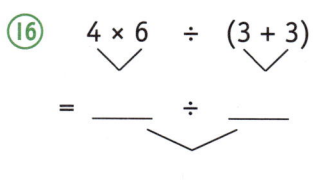

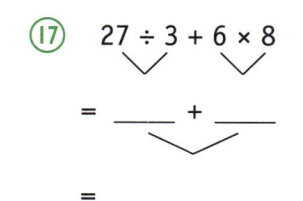

⑯ 4 × 6 ÷ (3 + 3)

= ___ ÷ ___

= ___

⑰ 27 ÷ 3 + 6 × 8

= ___ + ___

= ___

SCORE /17   0-8   9-15   16-17

36   TARGETING MATHS HOMEWORK: YEAR 6 © PASCAL PRESS ISBN: 9781925726596

Review: Unit 7 and Unit 8

AC9M6N02, AC9M6N09, AC9M6M04, AC9M6A03, AC9M6P01

Write the function rules for these machines.

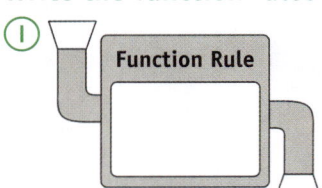

① Function Rule:

Input	Output
5	8
21	24
6	9

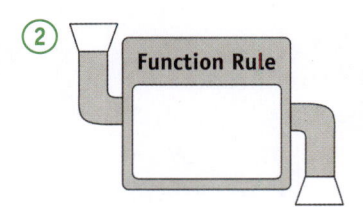

② Function Rule:

Input	Output
4	16
21	84
15	60

Complete the input and output lists for these function machines.

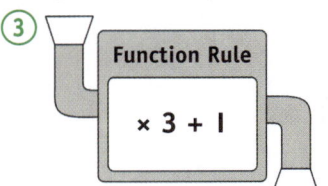

③ Function Rule: × 3 + 1

Input	Output
3	
	16
12	

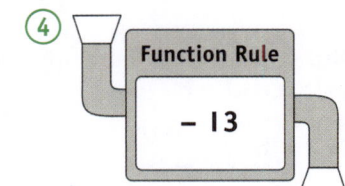

④ Function Rule: − 13

Input	Output
26	
	48
	98

⑤ Which of these numbers is not a square number?
○ 1   ○ 5   ○ 16

⑥ Which of these numbers is the next square number after 100?
○ 144   ○ 169   ○ 224   ○ 121

What is the angle marked ?

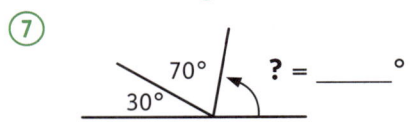

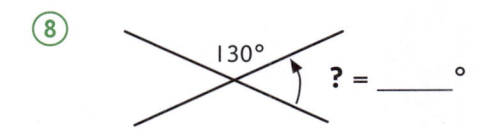

⑦ 70°, 30°   ? = _____°

⑧ 130°   ? = _____°

Tau has saved $186.

⑨ Tau wants to have $360 saved in 6 weeks' time. How much does he need to save each week?

$_____

⑩ If each week Tau stops spending $15 at the tuck shop and $6 on junk food, how much extra does he need to save to reach $360 in 6 weeks?

$_____

⑪ Which is the better buy: 6 oranges for $4·68 or 10 oranges for $8?

○ 6 for $4·68   ○ 10 for $8

Colour the probability spinner red, green, yellow, blue and purple to show these chances.

⑫ 30% chance of spinning red.

⑬ 15% chance of spinning green.

⑭ 20% chance of spinning yellow.

⑮ 5% chance of spinning blue.

⑯ What chance is there of spinning purple?

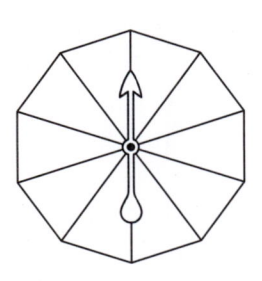

_____%

UNIT 9

Number & Algebra

AC9M6N01

Integers in the Context of Money

Bankrupt is a game that we invented.
You start with $100 and, on your turn, take a card from the pack.
We made two types of cards that look like this but have different amounts on them:

EARN $65   SPEND $65

The person who has the most money or least debt at the end of 4 rounds is the winner.

Here are the cards that Ruby, Sara and Min had in their game.
Use the number lines to work out who won.

	Ruby	Earn	Spend		Balance
①	Round 1		$45	Start with $100.	_____
②	Round 2		$100		_____
③	Round 3	$65		←————|————→	_____
④	Round 4		$35	$100	_____

	Sara	Earn	Spend		Balance
⑤	Round 1	$70		Start with $100.	_____
⑥	Round 2		$125		_____
⑦	Round 3		$45	←————|————→	_____
⑧	Round 4		$60	$100	_____

	Min	Earn	Spend		Balance
⑨	Round 1	$20		Start with $100.	_____
⑩	Round 2		$25		_____
⑪	Round 3		$125	←————|————→	_____
⑫	Round 4	$50		$100	_____

⑬ Who won that game? _____

SCORE /13   0-6   7-11   12-13

Quick Check

	Start	Spend	Balance
①	$100	$150	
②	$50	$65	
③	$50	$70	
④	$50	$150	
⑤	−$30	$70	

	Start	Earn	Balance
⑥	−$28	$30	
⑦	−$70	$45	
⑧	−$90	$85	
⑨	−$120	$95	
⑩	−$45	$120	

SCORE /10   0-4   5-8   9-10

Number & Algebra

UNIT 9
AC9M6N02

Prime Factors

You have learned about factors and prime numbers in the past. It is time to put those two together and work with prime factors.

You know that 12 has the factors **1, 2, 3, 4, 6** and **12** because all of those numbers divide 12 evenly, leaving no remainder. But only two of those factors are prime numbers: **2** and **3**.

When you make a factor tree, it shows that the prime factors of 12 are 2 and 3, even when you break 12 into its factors in different ways.

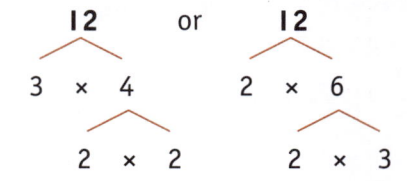

```
      12              or         12
     /  \                       /  \
    3  × 4                     2  × 6
        / \                         / \
       2 × 2                       2 × 3
```

Complete the factor trees to show prime factors.

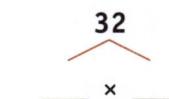

① 20
___ × ___

③ 16
___ × ___

⑤ 32
___ × ___

② 18
___ × ___

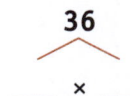

④ 24
___ × ___

⑥ 36
___ × ___

SCORE /6   0-2   3-4   5-6

Statistics & Probability

AC9M6ST03

What Is the Litter?

Every day, the school-yard at Sussex Primary School is full of litter. The school wants to do some research to find out what the litter is, how it gets there and what to do about it.

For example, are the bins close to where the litter is dropped?

Suggest five survey questions the class could ask about the litter problem.

① _____
② _____
③ _____
④ _____
⑤ _____

SCORE /6   0-2   3-4   5-6

TERM 2

UNIT 9

Measurement & Space

AC9M6SP02

The Cartesian Plane

Hai drew a triangle with point A at (−5, −5), point B at (0, −5) and point C at (−5, −1).

1. Use the grid to draw Hai's triangle.

2. Grow the triangle so that point A stays in the same position, but the triangle is twice as high and twice as wide.

3. List the new coordinates.

    B is now at (___, ___).

    C is now at (___, ___).

4. Draw a new triangle with point D at (1, 7), point E at (−2, 4) and point F at (4, 4).

5. Leaving point D in the same position, grow the triangle DEF to make it twice as wide and twice as high.

6. What are the new coordinates for points E and F?

    E is now at (___, ___).

    F is now at (___, ___).

7. Draw your own triangle ABC on the grid.

    List its coordinates: A (___, ___), B (___, ___), C (___, ___).

8. Grow your triangle by moving two of the vertices to make it twice as wide and twice as high.

    List its new coordinates: New B (___, ___), New C (___, ___).

SCORE /7   0-3   4-5   6-7

NAPLAN*-style Questions

1. A lift started at ground level and went down three floors to collect Liam from the car park. Liam pressed the button to go up 5 floors to his apartment.
   At which floor did Liam get out of the lift?

   _____ floor

2. Which of these numbers is not a prime factor of 126?

   ○ 2   ○ 3   ○ 7   ○ 9

3. The line AB is moved 3 units to the right and 3 units up.
   What are the coordinates of A and B after the move?

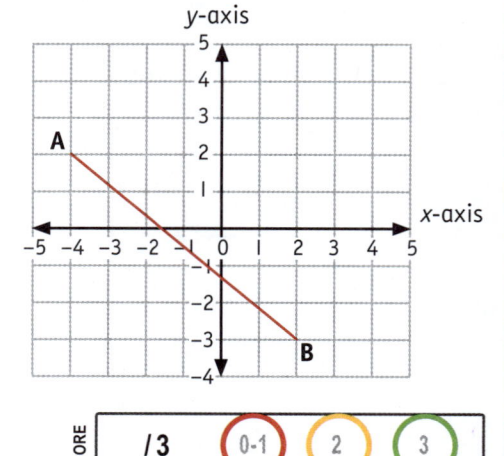

   A = (___, ___) and B = (___, ___)

SCORE /3   0-1   2   3

TARGETING MATHS HOMEWORK: YEAR 6 © PASCAL PRESS ISBN: 9781925726596

Problem of the Week

UNIT 9
AC9M6SP02

Draw Me a House

"My challenge to you, Tau, is to draw me a symmetrical house on the grid below.

"Start the roof by drawing a line from (−7, 3) to (−1, 7). Now draw in the rest of the roof, making it symmetrical."

"Got that, Elsa. So what do I do next?"

"Draw the left side of the house with a line from (−6, 3) to (−6, −6) and fill in the rest of the house.

"After that, you need a front door which you make symmetrical starting at (−2, −2). Then add in four windows, two upstairs and two either side of the front door."

The Challenge

Follow Elsa's instructions to make a symmetrical house.

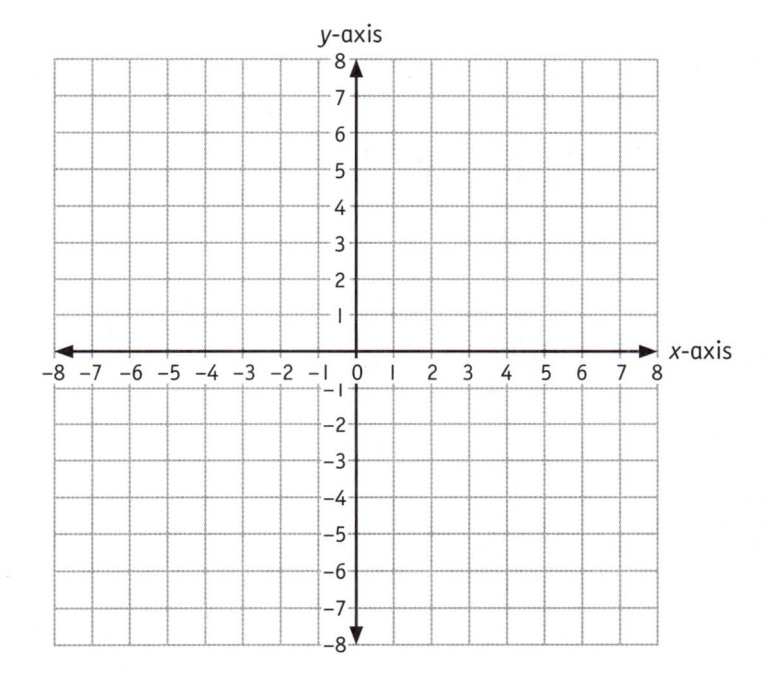

Extra Challenge

What are the coordinates of the top right corners of the windows?

Window 1 is at (___, ___).

Window 2 is at (___, ___).

Window 3 is at (___, ___).

Window 4 is at (___, ___).

TERM 2

UNIT 10 — Number & Algebra

AC9M6N04

Estimating and Rounding

I find I can make mistakes even when using a calculator. Maybe I've pressed a wrong number or put the decimal point in the wrong place.

I know that mistakes like that can happen which is why it is important to make an estimate of the answer before keying in the numbers.

In the following problems, the numbers go to three decimal places, so round up or down and estimate the answer before checking with your calculator.

	Example	Estimate	Check
①	36·759 + 27·285	37 + 27	36·759 + 27·285
②	28·369 − 17·856		28·369 − 17·856
③	18·359 + 17·543		18·359 + 17·543
④	39·763 + 27·835		39·763 + 27·835
⑤	56·754 − 27·836		56·754 − 27·836

	Example	Estimate	Check
⑥	74·439 − 36·872		74·439 − 36·872
⑦	39·496 + 27·878		39·496 + 27·878
⑧	56·989 − 17·635		56·989 − 17·635
⑨	56·747 + 101·835		56·747 + 101·835

SCORE /9   0-4   5-7   8-9

Quick Check

Round these decimals to the nearest whole number.

① 37·654 rounds to _____.
② 38·499 rounds to _____.
③ 46·756 rounds to _____.
④ 33·432 rounds to _____.
⑤ 18·099 rounds to _____.
⑥ 27·6584 rounds to _____.
⑦ 13·4896 rounds to _____.
⑧ 54·4359 rounds to _____.
⑨ 108·7366 rounds to _____.
⑩ 200·8932 rounds to _____.

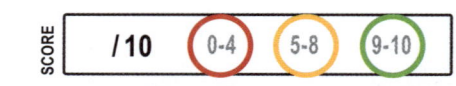

SCORE /10   0-4   5-8   9-10

Number & Algebra

UNIT 10
AC9M6N03

Which Fraction Is the Larger?

To show which of two fractions is the larger or the smaller, we use these symbols:
> to mean **greater than** and **<** to mean **less than**.

For example, you know that **6 is greater than 3** and that **5 is less than 9**. These are written as: **6 > 3** and **5 < 9**.

I like to think of the greater than symbol > as 'shrink me down' and the less than symbol < as 'grow me up'.

Use equivalent fractions to find which fraction is the larger.
Use the > symbol to show your answer. Sara has completed the first one for you.

	Fractions	Equivalent fractions	Show which is larger
①	$\frac{2}{5}$ or $\frac{1}{2}$	$\frac{4}{10}$ or $\frac{5}{10}$	$\frac{1}{2} > \frac{2}{5}$
②	$\frac{2}{3}$ or $\frac{3}{4}$		
③	$\frac{2}{3}$ or $\frac{5}{8}$		

Use equivalent fractions to find which fraction is the smaller.
Use the < symbol to show your answer.

	Fractions	Equivalent fractions	Show which is smaller
④	$\frac{2}{3}$ or $\frac{3}{5}$		
⑤	$\frac{5}{6}$ or $\frac{7}{9}$		
⑥	$\frac{3}{7}$ or $\frac{2}{5}$		

SCORE /6   0-2   3-4   5-6

Statistics & Probability

AC9M6ST03

Fake Data

You have heard of fake news.
Well, there is **fake data** as well.

It is not made-up data because the data is usually factual, but the way in which the data is presented gives a distorted view of the information.

The graph shows crowd sizes at the local women's soccer club.

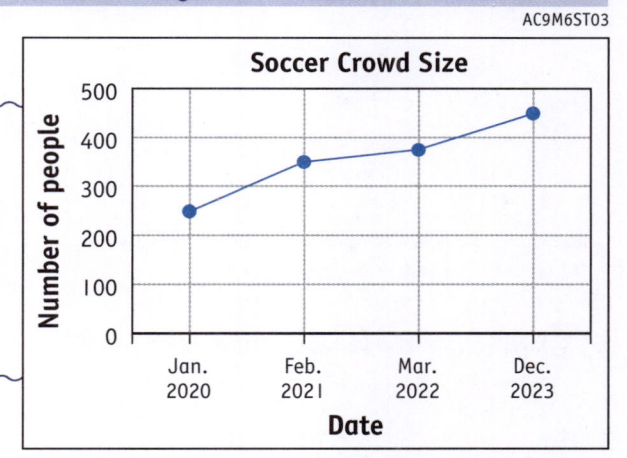

Soccer Crowd Size
(Line graph with Number of people on y-axis 0–500, Date on x-axis showing Jan. 2020 (~250), Feb. 2021 (~350), Mar. 2022 (~380), Dec. 2023 (~450))

① When did the crowd size increase the most? _____

② When did the crowd size increase the least? _____

③ Look again at the graph and notice that the timeline is misleading.

How is the timeline misleading? _____

④ How is the graph misrepresenting the data? _____

⑤ What would be a more accurate way of showing the timeline?

_____

SCORE /5   0-2   3-4   5

UNIT 10 — Measurement & Space

AC9M6SP01

Right Prisms

To understand and use the definition of a right prism, you need to know these words.

Two shapes are called **congruent** if they are the same shape and size.

Congruent 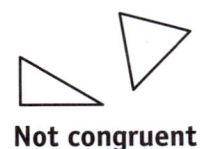 | **Not congruent**

Two lines or shapes are called **parallel** if they point in the same direction.

Parallel | **Not parallel**

Two shapes are **similar** to each other if they are the same shape, but not necessarily the same size.

Similar  | **Not similar**

TERM 2

When you make a slice parallel to the base of these solids, will the cross-section shape be similar or congruent to the base?

1. A square-based prism's cross-section is **similar / congruent** to the base.

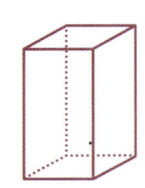

2. A square-based pyramid's cross-section is **similar / congruent** to the base.

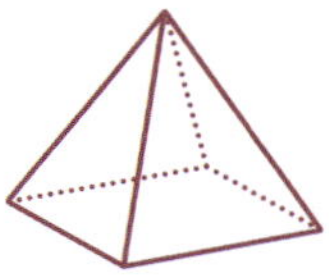

3. A hexagonal-based prism's cross-section is **similar / congruent** to the base.

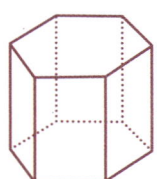

4. A parallellogram prism's cross-section is **similar / congruent** to the base.

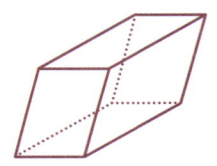

5. A cone's cross-section is **similar / congruent** to the base.

6. A pentagonal prism's cross-section is **similar / congruent** to the base.

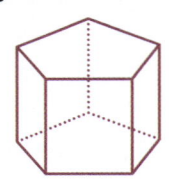

SCORE /6   0-2   3-4   5-6

NAPLAN*-style Questions

1. Which of these fractions has the largest value?
   ○ $\frac{5}{8}$ ○ $\frac{7}{12}$ ○ $\frac{1}{3}$ ○ $\frac{1}{2}$

2. Which is the most reasonable estimate for 36·957 − 18·499?
   ○ 18   ○ 55   ○ 19   ○ 17

3. 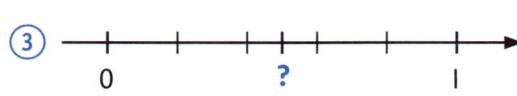
   ```
   +---+---+---?---+---+---+---+---+---+---+
   0           ?                           1
   ```
   Which of these fractions is represented by the ? on the number line?
   ○ $\frac{4}{10}$ ○ $\frac{5}{10}$ ○ $\frac{6}{10}$ ○ $\frac{7}{10}$

SCORE /3   0-1   2   3

TARGETING MATHS HOMEWORK: YEAR 6 © PASCAL PRESS ISBN: 9781925726596

Problem of the Week

UNIT 10

Matching Pairs

"Good morning, class," said Mr Green. "I was early to school today and so I had time to write these numbers on the board for you to work on.

"If you use rounding to the nearest whole number, you will find pairs of numbers that either add to 10 or whose difference is 10.

"Good luck finding six pairs.

"Please talk quietly to each other as you work on this challenge.

"Please start work now!"

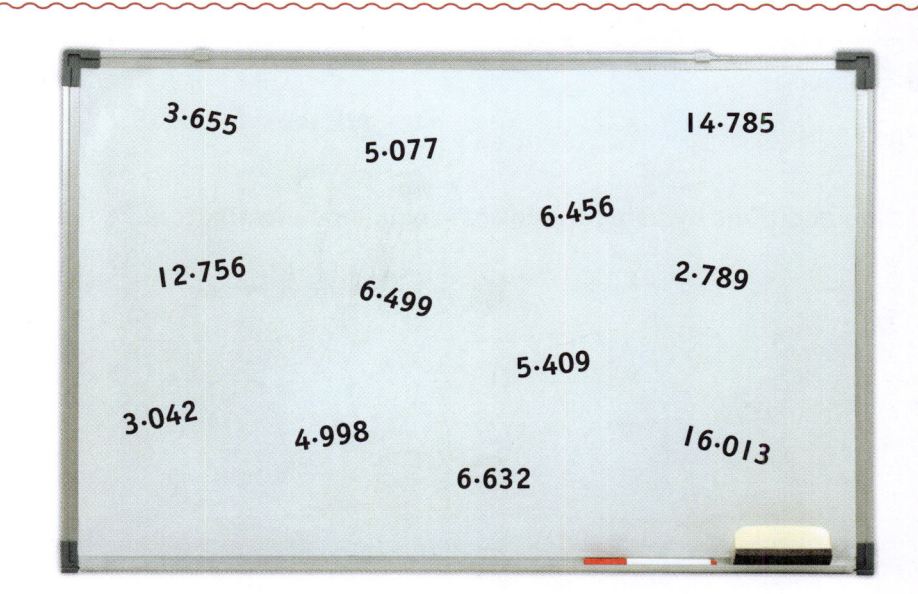

Numbers on the board:
3·655, 5·077, 14·785, 6·456, 12·756, 6·499, 2·789, 5·409, 3·042, 4·998, 16·013, 6·632

Find six pairs that either add to 10 or whose difference is 10.

Numbers on the board	Round and add or subtract
①	
②	
③	
④	
⑤	
⑥	

Extra Challenge

Make up three more pairs that add to 10 or whose difference is 10.

Pair 1: _____ and _____

Pair 2: _____ and _____

Pair 3: _____ and _____

UNIT 11 — Number & Algebra

AC9M6N05

Adding Fractions

If you have two fractions to add and they do not have the same denominator, you have to find the **lowest common denominator** of the two fractions.

For $\frac{3}{4} + \frac{1}{2}$ it is easy to see that 4 is the lowest common denominator.

For $\frac{3}{5} + \frac{2}{3}$ the lowest common denominator is not 5 or 3 but 3 × 5 which is 15.

To change 5ths to 15ths you have to multiply 5 by 3.
To change 3rds to 15ths you have to multiply 3 by 5.

But be careful! When you multiply the denominator, you also have to multiply the numerator by the same amount.

$\frac{3}{5}$ becomes $\frac{9}{15}$ and $\frac{2}{3}$ becomes $\frac{10}{15}$.

Now you can add the 15ths: $\frac{9}{15} + \frac{10}{15} = \frac{19}{15} = 1\frac{4}{15}$

Complete these fraction additions by using the lowest common denominators.

① $\frac{1}{4} + \frac{1}{2} = \underline{} + \underline{} = \underline{}$

② $\frac{2}{9} + \frac{2}{3} = \underline{} + \underline{} = \underline{}$

③ $\frac{3}{4} + \frac{5}{16} = \underline{} + \underline{} = \underline{}$

④ $\frac{3}{5} + \frac{4}{10} = \underline{} + \underline{} = \underline{}$

⑤ $\frac{3}{5} + \frac{8}{15} = \underline{} + \underline{} = \underline{}$

⑥ $\frac{3}{8} + \frac{7}{24} = \underline{} + \underline{} = \underline{}$

⑦ $\frac{1}{2} + \frac{2}{3} = \underline{} + \underline{} = \underline{}$

⑧ $\frac{3}{7} + \frac{1}{3} = \underline{} + \underline{} = \underline{}$

⑨ $\frac{2}{5} + \frac{5}{8} = \underline{} + \underline{} = \underline{}$

⑩ $\frac{5}{6} + \frac{7}{9} = \underline{} + \underline{} = \underline{}$

⑪ $\frac{4}{5} + \frac{2}{3} = \underline{} + \underline{} = \underline{}$

⑫ $\frac{5}{6} + \frac{5}{8} = \underline{} + \underline{} = \underline{}$

SCORE /12   0-5   6-10   11-12

Quick Check

What is the lowest common denominator of these fraction pairs?

① $\frac{1}{2}$ and $\frac{5}{6}$ ____

② $\frac{3}{5}$ and $\frac{7}{20}$ ____

③ $\frac{1}{2}$ and $\frac{5}{6}$ ____

④ $\frac{3}{7}$ and $\frac{5}{14}$ ____

⑤ $\frac{3}{8}$ and $\frac{7}{16}$ ____

⑥ $\frac{1}{5}$ and $\frac{5}{8}$ ____

⑦ $\frac{1}{14}$ and $\frac{5}{21}$ ____

⑧ $\frac{4}{15}$ and $\frac{7}{12}$ ____

⑨ $\frac{7}{18}$ and $\frac{11}{12}$ ____

⑩ $\frac{1}{25}$ and $\frac{9}{20}$ ____

SCORE /10   0-4   5-8   9-10

Number & Algebra

UNIT 11

AC9M6A01

Fraction Sequences

Draw and label the next fractions in these sequences.

	A	B	C	D	E	F
①	$\frac{1}{4}$	$\frac{3}{4}$	$1\frac{1}{4}$	$1\frac{3}{4}$		
②						
③						

Continue these fraction sequences.

④ $\frac{1}{2}, \frac{4}{6}, \frac{5}{6},$ ___, ___, ___

⑤ $3\frac{5}{8}, 3\frac{1}{2}, 3\frac{3}{8},$ ___, ___, ___

⑥ $2\frac{5}{10}, 2\frac{3}{10}, 2\frac{1}{10},$ ___, ___, ___

⑦ $4, 3\frac{1}{3}, 2\frac{2}{3},$ ___, ___, ___

SCORE /7   0-3   4-5   6-7

TERM 2

Statistics & Probability

AC9M6P01

A Colour Spinner

This is a five-sided colour spinner.

① Using this spinner, what is the chance of spinning red? ____%

② Is there an equal chance of spinning any of the colours? _____

③ Out of 9 spins, blue was the outcome in the first 4 spins. What is the chance of spinning a red in the next 5 spins?

___ in ___ chance

④ This is the tally chart of the outcomes of spins. Write the percentage of spins for each colour.

	Red	Yellow	Blue	Green	Black
Spins	||			|||		||||
Percentage					

⑤ Do the percentages add to 100%?

○ Yes   ○ No

SCORE /5   0-2   3-4   5

UNIT 11

Measurement & Space

AC9M6M01

Measurement Units

I really like it in the shows I watch when the police tape off a crime scene.
So I make up my own crime scene problems for my friends.
Here are some for you to work out.
The measurements written on the sides are actual measurements.
Use the scale to work out the missing measurement. The scale is 1 cm to 1 m.

TERM 2

① The police marked off this crime scene shape.
What is the length of the missing side?

_____ m

3750 mm
2·6 m   Scale: 1 cm = 1 m   ?
500 cm

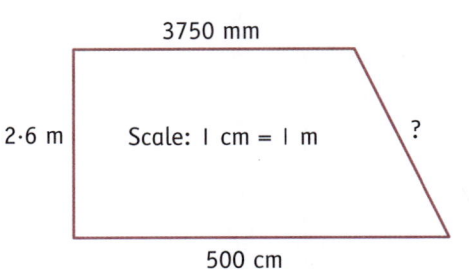

② How much tape did the police use altogether?

_____ m

③ The police marked off this crime scene shape.
What is the length of the missing side?

_____ m

420 cm
$2\frac{1}{2}$ m   Scale: 1 cm = 1 m   ?
3·75 m

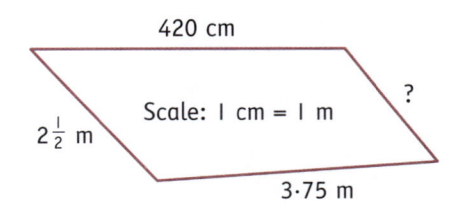

④ How much tape did the police use altogether?

_____ m

SCORE /4   0-1   2-3   4

NAPLAN*-style Questions

① What number must be added to $1\frac{3}{5}$ to make $2\frac{2}{5}$?

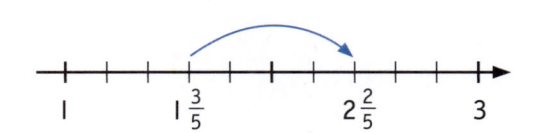

○ 1   ○ $1\frac{1}{5}$ ○ $\frac{4}{5}$ ○ $2\frac{1}{5}$

1    $1\frac{3}{5}$ $2\frac{2}{5}$ 3

② Hai made up this fraction addition rule: Add $\frac{1}{6}$ and double the result.
Using this rule, her pattern sequence starts as $\frac{1}{2}$, $1\frac{2}{6}$, 3.
What is the fourth number in Hai's sequence?

③ The perimeter of this shape is 11·75 m.
What is the length of the ? side?

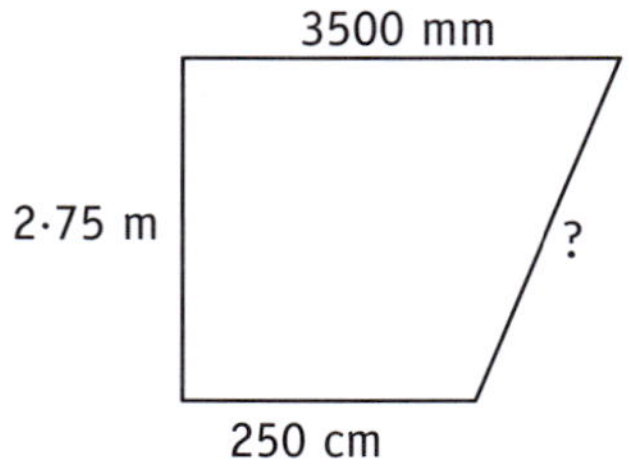

3500 mm
2·75 m   ?
250 cm

Note: This diagram is not
to the scale of 1 cm to 1 m.

SCORE /3   0-1   2   3

48   TARGETING MATHS HOMEWORK: YEAR 6 © PASCAL PRESS ISBN: 9781925726596

Problem of the Week

UNIT 11

Sequences of Fractions

Ruby, Elsa, Tau and Liam have been making fraction sequences.

Sequence 1	$\frac{3}{8}, \frac{10}{16}, \frac{7}{8}, 1\frac{1}{8}, 1\frac{6}{16}, 1\frac{5}{8}, \frac{15}{8}$
Sequence 2	$\frac{2}{8}, \frac{5}{10}, \frac{3}{4}, 1, \frac{6}{4}, 1\frac{4}{8}, \frac{14}{8}, \frac{10}{5}$
Sequence 3	$\frac{4}{8}, \frac{4}{6}, \frac{10}{12}, \frac{7}{7}, \frac{7}{6}, 1\frac{1}{3}, \frac{9}{6}$
Sequence 4	$\frac{3}{16}, \frac{2}{8}, \frac{5}{16}, \frac{3}{8}, \frac{14}{32}, \frac{12}{24}, \frac{9}{16}$

They also wrote two clues so that you can work out who made which fraction sequence.

Clue 1: Ruby does not have a half or the equivalent of a half in her sequences.

Clue 2: The first fraction in Liam's sequence is one-sixteenth smaller than the first fraction in Elsa's sequence.

The Challenge

Follow the clues that Ruby, Elsa, Tau and Liam left to identify who made up which sequence.

Ruby made up Sequence ___.

Elsa made up Sequence ___.

Tau made up Sequence ___.

Liam made up Sequence ___.

UNIT 12 — Number & Algebra

AC9M6N06

Multiplying Decimal Numbers

In Unit 4 you learnt about multiplying and dividing decimal numbers by 10 or 100. You can also use those rules when you have to multiply by a number such as 30.

Let's look at how you might find **33·2 × 30**.

Step 1: Split 30 into 10 × 3.
Step 2: 33·2 × 10 = 332
Step 3: 332 × 3 = 996

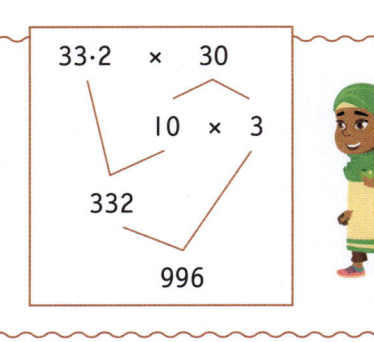

33·2 × 30
10 × 3
332
996

Use Sara's strategy to complete these multiplications.

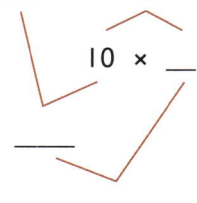

1. 42·5 × 40
   10 × ___

2. 31·3 × 30
   ___ × ___

3. 32·4 × 40
   ___ × ___

4. 56·5 × 200
   ___ × ___

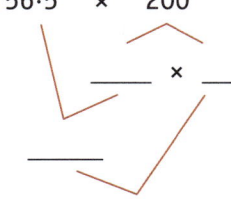

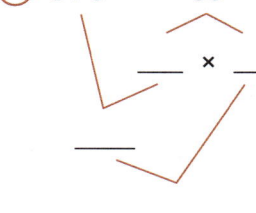

5. 50·5 × 300
   ___ × ___

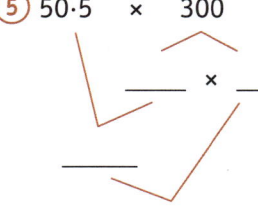

6. 3·45 × 400
   ___ × ___

7. 25·06 × 40
   ___ × ___

8. 150·7 × 70
   ___ × ___

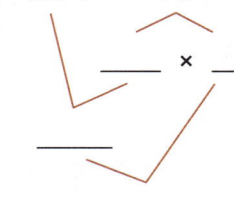

9. 24·7 × 300
   ___ × ___

SCORE /9   0-4   5-7   8-9

Quick Check

1. 3·5 × 20 = _____
2. 6·3 × 30 = _____
3. 7·6 × 200 = _____
4. 3·2 × 800 = _____
5. 4·5 × 400 = _____
6. 3·43 × 200 = _____
7. 1·26 × 200 = _____
8. 2·32 × 300 = _____
9. 5·05 × 700 = _____
10. 2·222 × 2000 = _____

SCORE /10   0-4   5-8   9-10

Number & Algebra

UNIT 12

Dividing Decimal Numbers

You have just learnt about multiplying decimal numbers. It's time to extend that strategy to dividing decimal numbers.

Let's look at how you might find **996 ÷ 30**.

Step 1: Split ÷ 30 into ÷ 3 and then ÷ 10.
Step 2: 996 ÷ 3 = 332.
Step 3: 332 ÷ 10 = 33·2

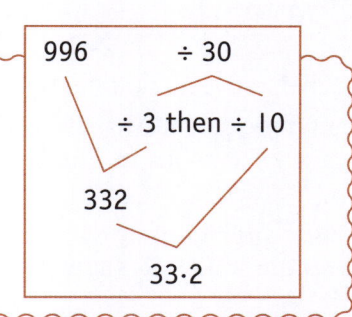

```
996    ÷ 30
   ÷ 3 then ÷ 10
332
      33·2
```

Use Sara's strategy to complete these divisions.

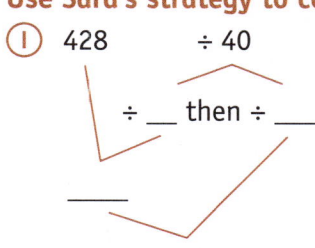

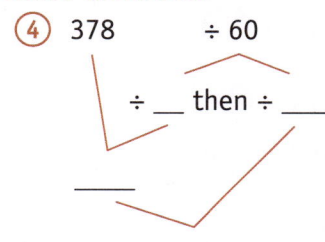

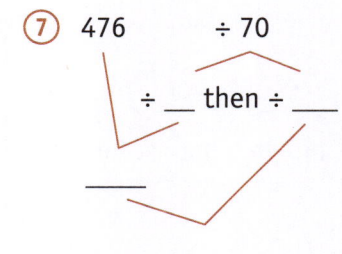

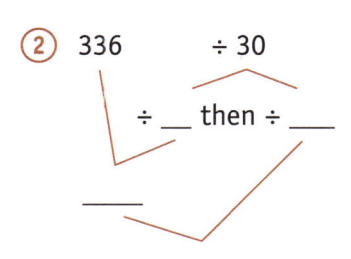

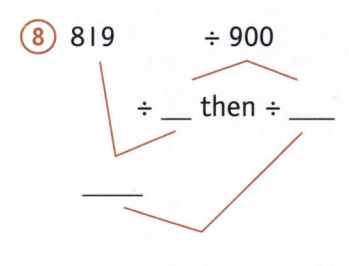

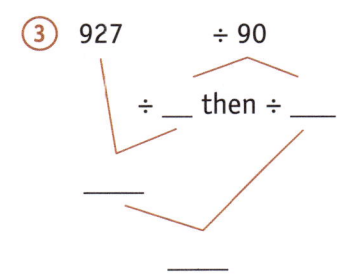

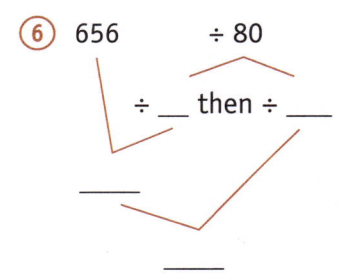

1. 428 ÷ 40
   ÷ __ then ÷ ___

2. 336 ÷ 30
   ÷ __ then ÷ ___

3. 927 ÷ 90
   ÷ __ then ÷ ___

4. 378 ÷ 60
   ÷ __ then ÷ ___

5. 427 ÷ 70
   ÷ __ then ÷ ___

6. 656 ÷ 80
   ÷ __ then ÷ ___

7. 476 ÷ 70
   ÷ __ then ÷ ___

8. 819 ÷ 900
   ÷ __ then ÷ ___

SCORE /8   0-3   4-6   7-8

Statistics & Probability

Rainfall Record

The chart shows the monthly rainfall for Adelaide and Brisbane from September to November.

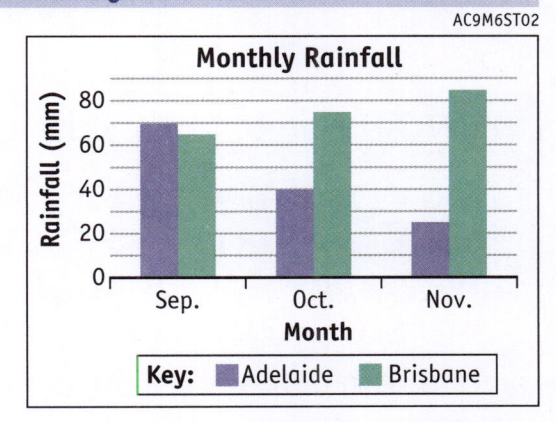

1. How much less rain did Brisbane have than Adelaide in September? ____ mm
2. How much more rain did Brisbane have than Adelaide in November? ____ mm
3. How much rain did Adelaide have in the three months? ____ mm
4. How much more rain did Brisbane have than Adelaide in the three months? ____ mm

Monthly Rainfall (Rainfall (mm) vs Month: Sep., Oct., Nov.)
Key: Adelaide, Brisbane

SCORE /4   0-1   2-3   4

TERM 2

51

UNIT 12

Measurement & Space

AC9M6M01

Converting Metric Units

Chefs have to be able to scale a recipe up or down to match an order.
If a recipe calls for 250 g of meat and Chef has to cook 5 servings, then she needs to find 5 × 250 g, which is 1250 g or 1·25 kg.

**Work out the quantities needed for these orders.
Use the boxes to show your thinking.**

① 75 g of flour for one pancake. How much flour for 12 pancakes?

_____ g or _____ kg

② 450 mL of stock for 4 soup servings. How much stock for 8 servings?

_____ mL or _____ L

③ 375 g sugar for 6 muffins. How much sugar for 2 dozen muffins?

_____ g or _____ kg

④ 0·75 kg of peanut butter for 3 dozen dog biscuits. How much peanut butter for 12 dog biscuits?

_____ kg or _____ g

⑤ $1\frac{1}{2}$ kg of flour for 6 loaves of bread. How much flour for 3 loaves?

_____ kg or _____ g

SCORE /5   0-2   3-4   5

NAPLAN*-style Questions

① Min bought 30 balloons at $1·75 each. How much did Min spend? $_____

② The farmer spent $968 on 40 laying chickens. How much was each chicken? $_____

③ The apprentice chef used a 250 mL measuring cup to measure out 3 L of stock. Which of these equations did she need to use?

○ 3000 ÷ 250   ○ 3000 − 250
○ 3000 × 250   ○ 3000 + 250

SCORE /3   0-1   2   3

TERM 2

Problem of the Week

UNIT 12

Shopping for Camp

> "Good morning, class. We need to prepare our food shopping list for the items that you have chosen for our school camp: damper, gourmet sausages, tomatoes and orange juice."
>
> The class has collected this data for their school camp.
>
> 24 students and 4 adults are going to camp.
>
> They plan on having:
> - damper, which takes 125 g flour for a loaf for 4 people
> - 375 g of sausage per person
> - 1 tomato each. Tomatoes are about 100 g each
> - pure orange juice which comes in 750 mL bottles. Allow two 250 mL glasses per person.
>
> **Help the class make their shopping list. Use your calculator.**

The First Challenge
Complete the shopping list.

You will need:
- _____ kg of flour
- _____ kg of sausages
- _____ kg of tomatoes
- _____ L of orange juice.

The Second Challenge

Yes, you guessed it – they need to work out how much it is all going to cost.

They will pay by cash so some amounts will need to be rounded.

They collected this information from the local supermarket:

Flour is $3·50 for a 1 kg packet.	$_____
Gourmet sausages are $14·25 a kilogram.	$_____
Tomatoes are $6·99 a kilogram.	$_____
Pure orange juice is $6·50 per 750 mL.	$_____
Total Cost:	$_____

Working space

UNIT 13 — Number & Algebra

AC9M6N08, AC9M6N09

Percentage Discounts

I am quite happy to get questions such as: **A jacket was $85 was marked down by 30%. What was the new price?**

It can seem quite daunting, but when I use the bar model I find it a lot easier than you might think. First, you draw a bar to represent 100%.

Then you can divide it into tenths because $\frac{1}{10}$ is 10%.

To mark off the discount, you can fill three of the spaces with $8·50 which is 10% of $85.

| $8·50 | $8·50 | $8·50 | | | | | | | |

The discount
3 × $8·50 = $25·50

The jacket is now
7 × $8·50 = $59·50

When the 30% discount is taken off the original price of $85, the bar model shows that it is now priced at $59·50.

Use the bar model to answer these questions.

① A $39 T-shirt was marked down 40%. What does the T-shirt cost now? $_____

② A $45 book has been reduced by 60%. What does the book cost now? $_____

③ Hai saved 40% on a $52 book. How much did Hai save? $_____

④ SuperAir Travel have reduced their $3330 flight to Europe by 60%. What does their flight to Europe cost now? $_____

⑤ Matinee movie tickets are 15% cheaper than the $24 evening tickets. How much do Liam and Elsa each save by going to the matinee? $_____

SCORE /5   0-2   3-4   5

Quick Check

① 10% of $65 = $_____
② 20% of $30 = $_____
③ 25% of $60 = $_____
④ 1% of $60 = _____
⑤ 11% of $34 = $_____
⑥ 70% of $350 = $_____
⑦ 15% of $120 = $_____
⑧ 22% of $200 = $_____
⑨ 35% of $300 = $_____
⑩ 20% of $300 = $_____

SCORE /10   0-4   5-8   9-10

Number & Algebra

UNIT 13

AC9M6N08

Fractions, Decimals and Percentages

Fractions, decimals and percentages are different ways of expressing the same mathematical idea.
$\frac{1}{2} = \frac{5}{10} = 0.5 = 50\%$
We can use these relationships to help work out percentages.
There are two ways of working out percentages using a calculator.
To solve **12% of 80**:
- If the calculator has a % key, then simply key in [8][0][×][1][2][%][=] (9.6).
- If the calculator does not have a % key, change the % to a decimal and multiply by the decimal, [8][0][×][0][.][1][2][=] (9.6).

Show both ways to work out these percentage questions.
Use your calculator to include the result each time.

Percentage to find	Calculator with a % key	Calculator without a % key
① 36% of 120	[1][2][0][×][3][6][%][=][=] (43.2)	[1][2][0][×][0][.][3][6][=][=] (43.2)
② 42% of 74		
③ 17% of 1300		
④ 58% of 4250		
⑤ 73% of 247		

SCORE /5   0-2   3-4   5

Statistics & Probability

AC9M6ST03

A Graph of Exercise Times

Stoke Primary School was concerned that students were spending more time in front of screens each day than outdoors exercising. So they did a survey. The chart shows the results of the survey.

Daily Exercise Time for 9–12 Years

0-5   6-15   16-25   26-35   36-45
Minutes

Key: ● = 10 students

① How many students were surveyed? _____

② What is the range of the data collected?

From ___ to ___

③ What is the mode of the data collected? _____

④ What does the shape of the data suggest?

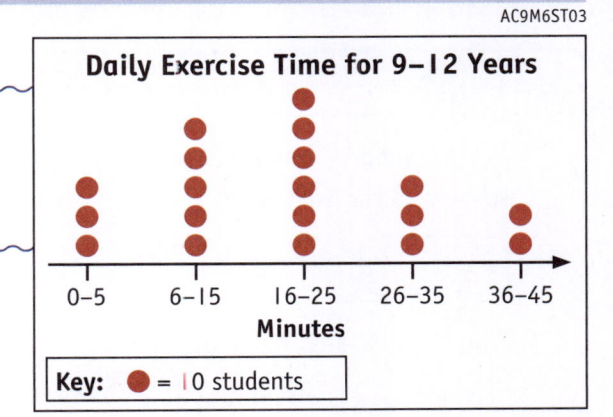

_____

⑤ How many more students do less than 16 minutes daily exercise than do more than 25 minutes daily?

___ students

SCORE /5   0-2   3-4   5

TERM 2

TARGETING MATHS HOMEWORK: YEAR 6 © PASCAL PRESS ISBN: 9781925726596

UNIT 13

Measurement & Space

AC9M6SP02, AC9M6SP03

Translation of a Shape

Ruby drew a quadrilateral ABCD in Quadrant 1 and then translated and reflected it into the other quadrants.

For the quadrilateral in Quadrant 2, Ruby translated ABCD eight units to the left and called it Shape 2.

For the quadrilateral in Quadrant 3, Ruby translated Shape 2 eight units down and called it Shape 3.

For the quadrilateral in Quadrant 4, Ruby reflected Shape 3 in the y-axis.

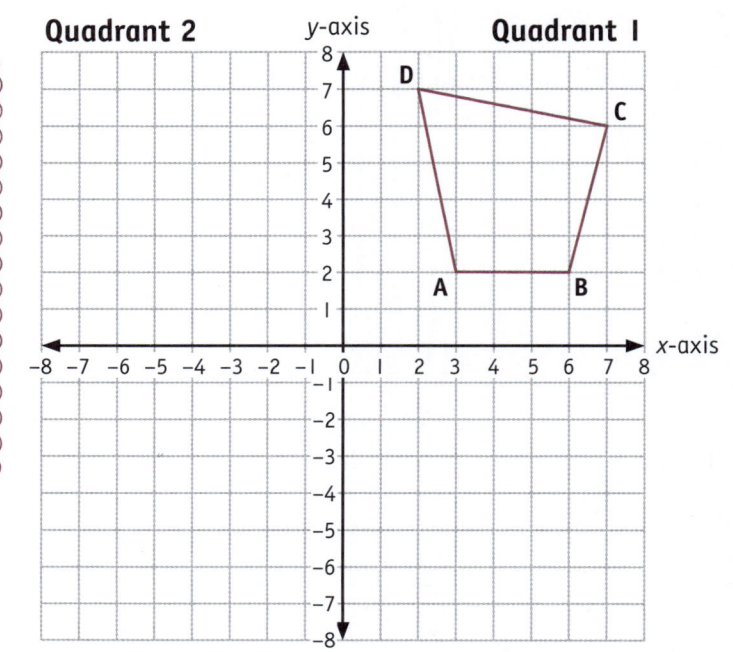

① What are the coordinate pairs for the original quadrilateral?

A = (___, ___)   C = (___, ___)
B = (___, ___)   D = (___, ___)

② Complete the quadrilaterals in the other quadrants.
Label the points A B C and D to show where they came from.

List the coordinate pairs for each of the new quadrilaterals.

③ **Quadrant 2, Shape 2** A = (___, ___), B = (___, ___), C = (___, ___) and D = (___, ___)

④ **Quadrant 3, Shape 3** A = (___, ___), B = (___, ___), C = (___, ___) and D = (___, ___)

⑤ **Quadrant 4, Shape 4** A = (___, ___), B = (___, ___), C = (___, ___) and D = (___, ___)

SCORE /5   0-2   3-4   5

NAPLAN*-style Questions

① A $125 scooter was reduced by 11% in the sale.
What was the sale price?

② What is 45% as a decimal fraction?
○ 4·5   ○ 4·50   ○ 4·05   ○ 0·45

③ Look at the triangle drawn on the Cartesian plane.
What are the coordinates of point C?

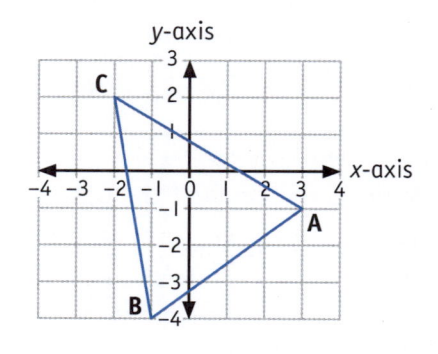

SCORE /3   0-1   2   3

56   TARGETING MATHS HOMEWORK: YEAR 6 © PASCAL PRESS ISBN: 9781925726596

Problem of the Week

UNIT 13

Best Buy

Four shops each have the same four items on special at the moment.

Shop 1

Items	Price	Discount	Amount Saved
Anorak	$135	25%	
Shorts	$65	25%	
Thongs	$48·60	25%	
T-shirt	$40	25%	

Shop 2

Items	Price	Discount	Amount Saved
Anorak	$135	30%	
Shorts	$65	10%	
Thongs	$48·60	15%	
T-shirt	$40	20%	

Shop 3

Items	Price	Discount	Amount Saved
Anorak	$135	12%	
Shorts	$65	Half price	
Thongs	$48·60	15%	
T-shirt	$40	22%	

Shop 4

Items	Price	Discount	Amount Saved
Anorak	$135	Save $15	
Shorts	$65	Save $19	
Thongs	$48·60	Save a third	
T-shirt	$40	Save $10	

TERM 2

How much would be saved by buying all four items at each shop?

	Amount saved
Shop 1	$
Shop 2	$
Shop 3	$
Shop 4	$

If you bought each item from the shop with the best deal, how much would you save from the original prices?

Items	From which shop?	Amount saved
Anorak		$
Shorts		$
Thongs		$
T-shirt		$
	Total saving	

TARGETING MATHS HOMEWORK: YEAR 6 © PASCAL PRESS ISBN: 9781925726596

UNIT 14 — Number & Algebra

AC9M6A02

Numerical Equations

In this equation, there are two unknown numbers that will make the equation balance:

2 × 6 + 4 = 3 × ☐ + ☐

Here is one way to solve this equation.

Step 1: Use **order of operations** to find the value of the first part of the equation by doing the multiplication and then the addition.
2 × 6 = 12, 12 + 4 = **16**

Step 2: Find a combination that matches the given numeral and operation in the second part of the equation to make the two parts balance. For example:
2 × 6 + 4 = 3 × **5** + **1**

There is more than just this one solution. 3 × 4 + 4 and 3 × 3 + 7 will also balance the equation.

Find the unknowns in these equations and give two possible solutions for each one.

1. 6 + 3 × 7 = 5 × ☐ + ☐
   = 5 × ☐ + ☐

2. 6 + 3 × 7 = 4 × ☐ − ☐
   = 4 × ☐ − ☐

3. 8 × 3 + 6 = 7 × ☐ + ☐
   = 7 × ☐ + ☐

4. 8 × 3 − 4 = 6 × ☐ + ☐
   = 6 × ☐ + ☐

5. 5 × 9 + 3 = 9 × ☐ + ☐
   = 9 × ☐ + ☐

6. 7 × 9 + 6 = 8 × ☐ − ☐
   = 8 × ☐ − ☐

7. 4 + 6 × 7 = 8 × ☐ + ☐
   = 8 × ☐ + ☐

8. 4 × 7 + 3 = 24 ÷ ☐ + ☐
   = 24 ÷ ☐ + ☐

9. 8 + 6 × 3 = 10 × ☐ − ☐
   = 10 × ☐ − ☐

10. 36 ÷ 9 + 4 = 24 ÷ ☐ + ☐
    = 24 ÷ ☐ + ☐

SCORE /10   0–4   5–8   9–10

Quick Check

1. 6 × 5 + 6 = ☐
2. 3 + 7 × 8 = ☐
3. 27 ÷ 9 + 6 = ☐
4. 36 ÷ 4 + ☐ = 13
5. 56 ÷ ☐ + 8 = 15
6. ☐ × 6 + 5 = 41
7. ☐ ÷ 8 + 3 = 6
8. 6 × ☐ + 3 = 51
9. 7 × ☐ + 4 = 53
10. 35 ÷ ☐ + 7 = 12

SCORE /10   0–4   5–8   9–10

Number & Algebra

UNIT 14

AC9M6A02, AC9M6N09

Sticky Word Problems

**Write the number sentences and answers for these word problems.
The first one has been started for you.**

1. Min had 6 packets of 8 butterfly stickers, 8 bird stickers and 3 packets of 6 bug stickers. How many stickers did Min have altogether?

    6 × 8 + 8 + 3 × 6   48 + 8 + 18 = _____   Min had _____ stickers.

2. Alex had 48 stickers and put $\frac{1}{3}$ of them in his sticker folder.
    Then he gave his 11 spider stickers to Hai because he doesn't like spiders.
    How many stickers does he have left to add to his folder?

    _____ Alex has _____ stickers left.

3. Liam bought 6 packets of 12 stickers which he then divided equally among 4 pages in his sticker folder. How many did he put on each page?

    _____ Liam put _____ stickers on each page.

4. Elsa had 6 truck stickers, 2 packets of 12 car stickers, 3 packets of 8 motorbike stickers and 3 super car stickers. How may stickers does Elsa have altogether?

    _____ Elsa has _____ stickers altogether.

5. Tau bought 3 packets of stickers at $3·50 a packet and 6 packets of stickers at $2·75 a packet. He started with $60. How much does he have left now?

    _____ Tau has $_____ left.

SCORE /5   0-2   3-4   5

Statistics & Probability

AC9M6P01

Weather Predictions

1. On the chart below, mark yesterday's weather and today's weather using symbols such as these:

	Yesterday	Today	Day 1	Day 2	Day 3	Day 4
Actual						
Predict						
Chance						

2. Now make an informed prediction for the next 4 days based on the weather of the last 2 days.

3. For each day, write a chance of between 1 and 10 to show how likely you think your prediction is. 1 means impossible and 10 means certain.

4. For the next 4 days, record the actual weather on the chart.

5. Compare your predictions with the actual weather. Explain why you think your predictions were or were not accurate.

    _____

    _____

SCORE /5   0-2   3-4   5

TERM 2

UNIT 14

Measurement & Space

AC9M6M04

Angles

There are specific terms and facts that are important in the study of angles. Two of these terms are **complementary** angles and **supplementary** angles.

Complementary angles are two angles that together equal a right angle or 90°.

Supplementary angles are two angles that together equal a straight-line angle or 180°.

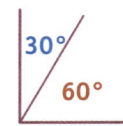

Complementary angles: 30°, 60°

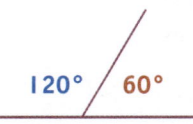

Supplementary angles: 120°, 60°

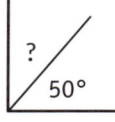

This diagram has an unlabelled angle.
The unmarked angle is the complement of 50°.
The complement to 50° that makes 90° is 40°.

TERM 2

Write the complement of these angles.

① _____° (50°)

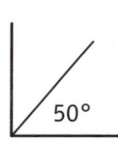

② _____° (15°)

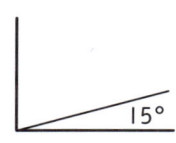

③ _____° (22°)

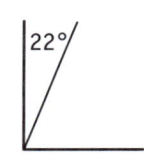

④ _____° (35°)

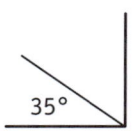

Write the supplement of these angles.

⑤ _____° (70°)

⑥ _____° (105°)

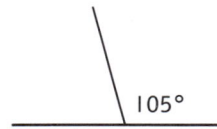

⑦ _____° (50°)

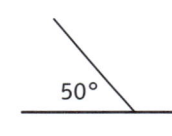

⑧ _____°

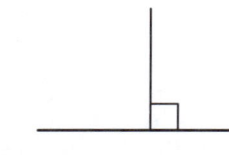

SCORE /8   0–3   4–6   7–8

NAPLAN*-style Questions

① What number does ☐ represent in this equation? _____

$3 \times \square + 6 = 21$

② Tau bought 3 sets of 12 car collector cards, 6 special cards and 4 sets of 8 truck collector cards. Which expression shows how to work out how many cards Tau bought altogether?

○ 3 + 12 + 6 + 6 + 4 + 8
○ 3 + 12 × 6 + 4 × 8
○ 3 × 12 + 6 + 4 × 8
○ 3 + 12 × 6 + 4 + 8

③ What is the size of angle A?

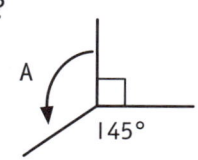

☐   A, 145°

SCORE /3   0–1   2   3

60   TARGETING MATHS HOMEWORK: YEAR 6 © PASCAL PRESS ISBN: 9781925726596

Problem of the Week

UNIT 14

Make the Number 30

Sara, Min, Alex and Hai have made up a new game that uses all the number cards from a normal pack of cards.

Rule 1: Shuffle the cards and place the top five cards face-up on the table.

Rule 2: Each player then uses the numbers that are on the table to make an expression with a value as close to 30 as possible.

Rule 3: The expression must include at least one of + and − as well as at least one of × and ÷.

Here are the five cards that were dealt in their last game:

[Cards: 4♥, 6♦, 3♥, 4♣, 5♠]

Sara: I got close with this expression:
6 × 4 − 5 + 4 + 3

Min: I got closer than Sara with my expression:
4 × 6 ÷ 3 × 4 − 3

Alex: I was nearly right with my expression:
4 × 3 + 6 + 4 + 5

Hai: I might be the winner with my expression:
(4 + 5) ÷ 3 × (6 + 4)

① Who was the winner? _____

Challenge

How close to 30 can you get with an expression that has the same numbers used by Sara, Min, Alex and Hai but is not the same expression as theirs?

② My expression is _____ = _____

Extra Challenge

What if these were the cards that were dealt?

[Cards: 8♦, 2♥, 6♥, 7♠, A♣]

Can you make an expression with these numbers that is close to or exactly 30?

③ My expression is _____ = _____

TERM 2

UNIT 15 — Number & Algebra

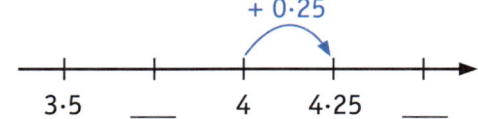

AC9M6A01, AC9M6A03

Number Sequences

To complete these missing number patterns, you need to look along the number line for hints. In the sequence below, there are two numbers that come right next to each other in the sequence: 4 and 4·25.

+ 0·25

3·5 ___ 4 4·25 ___

This hint tells us that the pattern rule is + 0·25 each time.
Using the hint, we can tell that the missing numbers are 3·75 and 4·5.

Complete these missing number pattern sequences. Write the rule for each sequence.

① 1·75, ___, 2·25, 2·5, ___, ___   The rule is _____

② 15, 3, 30, 6, ___, 12, ___, ___   The rule is _____

③ 6, 24, 12, ___, 24, ___, ___   The rule is _____

④ 0·075, 0·08, ___, 0·09, ___, ___   The rule is _____

⑤ 1, ___, 2⅓, 3, ___, ___, ___   The rule is _____

⑥ ⅗, ___, 1⅘, 2⅖, ___, ___, ___   The rule is _____

⑦ ½, ___, 1¼, 1⅝, ___, ___, ___   The rule is _____

⑧ ⅓, ___, 1⅙, 1 7/12, ___, ___, ___   The rule is _____

SCORE /8   0–3   4–6   7–8

Quick Check

Write the next two numbers in each of these sequences.

① ⅗, 7/10, ⅘, ___, ___

② 0·8, 0·84, 0·88, ___, ___

③ 27, 9, 18, ___, ___

④ 3½, 3⅜, 3¼, ___, ___

⑤ 10, 9·75, 9·5, ___, ___

⑥ 11·1, 11·075, 11·05, ___, ___

⑦ 6, 18, 30, ___, ___

⑧ 2, 4, 8, ___, ___

⑨ 21, 42, 63, ___, ___

⑩ 19, 21, 24, ___, ___

SCORE /10   0–4   5–8   9–10

Number & Algebra

UNIT 15
AC9M6N05

Subtracting Fractions

In Unit 11, I showed you how to find the **lowest common denominator** to make addition of fractions easier. You can use similar thinking with the subtraction of fractions.

To find $\frac{4}{5} - \frac{2}{3}$, you can use the lowest common denominator which in this case is 15.

$\frac{4}{5} - \frac{2}{3} = \frac{12}{15} - \frac{10}{15} = \frac{2}{15}$

Complete these fraction subtractions by using the lowest common denominator.

① $\frac{2}{3} - \frac{1}{2} = \underline{} - \underline{} = \underline{}$

② $\frac{3}{4} - \frac{2}{5} = \underline{} - \underline{} = \underline{}$

③ $\frac{5}{6} - \frac{4}{5} = \underline{} - \underline{} = \underline{}$

④ $\frac{3}{10} - \frac{1}{6} = \underline{} - \underline{} = \underline{}$

⑤ $\frac{2}{3} - \frac{3}{5} = \underline{} - \underline{} = \underline{}$

⑥ $\frac{5}{7} - \frac{2}{3} = \underline{} - \underline{} = \underline{}$

⑦ $\frac{3}{8} - \frac{1}{3} = \underline{} - \underline{} = \underline{}$

⑧ $\frac{3}{5} - \frac{1}{2} = \underline{} - \underline{} = \underline{}$

⑨ $\frac{7}{9} - \frac{4}{6} = \underline{} - \underline{} = \underline{}$

⑩ $\frac{3}{4} - \frac{5}{7} = \underline{} - \underline{} = \underline{}$

SCORE /10   0-5   6-8   9-10

Statistics & Probability

AC9M6ST03

Clown Dress-up Day

At the school clown dress-up day, people could choose combinations of hats, red noses, baggy pants and big shoes.

① Which item do you think would be the most popular? _____

Complete this diagram to find out how many people altogether had red noses.
- 6 people had only hats and 5 people had hats and red noses.
- 8 people had only baggy pants and 8 people had baggy pants and red noses.
- 3 people had baggy pants and hats.
- 9 people had only big shoes, and 10 people had big shoes and red noses.

	Hats	Red noses	Baggy pants	Big shoes
② **Hats**				
③ **Red noses**				
④ **Baggy pants**				
⑤ **Big shoes**				
⑥ **Totals**				

SCORE /6   0-2   3-4   5-6

TARGETING MATHS HOMEWORK: YEAR 6 © PASCAL PRESS ISBN: 9781925726596

UNIT 15

Measurement & Space

AC9M6M02

Area

The tiler has an interesting job to quote for. The floor of a kitchen and hall is to be covered in new tiles. He has been given the following plan, but it does not have every measurement.

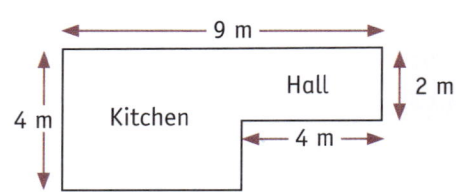

The tiler knows that he needs to divide the shape into two rectangles and find the lengths of the missing sides.

Use the tiler's plan to answer these questions.

1. How wide is the kitchen? _____ m

2. How wide is the hall? _____ m

3. How long is the kitchen? _____ m

4. How long is the hall? _____ m

5. What is the area of the kitchen? _____ m^2

6. What is the area of the hall? _____ m^2

7. What is the area of the hall and kitchen altogether? _____ m^2

8. The tiler has to allow 25% extra area because the tiles have a pattern that must be matched. The total area of tiles that he needs to order including the extra is how much?

    _____ m^2

9. The tiles are $69·95 per square metre. How much to the nearest dollar will the tiles cost?

    $_____

SCORE /9   0-4   5-7   8-9

NAPLAN*-style Questions

1. Tau jumped 2·25 m in the long jump competition. Ruby's jump was a tenth longer.

    How far did Ruby jump? _____ m

2. What is the difference between the fractions $\frac{2}{3}$ and $\frac{5}{8}$?

    ○ $\frac{3}{5}$ ○ $\frac{3}{8}$ ○ $\frac{7}{24}$ ○ $\frac{1}{24}$

3. What is the area of this shape?

    ○ 21 m^2
    ○ 22 m^2
    ○ 24 m^2
    ○ 28 m^2

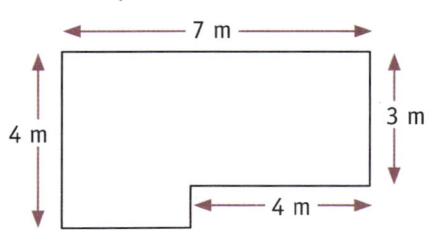

SCORE /3   0-1   2   3

TERM 2

64   TARGETING MATHS HOMEWORK: YEAR 6 © PASCAL PRESS ISBN: 9781925726596

Problem of the Week

UNIT 15

House Plans

Building a new house is expensive. Right at the end of the build there is even more expense because the floor coverings have to be bought.

Look at the house plan below. Notice how the measurements for each space have been written. 6 m × 5 m means that a room is a rectangle with sides of 6 metres and 5 metres.

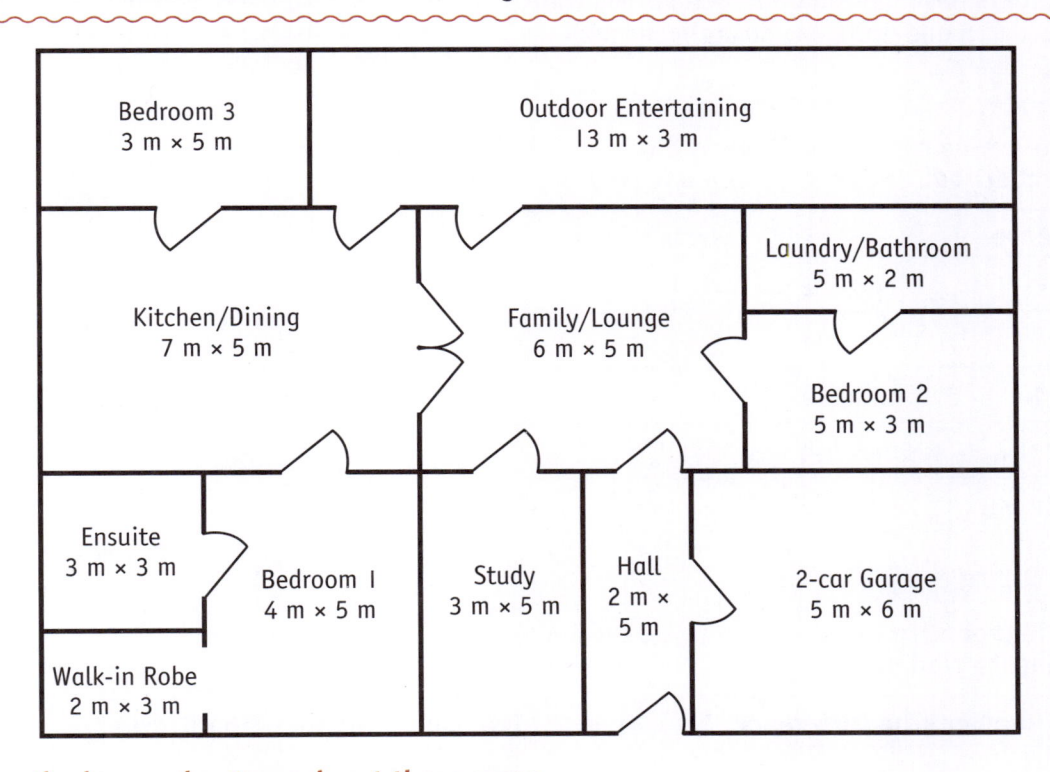

```
Bedroom 3        Outdoor Entertaining
3 m × 5 m        13 m × 3 m

Kitchen/Dining   Family/Lounge    Laundry/Bathroom
7 m × 5 m        6 m × 5 m        5 m × 2 m

                                  Bedroom 2
                                  5 m × 3 m

Ensuite
3 m × 3 m   Bedroom 1   Study     Hall       2-car Garage
            4 m × 5 m   3 m × 5 m 2 m × 5 m  5 m × 6 m

Walk-in Robe
2 m × 3 m
```

Use the house plan to work out these areas.

① The area of tiles needed altogether to tile the Hall, Kitchen/Dining, Laundry/Bathroom and Ensuite

② The area of carpet needed altogether for the Family/Lounge, Bedrooms, Walk-in Robe and Study

③ The outdoor entertaining area is going to be paved and there has to be a paved pathway 1 metre wide all the way around the outside of the house. What area of pavers will be needed?

Extra Challenge

To find out just how expensive this is all going to be, go online and choose tiles, carpets and pavers. Work out the total price for each and then the combined price. Remember to show your prices per square metre and your working out.

TERM 2

UNIT 16 — Number & Algebra

AC9M6N02

Prime, Composite and Square Numbers

> **Just a reminder!**
> **Prime numbers** only have 1 and themselves as factors. You will remember that 2, 3, 5 and 7 are prime numbers.
> **Composite numbers** have more than 2 factors. You will remember that 4, 6, 8 and 9 are composite numbers.
>
> **Square numbers** are the product of one number by itself. As an example, 9 is a square number because $3 \times 3 = 9$. Often 3×3 is written as 3^2 which is said as 'three squared'.

In each of the following sequences there is a number that does not belong. Which is the number that does not belong and why does it not belong?

Number Sequence	Doesn't Belong
① 1, 4, 9, 24, 49	because
② 5, 38, 9, 15, 22	because
③ 9, 18, 6, 23, 81	because
④ 7, 17, 27, 37, 47	because
⑤ 32, 64, 16, 62, 48	because

Spotting Patterns

There seems to be a pattern in the difference between two consecutive square numbers. Complete the chart to find out what it is.

The Square Number	The Difference
$1^2 =$ ____	
⑥ $2^2 =$ ____	____
⑦ $3^2 =$ ____	____
⑧ $4^2 =$ ____	____
⑨ $5^2 =$ ____	____
⑩ $6^2 =$ ____	____

The Square Number	The Difference
$6^2 =$ ____	
⑪ $7^2 =$ ____	____
⑫ $8^2 =$ ____	____
⑬ $9^2 =$ ____	____
⑭ $10^2 =$ ____	____
⑮ $11^2 =$ ____	____

⑯ The difference between two square numbers is _____.

SCORE /16   0-7   8-14   15-16

Quick Check

① $5^2 =$ ____
② $6^2 =$ ____
③ $11^2 =$ ____
④ $9^2 =$ ____
⑤ $12^2 =$ ____

⑥ The third prime number is ____.
⑦ The first composite number is ____.
⑧ The prime number between 4^2 and 3×6 is ____.
⑨ The square number in the 30s is ____.
⑩ The prime number between 2×10 and 2×14 is ____.

SCORE /10   0-4   5-8   9-10

Number & Algebra

UNIT 16

AC9M6N01

Measuring Temperatures

In most countries, temperatures are measured in degrees Celsius and written with a degrees symbol and a capital C like this: 48 °C.

Temperatures are measured on a scale from 0 to 100, but can be below 0 °C or above 100 °C.

- 100 °C is the boiling temperature for water.
- 0 °C is the freezing temperature for water.
- −10 °C is below freezing. It is a minus temperature and is very cold.

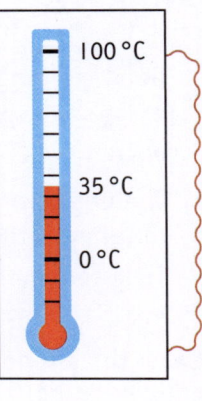

Mark these temperatures on the thermometers.

① Normal body temperature is 37 °C. Where on the thermometer would that be?

② The average fridge temperature is 5 °C. Where on the thermometer would that be?

③ The average freezer temperature is −8 °C. Where on the thermometer would that be?

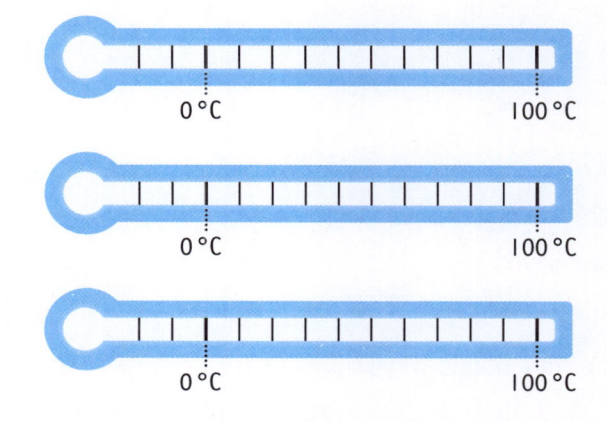

Find the difference in temperature.

④ What is the difference in degrees between the fridge temperature and the freezer temperature?

_____

⑤ What is the difference in temperature between a daytime temperature of 12° and an overnight temperature of −4 °C?

_____

SCORE /5   0-2   3-4   5

Statistics & Probability

AC9M6P01

Fractions, Decimals, Percentages

The chance of something occurring can be stated using fractions, decimals or percentages. Complete this chance table to show each way of expressing probability.

	The chance	As a fraction	As a decimal	As a percentage
①	1 in 8	$\frac{1}{8}$	0.125	
②	25 in 100			
③	2 in 5			
④	6 in 8			
⑤	37 in 50			

SCORE /5   0-2   3-4   5

TARGETING MATHS HOMEWORK: YEAR 6 © PASCAL PRESS ISBN: 9781925726596

67

UNIT 16 — Measurement & Space

AC9M6SP02, AC9M6M04

Angles of a Polygon

"Good morning, class! I have a list of coordinates for you to plot.
(1, 5)   (7, 2)   (5, –5)   (0, –6)   (–4, 2)
"What shape will be made by joining those points?
"The angles of a quadrilateral add to 360° and the angles of a hexagon add to 720°. What might the angles of your shape add to?
"Time for you to get out your protractors, rulers and pencils."

Draw the shape on this graph and label the above points A–E in the order given. Measure the angles and find their total.

① Angle A = _____°

② Angle B = _____°

③ Angle C = _____°

④ Angle D = _____°

⑤ Angle E = _____°

⑥ The shape is a _____

⑦ The angles add to _____°

⑧ Make up your own list of coordinates and draw the shape they make on the graph.
Coordinate List: _____

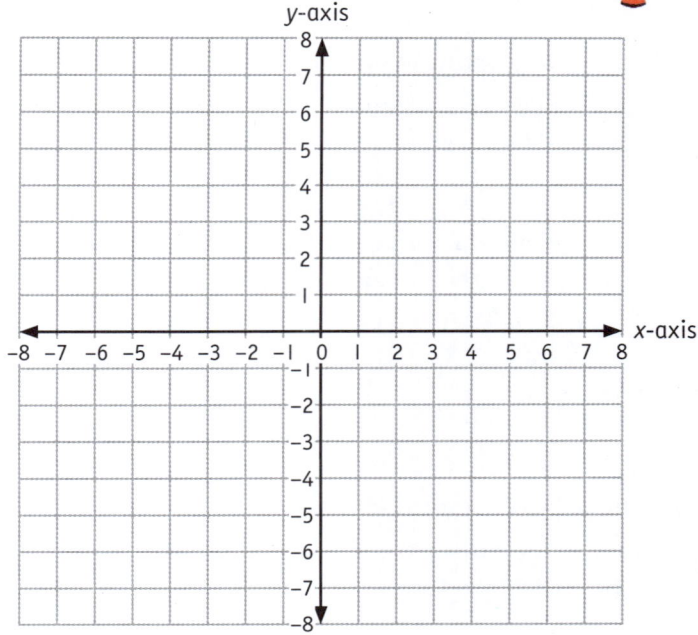

⑨ Angle List: _____
Total: _____°

SCORE /9   0-4   5-7   8-9

NAPLAN*-style Questions

① Which of the following numbers follows these rules?
The number must be composite, lie between 6^2 and 6×7 and have more than 4 factors.
○ 37   ○ 38   ○ 39   ○ 40   ○ 41

② On 24 January, the temperature in Marree, South Australia, was 45 °C which made it the hottest place in the world on that day. Antarctica was –95 °C on the same day, making it the coldest place in the world.
What was the temperature difference between Marree and Antarctica on 24 January?

③ Look at the Cartesian plane.
Which shape is at (–3, 1)?
○ ■   ○ ★   ○ ◆   ○ ▲

SCORE /3   0-1   2   3

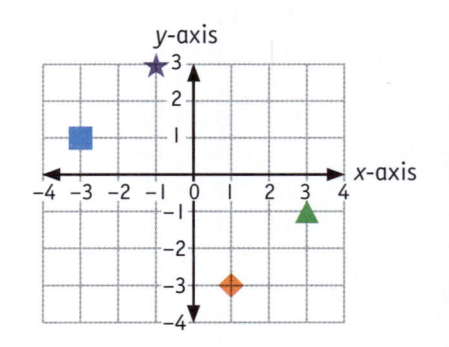

TARGETING MATHS HOMEWORK: YEAR 6 © PASCAL PRESS ISBN: 9781925726596

Problem of the Week

UNIT 16

A Numbers Game

Min and Alex have been really enjoying the **Prime or Square** game that they invented.

- Using only the number cards from a pack, you shuffle the cards and then deal three cards to each player.
- Score 5 points for each prime number or square number that you can make with the cards.

These are the cards that Min was dealt.

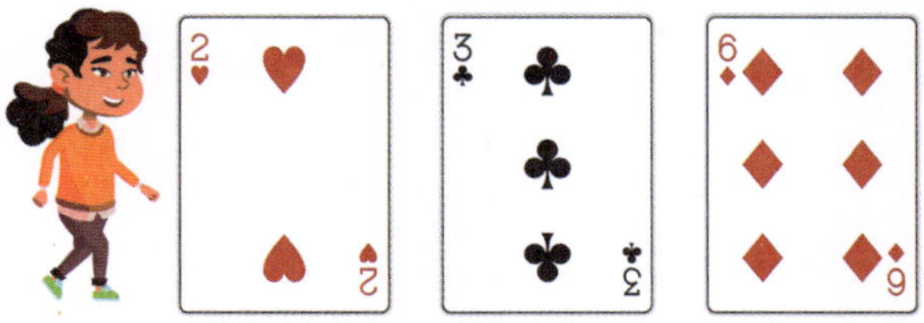

These are the cards that Alex was dealt.

Min found that she could make three prime numbers which were 2, 3 and 23 and a square number 36 so she scored 20.

Alex found that he could make two prime numbers which were 3 and 43 and three square numbers which were 4, 9 and 49 so he scored 25.

The Challenge

What Min and Alex didn't realise was that there are some 3-digit numbers that their cards could make, which might have scored points for them.

Here is how to check on your calculator.

- First, make an odd 3-digit number with the cards, like 623 for Min.
- Then on your calculator divide that number by the prime numbers up to 31, which are:

    2, 3, 5, 7, 11, 13, 17, 19, 23, 29 and 31

    Here is one to get you started: [6] [2] [3] [÷] [3] [=] (207·6666667)

    The display includes the decimal point, which shows that 3 is not a factor of 623. However, if the decimal point is not in the display, then that prime number is a factor of 623, which shows that 623 is not a prime number.

- Press the Clear button and repeat the key sequence with the next prime number.

The extra primes that Min and Alex could have found are: _____, _____, _____

Extra Challenge

If you were dealt these three cards, what score could you make?
List the possibilities here.

Square Numbers	
Prime Numbers	
Score:	

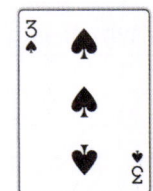

TERM 2

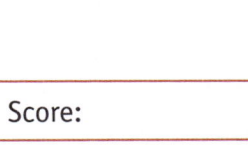

Review: Unit 9 and Unit 10

AC9M6N01, AC9M6N02, AC9M6N03, AC9M6N04, AC9M6SP02

Hai started a Bankrupt game with $75. He drew these cards in the first four rounds.
Complete this table to show his balances during the game.

	Ruby	Earn	Spend		Balance
①	Round 1		$125	Start with $75.	_____
②	Round 2	$25			_____
③	Round 3	$135		$75	_____
④	Round 4		$45		_____

Complete these prime factor trees.

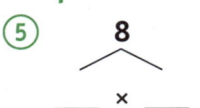

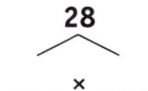

⑤ 8
___ × ___

⑥ 28
___ × ___

⑦ 42
___ × ___

What are the coordinates for the quadrilateral ABCD?

⑧ A is at (___, ___)

⑨ B is at (___, ___)

⑩ C is at (___, ___)

⑪ D is at (___, ___)

Round these decimal numbers to the nearest whole number.

⑫ 36·504 rounds to _____

⑬ 49·678 rounds to _____

⑭ 37·496 rounds to _____

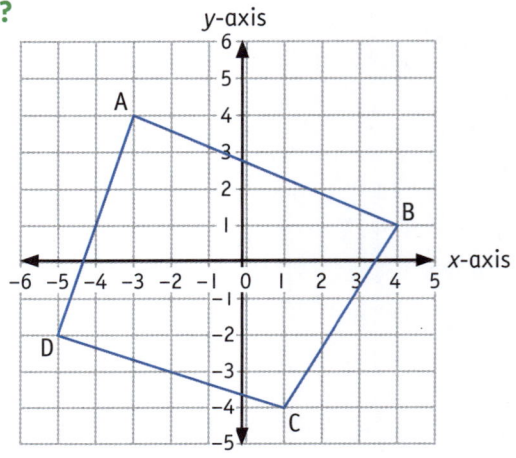

Estimate first and then write the answers to these additions.

⑮ 47·365 + 28·469

Estimate: _____

Check: 47·365
      + 28·469
      _____

⑯ 39·865 + 43·738

Estimate: _____

Check: 39·865
      + 43·738
      _____

Use equivalent fractions to find the larger fraction. Use the > or < symbols to show your answer.

	Fractions	Equivalent fractions	Show which is larger
⑰	$\frac{5}{6}$ or $\frac{9}{12}$		
⑱	$\frac{3}{4}$ or $\frac{13}{16}$		
⑲	$\frac{3}{5}$ or $\frac{11}{15}$		

Review: Unit 11 and Unit 12

AC9M6N05, AC9M6N06, AC9M6A01, AC9M6M01, AC9M6P01

Complete these fraction additions by using the lowest common denominators.

① $\frac{3}{4} + \frac{3}{5} = \frac{}{} + \frac{}{} = \frac{}{}$

② $\frac{5}{16} + \frac{3}{4} = \frac{}{} + \frac{}{} = \frac{}{}$

③ $\frac{3}{9} + \frac{2}{3} = \frac{}{} + \frac{}{} = \frac{}{}$

④ $\frac{3}{15} + \frac{3}{6} = \frac{}{} + \frac{}{} = \frac{}{}$

Continue these fraction sequences.

⑤ $\frac{1}{2}, \frac{4}{6}, \frac{5}{6}, \underline{}, \underline{}, \underline{}$

⑥ $\frac{2}{3}, 1, 1\frac{1}{3}, \underline{}, \underline{}, \underline{}$

⑦ $\frac{1}{8}, \frac{1}{2}, \frac{7}{8}, \underline{}, \underline{}, \underline{}$

⑧ $\frac{2}{9}, \frac{1}{3}, \frac{4}{9}, \underline{}, \underline{}, \underline{}$

The tally chart shows the outcomes for 10 spins of this spinner.

	Red	White	Yellow	Green	Blue
Spins	||	||		|||		
Percentage					

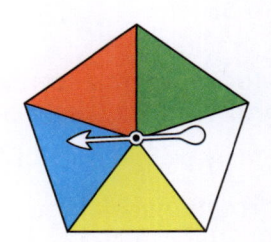

⑨ The data for yellow was not included. What should it be? _____

⑩ Write the percentage of spins for each colour in the tally chart.

Complete these multiplications.

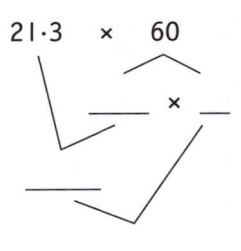

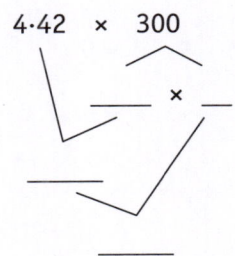

⑪ 36·2 × 40
   10 × ___

⑫ 21·3 × 60
   ___ × ___

⑬ 4·42 × 300
   ___ × ___

Complete these divisions.

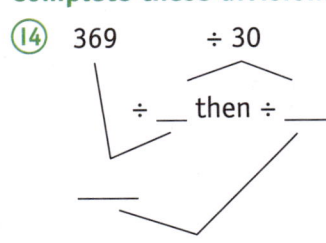

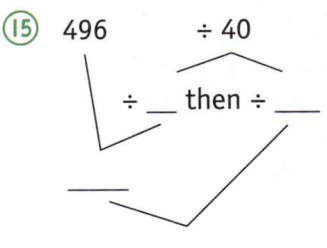

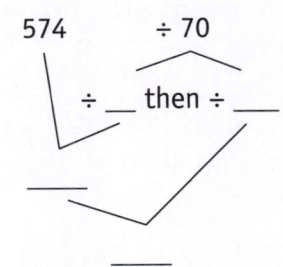

⑭ 369 ÷ 30
   ÷ __ then ÷ __

⑮ 496 ÷ 40
   ÷ __ then ÷ __

⑯ 574 ÷ 70
   ÷ __ then ÷ __

⑰ How much flour is needed to make 5 pancakes if each pancake uses 85 g of flour?
   _____ g

⑱ How much juice is needed to fill 6 glasses if each glass holds 325 mL?
   _____ mL

Review: Unit 13 and Unit 14

AC9M6N08, AC9M6N09, AC9M6A02, AC9M6ST03

Use the bar model to answer these percentage questions.

① The shop offered 40% off a $45 T-shirt. What does the T-shirt cost now? $____

② A $17·50 book was reduced by 30%. What does the book cost now? $____

Use a calculator to answer these percentage questions.

③ 27% of $345 = $_____
④ 36% of $87 = $_____
⑤ 44% of $1320 = $_____
⑥ 18% of $96 = $_____

The dot plot shows the scores out of 100 at the trivia night.

⑦ How many people were at the trivia night? ____

⑧ What is the range of the data?
From ____ to ____

⑨ What is the mode of the data? _____

Trivia Night Scores

30–35   36–45   46–55   56–65   66–75
Points

Key: ● = 4 people

Give two possible solutions to these equations with unknowns.

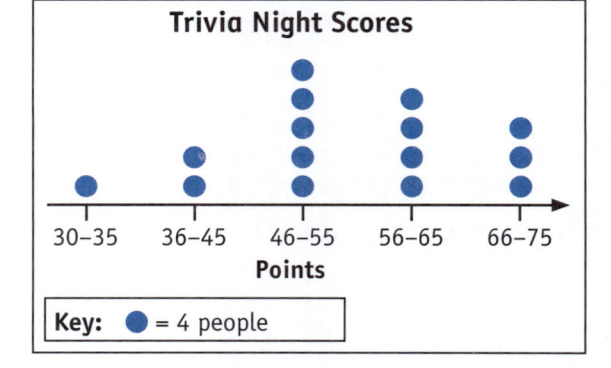

⑩ 6 × 4 + 3 = 5 × ☐ + ☐
    = 5 × ☐ + ☐

⑪ 7 + 3 × 9 = 6 × ☐ − ☐
    = 6 × ☐ − ☐

⑫ 63 ÷ 9 + 8 = 56 ÷ ☐ + ☐
    = 56 ÷ ☐ + ☐

⑬ 72 ÷ 8 + 4 = ☐ ÷ 7 + ☐
    = ☐ ÷ 8 + ☐

Write the number expression and answer for these word problems.

Expression	Working Out	Answer

⑭ How much would a family meal of 6 burgers at $4·95 each, 4 coffees at $4·20 each and 2 drinks at $3·20 each cost?

The meal would cost $_____.

⑮ How much would the family have to pay for 6 movie tickets at $22·50 each, 4 bags of popcorn at $4·50 each and a bag of jelly snakes at $6?

The family has to pay $_____.

⑯ Liam bought 6 packets of 4 stickers and 1 packet of 9 stickers which he then divided equally among 3 pages in his sticker folder. How many did he put on each page?

____ stickers on each page

Review: Unit 15 and Unit 16

Complete these missing pattern sequences. Write the rules for each sequence.

① 1·65, ____, 2·15, 2·4, ____, ____   The rule is _____

② $\frac{7}{16}$, ___, $\frac{11}{16}$, $\frac{13}{16}$, ___, ___   The rule is _____

Write the next two numbers in each of these sequences.

③ 0·5, $\frac{3}{4}$, 1, ____, ____

④ 15·9, 15·6, 15·3, ____, ____

Complete these fraction subtractions by finding the lowest common denominator each time.

⑤ $\frac{3}{4} - \frac{3}{6} = \frac{}{} - \frac{}{} = \frac{}{}$

⑥ $\frac{7}{12} - \frac{1}{6} = \frac{}{} - \frac{}{} = \frac{}{}$

Use the kitchen plan to answer the questions below.

⑦ How wide is the kitchen at its widest point? ____ m

⑧ What is the area of the kitchen? ____ m²

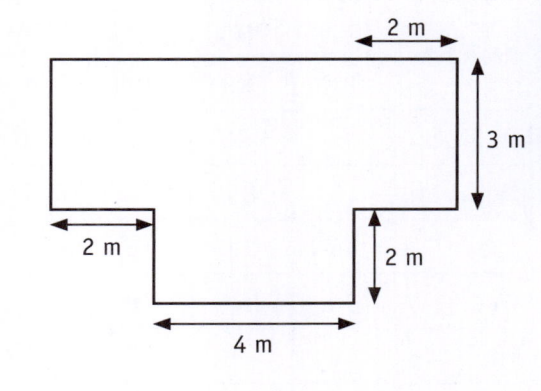

⑨ Circle the square numbers.

   64   1   16   2   7   121

⑩ Circle the prime numbers.

   15   1   7   11   27   2

As accurately as you can, mark these temperatures on the thermometers.

⑪ Boiling point of water

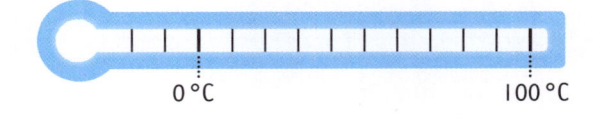

⑫ Freezing point of water

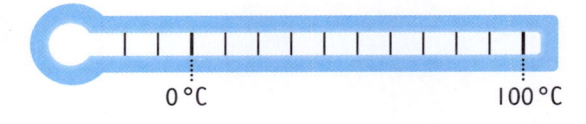

⑬ 16° warmer than −3°

⑭ 26° colder than 13°

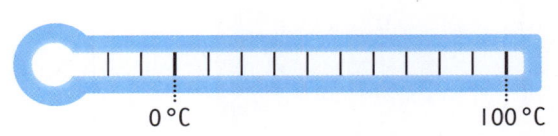

Express these chances as percentages.

⑮ 1 in 4 chance = ____%

⑯ 1 in 8 chance = ____%

⑰ 1 in 20 chance = ____%

⑱ 1 in 100 chance = ____%

UNIT 17 — Number & Algebra

AC9M6N01

Integer Addition and Subtraction

The online gardening warehouse No-More-Pests begins each Monday with 100 of every product in stock.

Sometimes their online orders mean that they run out of stock, so that is recorded as a negative on the stock list and has to be made up in the next order.

On Friday afternoon they create an order list so they can restock for Monday.

The In Stock amounts for Insect Spray have been filled in for you.
Complete the warehouse stock list chart to work out what they need to order this Friday.

Products	Insect Spray Out	Insect Spray In	Rose Spray Out	Rose Spray In	Ant Dust Out	Ant Dust In	Slug Bait Out	Slug Bait In	Snail Pellets Out	Snail Pellets In
In Stock		100		100		100		100		100
Mon.	15	85	26		39		6		24	
Tue.	46	39	16		18		15		12	
Wed.	35	4	18		24		22		28	
Thu.	49	-45	17		13		26		37	
Fri.	12	-57	24		21		14		25	
Reorder Quantity	157									

Score one point for each correct reorder amount.

SCORE /4   0-1   2-3   4

Quick Check

Start with 30.
1. Add 12, subtract 40 = _____
2. Subtract 21, subtract 15 = _____
3. Subtract 35, add 8 = _____
4. Add 20, subtract 65 = _____
5. Subtract 45, add 6 = _____

Start with −30.
6. Add 24, subtract 6 = _____
7. Add 6, subtract 24 = _____
8. Add 50, subtract 16 = _____
9. Add 14, subtract 70 = _____
10. Add 27, subtract 14 = _____

SCORE /10   0-4   5-8   9-10

Number & Algebra

UNIT 17

Solving Equations with Square Numbers

In class today, we had to write two equations to match the clues that Mr Green set us. First, he gave us this example:

The Clue: a square number + 6 = 42

The Solution: $6^2 + 6 = 42$ and $6 × 6 + 6 = 42$

Then he wrote more clues on the board for us to solve.

Here are the clues that Mr Green wrote on the board. Please help us solve them.

① a square number + 6 = 22

____ + ____ = ____ or ____ × ____ + ____ = ____

② a square number + 4 = 13

____ + ____ = ____ or ____ × ____ + ____ = ____

③ a square number + 4 = 53

____ + ____ = ____ or ____ × ____ + ____ = ____

④ a square number − 3 = 61

____ − ____ = ____ or ____ × ____ − ____ = ____

⑤ a square number + 11 = another square number

____ + ____ = ____ or ____ × ____ + ____ = ____ × ____

SCORE /5   0-2   3-4   5

Statistics & Probability

Pizza Toppings

60 people were interviewed about their favourite pizza toppings and each person had one vote.

Complete the graph to match these clues about favourite pizza toppings.

The Clues

① 20% voted for Pepperoni.

② A third of the rest voted for Meat Lovers.

③ 3-cheese was three times as popular as Seafood.

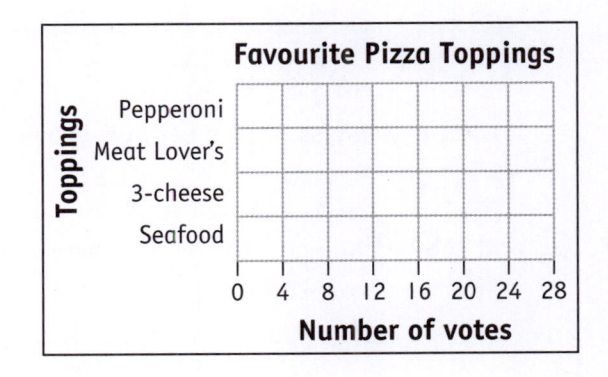

Favourite Pizza Toppings

Toppings: Pepperoni, Meat Lover's, 3-cheese, Seafood

Number of votes: 0 4 8 12 16 20 24 28

Use the graph to answer these questions.

④ How many more people preferred 3-cheese to Seafood?

____

⑤ How many fewer people preferred Meat Lovers than 3-cheese and Seafood together?

____

SCORE /5   0-3   4   5

TERM 3

TARGETING MATHS HOMEWORK: YEAR 6 © PASCAL PRESS ISBN: 9781925726596

75

UNIT 17 — Measurement & Space

AC9M6M03

Time

Timetables are often written in 24-hour time.
Write these times in 24-hour format and say how long it is between them.

From	To	24-hour time
① Clock showing approx 3:20 am	7:40 pm	__:__ to __:__ is __ h __ min
② Clock showing approx 10:55 pm	7:30 am	__:__ to __:__ is __ h __ min
③ Clock showing approx 7:25 am	4:15 pm	__:__ to __:__ is __ h __ min
④ Clock showing approx 10:20 pm	1:15 am	__:__ to __:__ is __ h __ min

What time will it be in 24-hour time?

⑥ $3\frac{1}{2}$ hours after 10:15 am
_____

⑦ 15 hours after 1:25 am
_____

⑧ 3 hours 35 minutes before 1:35 am
_____

⑨ 4 hours 25 minutes before 2:10 pm
_____

⑩ 270 minutes after 11:15 am
_____

SCORE /10   0-4   5-8   9-10

NAPLAN*-style Questions

① What is the missing number in this equation? $3^2 + 7 = \boxed{}$

$\boxed{} = $ ___

② At the beginning of the month there was $165 in the flexi account.
After paying $220 for electricity, the account was overdrawn by how much?

$_____

③ Min's family are flying from Brisbane to Melbourne for their winter holiday. They couldn't get a direct flight so they have a stop-over in Sydney. The table shows their flight schedule.

	Brisbane	Sydney	Melbourne
Arrive		9:25 am	12:10 pm
Depart	8:15 am	10:35 am	

What is the actual flight time in hours and minutes?

_____

SCORE /3   0-1   2   3

Problem of the Week

UNIT 17
AC9M6N09

The Gardener's Daily Schedule

A gardener works a 6-hour day and she needs to plan her jobs and her breaks.
- She must have a 15-minute break and a 45-minute lunch break through the day.
- She is not allowed to work for more than $2\frac{1}{2}$ hours before having a break.
- The gardener has two lawns to mow. The large lawn takes $1\frac{1}{2}$ hours and the other takes 30 minutes.
- It takes 30 minutes of backbreaking weeding for each of the two flower beds so the gardener likes to spread them out through the day.
- The gardener has a tree-lopping task which will take about 45 minutes.
- There are 30 seedlings to be planted and they take about 2 minutes each to plant.
- Finally, she has to tidy up, water the garden and pack up all the gear so she can leave by 3 o'clock to collect the children from school.

Challenge 1
Complete the Activity List for the gardener. Show how long each activity will take in minutes and how much time there will be for the tidy up.

Challenge 2
Use your Activity List to help create a timetable for the gardener that meets all the requirements.

Your table should show the time of day that the gardener will need to start work and when she might take those two breaks.

Gardener's Timetable

Activity	Duration	Start	Finish

Activity List

Activity	Duration (min)
Break 1	
Break 2	
Lawn 1	
Lawn 2	
Weed 1	
Weed 2	
Tree-lop	
Seedlings	
Tidy up	

TERM 3

Check Point
Does your timetable make sure that the gardener does not get too tired weeding?

Your suggestions will be very much appreciated.

UNIT 18

Number & Algebra

AC9M6N03

Fractions

The number lines below only have the 0 position marked.
Choose where to place 1 on each number line to help you mark the given fractions.

① $\frac{3}{4}$ and $\frac{3}{8}$

② $\frac{3}{5}$ and $\frac{2}{10}$

③ $\frac{5}{6}$ and $\frac{1}{4}$

④ $\frac{2}{7}$ and $\frac{1}{2}$

⑤ $\frac{1}{3}$ and $\frac{4}{5}$

⑥ $\frac{3}{16}$ and $\frac{3}{4}$

⑦ $\frac{1}{4}$ and $\frac{7}{8}$

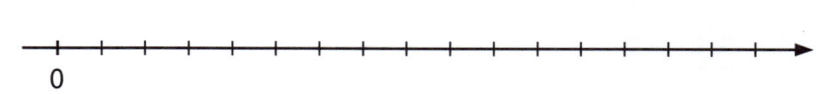

⑧ $\frac{1}{5}$ and $\frac{2}{3}$

SCORE /8   0–3   4–6   7–8

Quick Check

Write the lowest common denominator for each of these fraction pairs.

① $\frac{7}{8}$ and $\frac{3}{5}$ _____

② $\frac{4}{5}$ and $\frac{3}{6}$ _____

③ $\frac{2}{3}$ and $\frac{2}{9}$ _____

④ $\frac{2}{3}$ and $\frac{3}{8}$ _____

⑤ $\frac{7}{10}$ and $\frac{2}{15}$ _____

⑥ $\frac{3}{12}$ and $\frac{3}{4}$ _____

⑦ $\frac{4}{7}$ and $\frac{2}{5}$ _____

⑧ $\frac{3}{8}$ and $\frac{1}{6}$ _____

⑨ $\frac{1}{4}$ and $\frac{2}{9}$ _____

⑩ $\frac{3}{4}$ and $\frac{3}{24}$ _____

SCORE /10   0–4   5–8   9–10

TERM 3

Number & Algebra

UNIT 18

AC9M6N04

Decimal Additions

When adding decimals, it is really important to line up the numbers correctly using their place value.
For 3·6 + 4·73 + 15·65, write this:

```
    3 · 6
    4 · 7 3
+  15 · 6 5
----------
   23 · 9 8
```

Write each of the decimal addition strings in vertical format as shown by Ruby. Then work out the totals.

① 13·05 + 6·45 + 4·3

③ 14·36 + 127·65 + 1·06

⑤ 33·39 + 12·65 + 126·12

② 6·83 + 12·06 + 3·756

④ 37·6 + 12·08 + 31·76

⑥ 13·455 + 7·51 + 4·035

SCORE /6   0-2   3-4   5-6

Statistics & Probability

AC9M6ST02

The Family Journey

① At what time does the journey begin? _____

② At what time does the journey end? _____

③ How far along the journey were the family at 11:45? _____

④ How far along the journey were the family at 12:30? _____

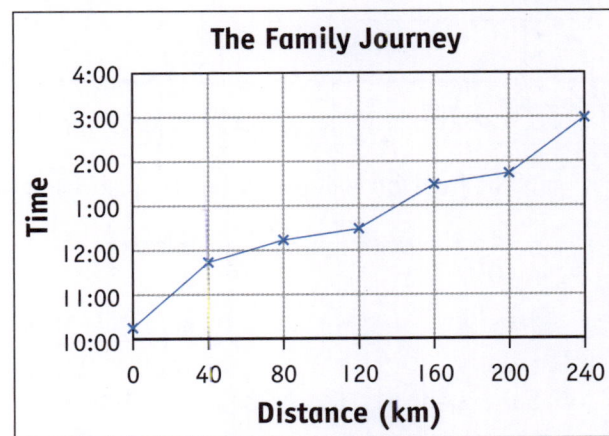

⑤ Which were the two slowest parts of the journey? _____

⑥ Why do you think they were so slow? _____

SCORE /6   0-2   3-4   5-6

TARGETING MATHS HOMEWORK: YEAR 6 © PASCAL PRESS ISBN: 9781925726596

79

UNIT 18 — Measurement & Space

AC9M6M01

The Water Bucket Relay

The water bucket relay is a popular race at the country show.
Teams can choose the buckets that they use and how full they fill them.
The goal is to be the team who carries the most water and pours it into their tank in the 5 minutes allowed.

① Team 1 used a 5-litre bucket filled only to the $4\frac{3}{4}$ litre mark because they didn't want to spill any as they ran. They made 6 successful journeys.

Total amount of water carried: _____ litres

② Team 2 also used a 5-litre bucket which they filled to the top. They made 6 journeys but spilt $\frac{1}{2}$ litre, then 365 mL, then 270 mL, then 90 mL, then 80 mL and finally 125 mL.

Total amount of water carried: _____ litres

③ Team 3 used a 6-litre bucket which they filled to the $\frac{5}{6}$ mark each time because they were strong but didn't run very fast. They made 4 journeys in the time limit.

Total amount of water carried: _____ litres

The Challenge

④ Who won the relay? By how much?

_____

Don't forget! The winner was the team that carried the most water in the 5 minutes.

SCORE /4   0-1   2-3   4

NAPLAN*-style Questions

① What fraction is represented by ? on the number line?

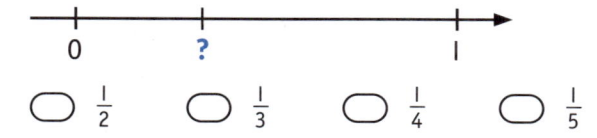

0 ——— ? ——— 1

◯ $\frac{1}{2}$ ◯ $\frac{1}{3}$ ◯ $\frac{1}{4}$ ◯ $\frac{1}{5}$

② Sara spent $1·75 on a pencil, $15·90 on a sketch book and $6·05 on a marker. How much did Sara spend altogether?

$_____

③ The canteen sold four glasses of orange juice. There is 425 mL in each glass. How much orange juice did the canteen sell?

_____ L

SCORE /3   0-1   2   3

TERM 3

Problem of the Week

UNIT 18

AC9M6N09

Decimal Target

Alex and Hai have made up a game with dice and decimals.
- Players take it in turns to throw two dice.
- The dice are then used to make a number to two decimal places. For example, a throw of 5 and 1 can be used to make 0·51 or 0·15.

To start:
- Each player starts with a total of 1 and adds or subtracts their choice of decimal from their total.
- The player closest to zero at the end of 4 turns wins that round.

Here is the twist:
A player can decide to round the decimal number up or down to the nearest tenth.

• [dice 1 and 5] 0·15
• [dice 5 and 1] 0·51

Liam and Min joined Alex and Hai for a game. Here are the throws they all made.

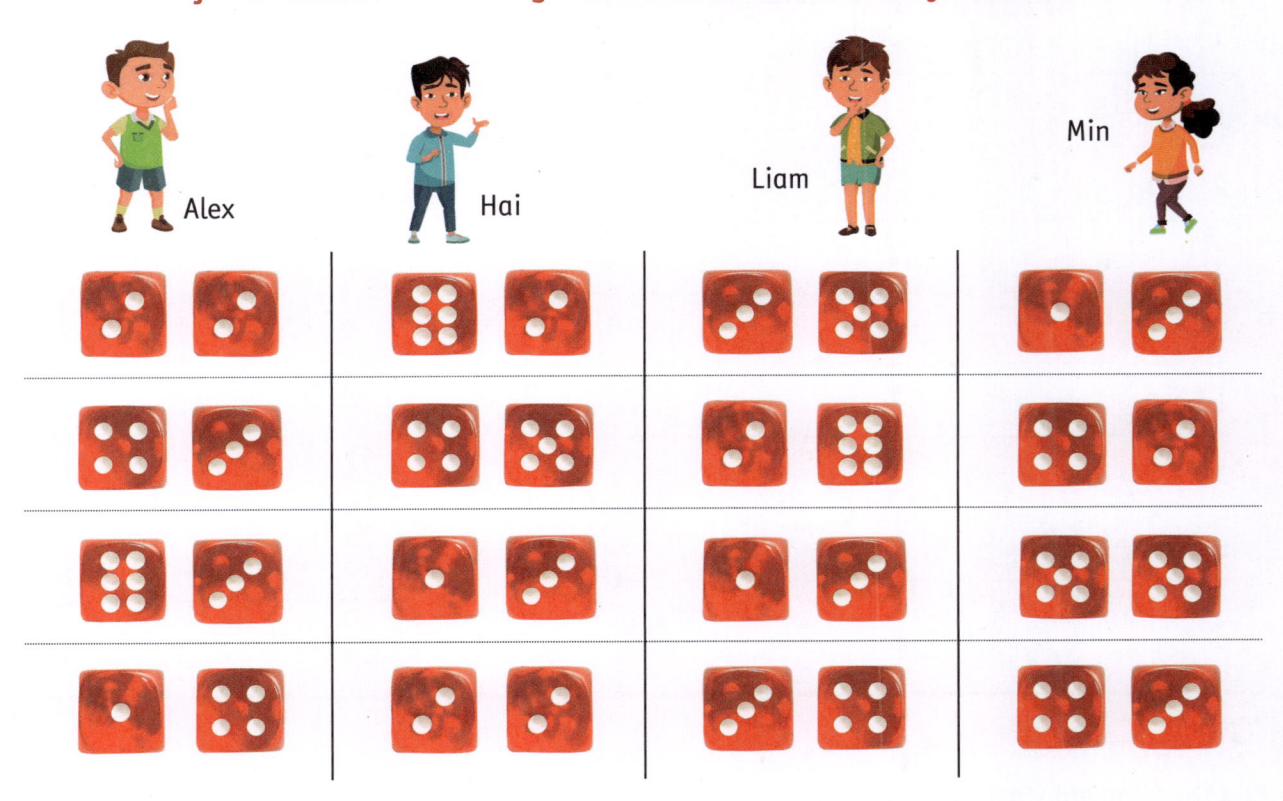

Alex | Hai | Liam | Min

The Challenge

How close to zero could each player get?
- Alex _____
- Hai _____
- Liam _____
- Min _____

Who could win the game? _____

Working Space

TERM 3

TARGETING MATHS HOMEWORK: YEAR 6 © PASCAL PRESS ISBN: 9781925726596

81

UNIT 19 — Number & Algebra

AC9M6N05

Addition of Mixed Fractions

In earlier units we learned about the addition of fractions, but mixed fractions were not included.
So it is time to give them a try.

Here is an example: $1\frac{1}{2} + 2\frac{3}{4}$

Add the whole numbers first: $1 + 2 = 3$

Next, use the lowest common denominator method to add the fractions: $\frac{1}{2} + \frac{3}{4} = \frac{2}{4} + \frac{3}{4} = \frac{5}{4} = 1\frac{1}{4}$

And to finish off, add those two results: $3 + 1\frac{1}{4} = 4\frac{1}{4}$

Show the steps needed to add these mixed fractions and work out the answers. Elsa has completed the first one for you to show you the steps to take.

① $2\frac{3}{4} + 1\frac{3}{8} = 3 + \frac{6}{8} + \frac{3}{8} = 3 + 1\frac{1}{8} = 4\frac{1}{8}$

② $1\frac{5}{6} + 2\frac{5}{12} =$

③ $2\frac{2}{3} + 1\frac{5}{6} =$

④ $4\frac{1}{2} + 3\frac{1}{3} =$

⑤ $3\frac{3}{12} + 1\frac{1}{3} =$

⑥ $1\frac{5}{8} + 2\frac{3}{24} =$

⑦ $3\frac{1}{6} + 2\frac{1}{5} =$

⑧ $5\frac{5}{12} + 2\frac{1}{9} =$

SCORE /8   0-3   4-6   7-8

Quick Check

Add these mixed fractions.

① $1\frac{1}{4} + \frac{1}{2} =$

② $2\frac{2}{3} + 1\frac{2}{3} =$

③ $4\frac{1}{2} + 1\frac{1}{5} =$

④ $1\frac{3}{5} + 1\frac{1}{10} =$

⑤ $2\frac{1}{4} + 3\frac{3}{8} =$

⑥ $3\frac{1}{6} + 1\frac{1}{9} =$

⑦ $2\frac{5}{6} + \frac{5}{12} =$

⑧ $3\frac{1}{5} + 1\frac{5}{6} =$

⑨ $2\frac{1}{8} + 1\frac{1}{12} =$

⑩ $2\frac{3}{7} + 1\frac{5}{14} =$

SCORE /10   0-4   5-8   9-10

TERM 3

TARGETING MATHS HOMEWORK: YEAR 6 © PASCAL PRESS ISBN: 9781925726596

Number & Algebra

UNIT 19

Subtraction of Mixed Fractions

Our last page was about the addition of mixed fractions. Now it is time to look at subtraction of mixed fractions.

Here is an example: $2\frac{1}{2} - 1\frac{1}{8}$

With subtraction, it is safest to convert both mixed fractions before subtracting: $2\frac{1}{2} - 1\frac{1}{8} = \frac{20}{8} - \frac{9}{8}$

Next, the numerators can be subtracted: $2\frac{1}{2} - 1\frac{1}{8} = \frac{20}{8} - \frac{9}{8} = \frac{11}{8}$

To finish off, convert the answer to a mixed fraction if possible: $2\frac{1}{2} - 1\frac{1}{8} = \frac{20}{8} - \frac{9}{8} = \frac{11}{8} = 1\frac{3}{8}$

Complete these mixed fraction subtractions using the method that Elsa showed you.

① $2\frac{1}{2} - 1\frac{1}{4} = \frac{10}{4} - \frac{5}{4} =$

② $2\frac{3}{5} - 1\frac{7}{10} = \quad - \quad =$

③ $4\frac{3}{4} - 2\frac{1}{2} = \quad - \quad =$

④ $3\frac{3}{10} - 2\frac{3}{5} = \quad - \quad =$

⑤ $2\frac{4}{5} - 1\frac{1}{2} = \quad - \quad =$

SCORE /5   0-2   3-4   5

Statistics & Probability

Measuring Chance Events

Chance can be shown using percentages from 0% to 100% on a number line:

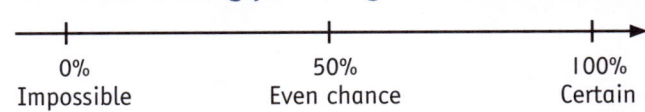

0% — Impossible
50% — Even chance
100% — Certain

Use the number lines to show the percentage chance of the following events.

① A tossed coin will land on heads.   0% ——— 100%

② A six-faced dice will roll a number less than 7.   0% ——— 100%

③ It will snow tonight.   0% ——— 100%

④ You will get full marks on your next test at school.   0% ——— 100%

⑤ You will go to the beach this weekend.   0% ——— 100%

SCORE /5   0-2   3-4   5

TERM 3

UNIT 19 — Measurement & Space

AC9M6SP03

Tessellations with a Shape

I started with a square tile, marked an off-cut and used that to make a new shape which I coloured differently to the tile that I started with.

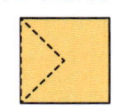

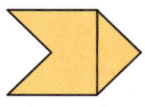

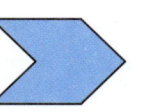

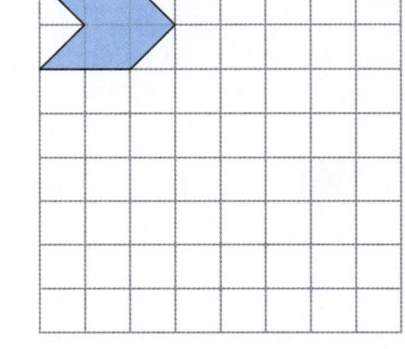

- Starting shape
- Mark an off-cut.
- Cut and move.
- Change colour.

① Use Tau's shape to make a tessellating pattern on the top grid. Colour your pattern.

I followed Tau's method to make a shape that will tessellate.

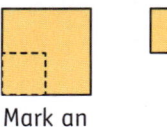

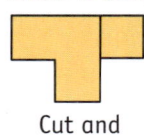

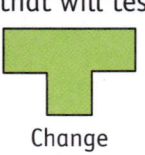

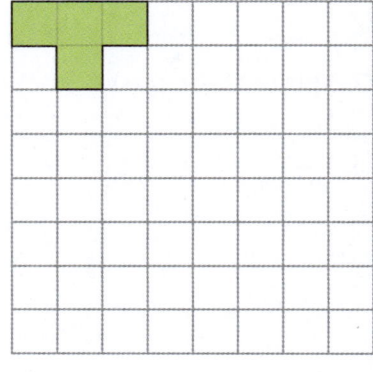

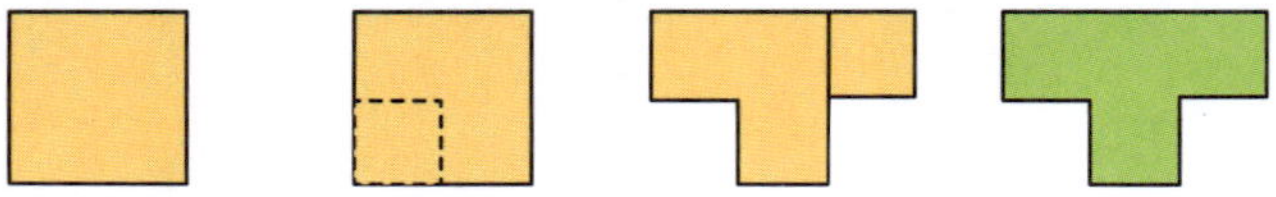

- Starting shape
- Mark an off-cut.
- Cut and move.
- Change colour.

② What does a tessellating pattern made on the middle grid with my shape look like?

③ What would happen if you used Tau's method but started with a shape like this?

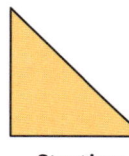

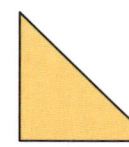

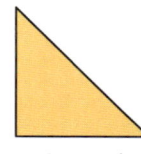

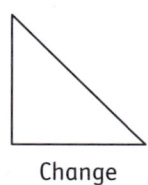

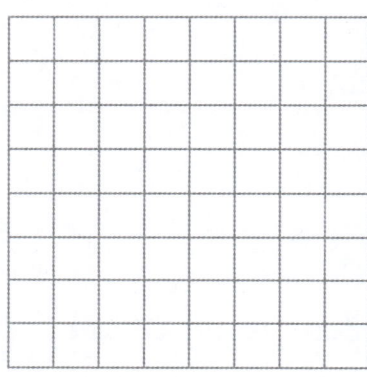

- Starting shape
- Mark an off-cut.
- Cut and move.
- Change colour.

Use your new shape in a tessellating pattern on the last grid.

SCORE /3   0–1   2   3

NAPLAN*-style Questions

① What is $3\frac{1}{4} - 1\frac{3}{8}$? _____

② You are given a piece of fruit from this bowl.
Show on this percentage line the chance of it being a banana.

0% ——————————— 100%

③ Which of these shapes will not tessellate?

○   ○   ○   ○

SCORE /3   0–1   2   3

84 TARGETING MATHS HOMEWORK: YEAR 6 © PASCAL PRESS ISBN: 9781925726596

Problem of the Week

UNIT 19

AC9M6N09

A Chance Experiment

① Write the numbers 1–10 on small pieces of paper or card like this:

| 1 | 2 | 3 | 4 | 5 | 6 | 7 | 8 | 9 | 10 |

② Put the cards into a bag or container that you can't see through.

Predict

What is the chance that, without looking, you will pull out a 3?

_____%

If you repeated the experiment 10 times, what is the chance that you will pull out a 3 in one of those experiments?

_____%

The Experiment

Take out 10 cards, one at a time and always putting the card back into the container before the next turn. Record the numbers that you pull out as a dot plot on the chart below.

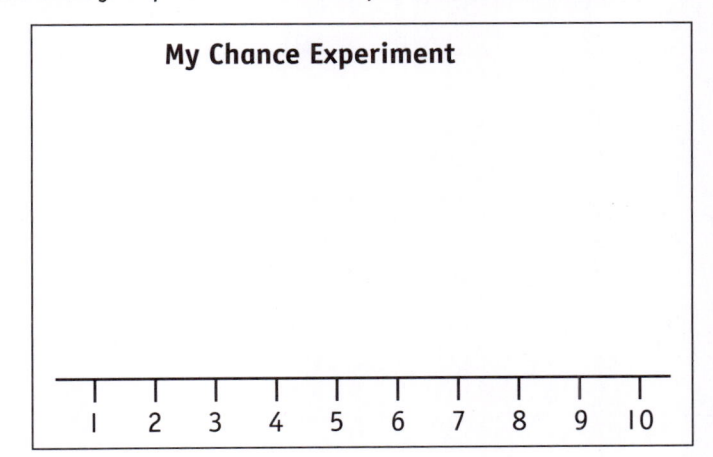

My Chance Experiment

1 2 3 4 5 6 7 8 9 10

The Questions

③ What percentage of the cards you pulled out was 3?

_____%

④ If you were to repeat the experiment, would the shape of the data be the same?

_____

⑤ Repeat the experiment and record the data as before.
Add the dots to the same dot plot in a different colour.

⑥ What percentage of the dots were in the 3 column this time?

_____%

UNIT 20 — Number & Algebra

Multiplication by a Decimal

To do decimal multiplications, convert them to ordinary multiplications and then do the decimal part.

For 6 × 0·5, convert to 6 × 5 ÷ 10 = 30 ÷ 10 = 3 so 6 × 0·5 = 3.

Note how the decimal number 0·5 has the same value as $\frac{5}{10}$, so × 0·5 is the same as × 5 ÷ 10.

The same strategy can be used with other decimal multiplications.
For 6 × 0·4, convert to 6 × 4 ÷ 10 = 24 ÷ 10 = 2·4 so 6 × 0·4 = 2·4.
For 6 × 0·3, convert to 6 × 3 ÷ 10 = 18 ÷ 10 = 1·8 so 6 × 0·3 = 1·8.
For 6 × 0·2, convert to 6 × 2 ÷ 10 = 12 ÷ 10 = 1·2 so 6 × 0·2 = 1·2.
For 6 × 0·1, convert to 6 × 1 ÷ 10 = 6 ÷ 10 = 0·6 so 6 × 0·1 = 0·6.

Show the steps for working out these decimal multiplications.

	The multiplication	Converts to	The answer
①	8 × 0·5	8 × 5 ÷ 10 = _____	= _____
②	10 × 0·4		
③	9 × 0·3		
④	15 × 0·2		
⑤	27 × 0·3		
⑥	165 × 0·2		
⑦	122 × 0·6		
⑧	125 × 0·8		

SCORE /8   0-3   4-6   7-8

Quick Check

Try to do these examples in your head.

① 13 × 0·2 = _____
② 6 × 0·7 = _____
③ 5 × 0·4 = _____
④ 12 × 0·7 = _____
⑤ 14 × 0·3 = _____
⑥ 8 × 0·9 = _____
⑦ 7 × 0·8 = _____
⑧ 25 × 0·4 = _____
⑨ 13 × 0·3 = _____
⑩ 38 × 0·2 = _____

SCORE /10   0-4   5-8   9-10

Number & Algebra

UNIT 20

AC9M6N07, AC9M6N08, AC9M6N09

Percentage Problems

Earlier units looked at money percentage problems, but there are many other applications of percentages in the real world. Here is an example:

The fuel tank holds 38 L of petrol. The gauge is showing that the tank is currently only 15% full. How much petrol is left in the tank?

Find 10% of 38 L = 3·8 L

Find 5% which is half of 10% = 1·9 L.

Add the 10% and 5% answers: 3·8 L + 1·9 L = 5·7 L

There is 5·7 litres of petrol left in the tank.

Answer these questions and show your thinking.

1. The carton holds 2 L of orange juice. 30% has already been poured. How much is left in the carton?

   _____ litres

2. There were 80 spelling words in the test. Alex scored 60%. How many did Alex get wrong?

   _____ wrong answers

3. 120 people took part in a Yes/No vote. 40% voted Yes. How many people voted No?

   _____

4. $1450 TV sets are 35% off in the end of year sale. How much saving is that?

   $_____

5. Yesterday, petrol was $1·90 a litre. Petrol went up 10% overnight. How much a litre is petrol today?

   $_____

6. It takes 15 litres of water to fill the bird bath. In the summer, the water evaporates by 20% every day. How much water has to be added to the bird bath every evening to keep it full?

   ___ litres

SCORE /6   0-2   3-4   5-6

Statistics & Probability

AC9M6ST03

Stadium Statistics

Statistical data is not always presented visually.
Sometimes it is only presented in percentages like the football crowd data below.
Answer these statistical questions that use percentages.

1. The local football stadium has a capacity of 20 000 spectators. On Saturday, the stadium was at 70% capacity. How many spectators were at the game?

   _____

2. 30% of the spectators were the away-team supporters. How many away-team supporters were at the game?

   _____

3. 40% of the away-team supporters were under 16. How many away-team under-16 supporters were at the game?

   _____

4. The home team had 30% under-16s at the game. How many under-16 home supporters were at the game?

   _____

5. How many more over-16 home-team supporters were there than over-16 away-team supporters?

   _____

6. How many more under-16 home-team supporters were there than away-team under-16 supporters?

   _____

SCORE /6   0-2   3-4   5-6

TERM 3

TARGETING MATHS HOMEWORK: YEAR 6 © PASCAL PRESS ISBN: 9781925726596

UNIT 20 — Measurement & Space

AC9M6N07, AC9M6M01

Measurement Percentages

The metric system for measurement works really well with percentages.
For example, to find 10% of 1 kilometre:
  use 1 kilometre = 1000 metres
  10% of 1000 m = 100 m

Use your knowledge of the metric system for measurement to find these percentages.

	To find	Measure to use	Result
1	10% of 3 kilometres	3 km = 3000 m	10% of 3000 m =
2	15% of 8 metres		
3	70% of 4 litres		
4	15% of 2 kilograms		
5	11% of 3 metres		
6	26% of 1 kilogram		
7	21% of 3 tonnes		
8	34% of 5 kilometres		
9	2% of 120 millilitres		
10	18% of 3 grams		

TERM 3

SCORE /10   0-4   5-8   9-10

NAPLAN*-style Questions

1. 64·5 × 0·3 = ?
   ○ 1935   ○ 193·5   ○ 19·35   ○ 1·935

2. The family stopped for lunch 55% of the way through their 650-kilometre journey. How far did they have left to travel after lunch?
   _____ km

3. There were 60 000 people at the football match and 70% of them were under cover. How many were not under cover?
   _____

SCORE /3   0-1   2   3

Problem of the Week

UNIT 20

AC9M6N09

Fraction and Percentage Clues

Elsa and Liam each have a bag of blocks, which they have used to make up these challenges.

I have made up these clues about how many blocks of each colour there are in my bag of 60 blocks.

- There are twice as many white blocks as all the other colours put together.
- There are twice as many red as purple.
- There are five more blue than yellow.
- 10% of the blocks are yellow.

How many of each colour do I have?

How many blocks?
___ White
___ Red
___ Purple
___ Blue
___ Yellow

I have made up these clues about how many blocks of each colour there are in my bag of 80 blocks.

- 35% of my blocks are red.
- A quarter of the rest are blue.
- A third of the others are white.
- There are five more blue than yellow.
- The rest of the blocks in my bag are purple.

How many of each colour do I have?

How many blocks?
___ White
___ Red
___ Purple
___ Blue
___ Yellow

The Challenge

Imagine that you too have a bag of coloured blocks.

① How many blocks are in your bag? _____ blocks

② What different colours are your blocks?
_____

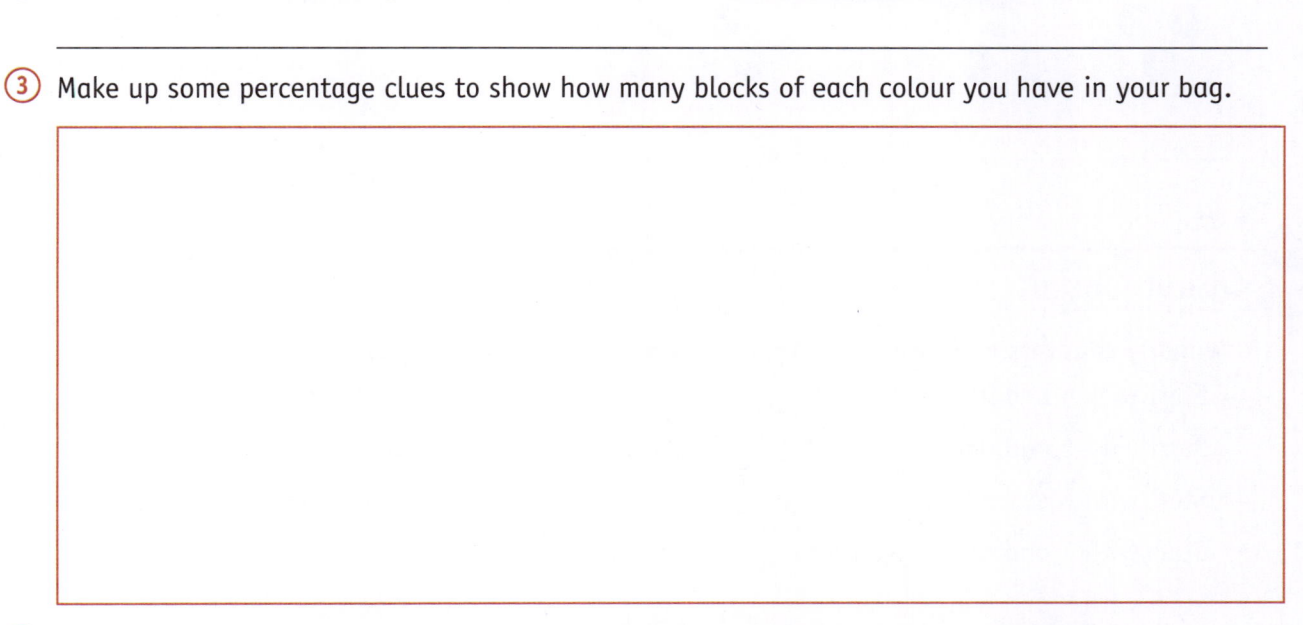

③ Make up some percentage clues to show how many blocks of each colour you have in your bag.

④ Challenge a friend to work out how many of each colour you have in your bag of blocks.

TERM 3

UNIT 21 — Number & Algebra

AC9M6A01

Growing Patterns

Here is the beginning of a growing pattern that I made with counters.

1	1 + 2	1 + 2 + 2
●	● ● ●	● ● ● ● ●
First unit	Second unit	Third unit

You can use addition to work out how many counters will be in the next pattern units. But you can also use multiplication. The sequence goes:

1,   1 + 2,   1 + 2 + 2,   1 + 2 + 2 + 2,   1 + 2 + 2 + 2 + 2

or   1,   1 + 1 × 2,   1 + 2 × 2,   1 + 3 × 2,   1 + 4 × 2

Write the pattern sequence and the multiplication rule for working out how many counters will be in the 10th unit for these patterns.

	Beginning of the pattern			Pattern sequence and multiplication rule	10th unit
	First unit	Second unit	Third unit		
①	(1 counter)	(4 counters)	(7 counters)		The 10th unit will use _____ counters.
②	(2 counters)	(5 counters)	(8 counters)		The 10th unit will use _____ counters.
③	(4 counters)	(7 counters)	(10 counters)		The 10th unit will use _____ counters.

SCORE /3   0-1   2   3

Quick Check

How many counters will be in the last unit of each of these patterns?

① Start with 4 and add 3 five times. _____
② Start with 5 and add 3 six times. _____
③ Start with 6 and add 4 seven times. _____
④ Start with 7 and add 4 five times. _____
⑤ Start with 2 and add 5 seven times. _____
⑥ Start with 8 and add 4 eight times. _____
⑦ Start with 9 and add 3 six times. _____
⑧ Start with 17 and add 12 six times. _____
⑨ Start with 24 and add 9 seven times. _____
⑩ Start with 12 and add 22 ten times. _____

SCORE /10   0-4   5-8   9-10

Number & Algebra

UNIT 21

AC9M6N08, AC9M6A03

Order of Operations Revisited

In Unit 6 you learned about BODMAS, which gives the order of operations as: 
- **B**rackets
- **O**ver
- **D**ivision and
- **M**ultiplication, then
- **A**ddition and
- **S**ubtraction.

It is time to practise order of operations again as it is really important to know how to work out the value of an arithmetical expression.

Use BODMAS to find the value of these expressions by using a tree diagram as we did in Unit 6. Question 1 shows you the steps.

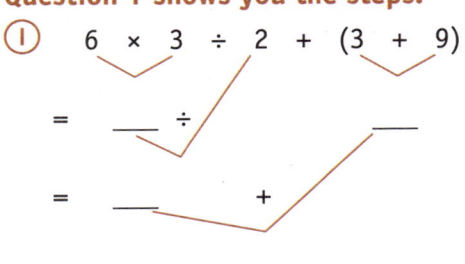

① 6 × 3 ÷ 2 + (3 + 9)

= ___ ÷ ___

= ___ + ___

= ___

④ 6 + (12 − 7) × 4 + 3

② 3 × 7 + (6 − 4) × 10

⑤ 36 ÷ 9 + 48 ÷ 8

③ 28 ÷ 4 + 27 ÷ 9

⑥ 31 × 4 − 24 + 6 × 3

SCORE /6   0-2   3-4   5-6

Statistics & Probability

AC9M6P01

Sara's Socks

Would you believe it? I have 30 pairs of socks but only three different types. I keep them all in the same drawer.

What I would like to know is:

How many socks do I need to take out of the drawer each morning so that I have a 100% chance of taking out a matching pair to wear that day?

Sara needs to take out ___ socks.

UNIT 21 — Measurement & Space

AC9M6SP03

Transformations

① Draw the three shapes in column A of the grid.
Then list the coordinates of the corners of the shapes.

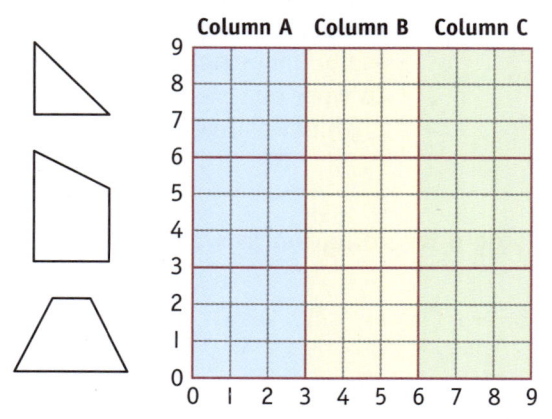

Column A Column B Column C

Shape 1	Shape 2	Shape 3
(___, ___)	(___, ___)	(___, ___)
(___, ___)	(___, ___)	(___, ___)
(___, ___)	(___, ___)	(___, ___)
	(___, ___)	(___, ___)

② Transform each shape by changing just one corner. Draw the new shapes in column B. List the corner coordinates for each new shape.

Shape 1	Shape 2	Shape 3
(___, ___)	(___, ___)	(___, ___)
(___, ___)	(___, ___)	(___, ___)
(___, ___)	(___, ___)	(___, ___)
	(___, ___)	(___, ___)

③ Transform each shape by changing one more corner. Draw the new shapes in column C. List the corner coordinates for each new shape.

Shape 1	Shape 2	Shape 3
(___, ___)	(___, ___)	(___, ___)
(___, ___)	(___, ___)	(___, ___)
(___, ___)	(___, ___)	(___, ___)
	(___, ___)	(___, ___)

SCORE /9   0–4   5–7   8–9

NAPLAN*-style Questions

① What is the answer to 6 × 7 + 8 ÷ 2?
○ 25   ○ 46   ○ 23   ○ 66

② Which equation matches this word problem?
Min made 4 fruit salads with 6 strawberries for each bowl and 5 fruit salads with 8 strawberries for each bowl. How many strawberries did Min use?
○ 4 + 6 + 5 + 8 = 23   ○ 4 × 6 + 5 + 8 = 37
○ 4 × 6 + 5 × 8 = 64   ○ 4 × 6 × 5 × 8 = 960

③ How many counters will be used in the 10th unit of this growing pattern?

_____ counters

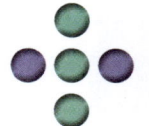

First unit   Second unit   Third unit

SCORE /3   0–1   2   3

TERM 3

92   TARGETING MATHS HOMEWORK: YEAR 6 © PASCAL PRESS ISBN: 9781925726596

Problem of the Week

UNIT 21

AC9M6N09

Figurate Numbers

When you make a sequence of pattern units that make a particular shape, the numbers are called figurate numbers.

Here is a sequence that uses a shape you know well:

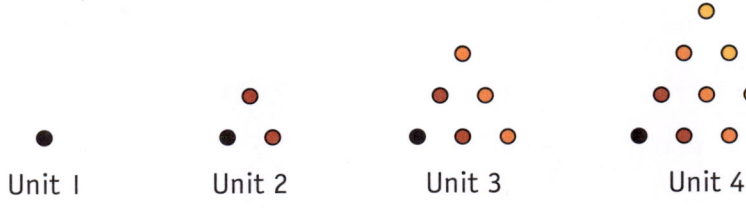

Unit 1   Unit 2   Unit 3   Unit 4

The sequence is 1, 3, 6, 10 and these are called **triangular numbers**.
The sequence is also made by adding the numbers like this: 1, 1 + 2, 1 + 2 + 3, and so on.

① Make a list of the first 10 triangular numbers.

_____, _____, _____, _____, _____, _____, _____, _____, _____, _____.

Here is another shape that you will recognise.

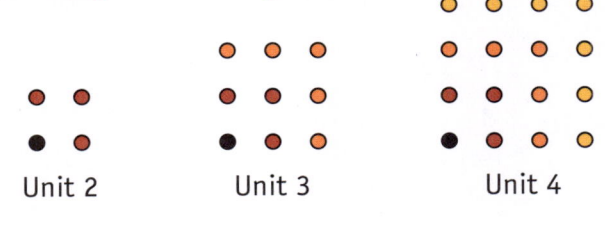

Unit 1   Unit 2   Unit 3   Unit 4

② What are these numbers called? _____

③ What sequence do the numbers of counters in these shapes make? List the first 10 numbers.
   _____

④ These are the numbers that are added to make this sequence: 1, 1 + 3, 1 + 3 + 5, and so on. What type of numbers are they?
   _____

Now for something really strange!

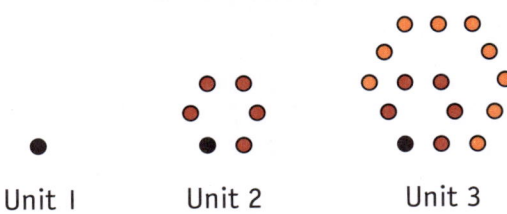

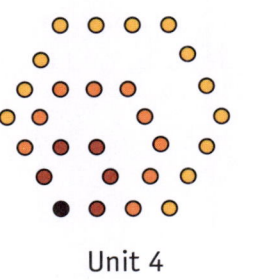

Unit 1   Unit 2   Unit 3   Unit 4

⑤ What shape do the counters in this sequence make? _____

⑥ Make a list of the first five numbers in this sequence.

   1, _____, _____, _____, _____

⑦ Where have you seen those numbers before? _____

TARGETING MATHS HOMEWORK: YEAR 6 © PASCAL PRESS ISBN: 9781925726596

93

UNIT 22

Number & Algebra

AC9M6N06

Multiplying Decimals

The decimal equations on this page have been designed so that you can work out the first example in a set using a calculator if you want to. For the remaining equations in each set, use your knowledge of place value to work out the answers.

Here is an example to get you started.

27·6 × 3 = 82·8

37·6 × 3 = 27·6 × 3 + 10 × 3 (because 37·6 is 10 more than 27·6)
= 82·8 + 30 = 112·8

37·7 × 3 = 112·8 + 0·1 × 3 (because 37·7 is 0·1 more than 37·6)
= 112·8 + 0·3 = 113·1

Complete these equations sets.

① 23·4 × 4 = _____

② 23·5 × 4 = _____ + _____ = _____

③ 33·5 × 4 = _____ + _____ = _____

④ 33·6 × 4 = _____ + _____ = _____

⑤ 43·6 × 4 = _____ + _____ = _____

⑥ 38·4 × 6 = _____

⑦ 38·5 × 6 = _____ + _____ = _____

⑧ 28·5 × 6 = _____ − _____ = _____

⑨ 48·5 × 6 = _____ + _____ = _____

⑩ 48·7 × 6 = _____ + _____ = _____

SCORE /10 0-4 5-8 9-10

Quick Check

Complete the multiplications in this table.
If you want to, use a calculator to find the answer to the multiplications in the first column.

① 23·2 × 7 = _____   23·3 × 7 = _____   33·3 × 7 = _____

② 38·3 × 4 = _____   36·3 × 4 = _____   56·3 × 4 = _____

③ 18·7 × 5 = _____   18·8 × 5 = _____   28·8 × 5 = _____

④ 36·4 × 3 = _____   36·6 × 3 = _____   46·6 × 3 = _____

⑤ 29·6 × 4 = _____   29·5 × 4 = _____   19·5 × 4 = _____

SCORE /15 0-7 8-13 14-15

Number & Algebra

UNIT 22

AC9M6N06

Multiplying Money Amounts

Multiplying money amounts by 10, 100 or 1000 is very similar to multiplying decimals by 10, 100 or 1000.

To multiply $36·50 by 10, the numerals move one place to the left.
$36·50 × 10 = $365

To multiply $36·50 by 100, the numerals move two places to the left.
$36·50 × 100 = $3650

To multiply $36·50 by 1000, the numerals move three places to the left.
$36·50 × 1000 = $36 500

Use your place value knowledge to solve these money problems.

1. How much are 10 cartons of juice at $12·50 a carton?

    $_____

2. How much are 100 tournament tennis balls at $3·75 each?

    $_____

3. Tau has saved $1·75 a day for the last 100 days. How much has he saved so far?

    $_____

4. The greengrocer bought 100 boxes of apples at the wholesale market at $38·60 a box. How much did he pay for the apples?

    $_____

5. The stamp dealer bought 1000 rare stamps at the stamp auction for $13·75 a stamp. How much did the stamp dealer pay for the stamps?

    $_____

SCORE /5   0-2   3-4   5

Statistics & Probability

AC9M6P02

10 Counters in the Bag

I have made up a bag with these 10 counters.

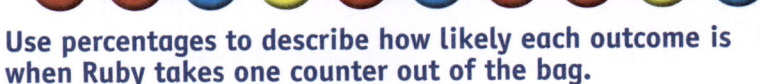

Use percentages to describe how likely each outcome is when Ruby takes one counter out of the bag.

1. It will be a green counter. _____

2. It will be a red counter. _____

3. It will not be a yellow counter. _____

4. It will not be a black counter. _____

5. It will be either a blue or a red counter. _____

SCORE /5   0-2   3-4   5

TERM 3

UNIT 22 — Measurement & Space

AC9M6M02

Hidden Areas

Sara and Min have been making area puzzles.
They draw a grid and then colour over part of it. Then they swap their puzzles.
Here are some of their puzzles for you to solve.

What is the area of the grid that has not been coloured? Note: 1 square = 1 cm²

1. Area = ___ cm²

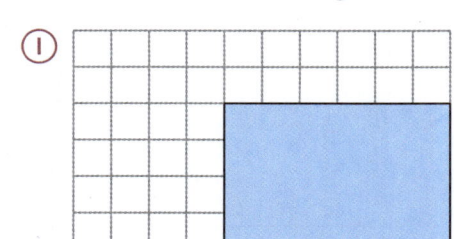

2. Area = ___ cm²

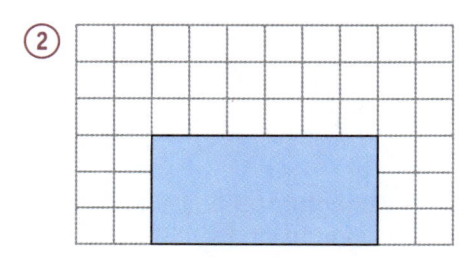

3. Area = ___ cm²

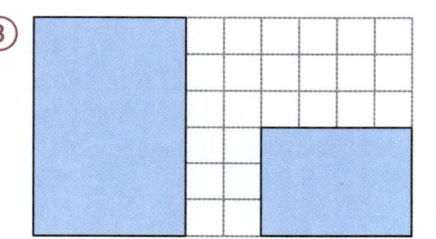

4. Area = ___ cm²

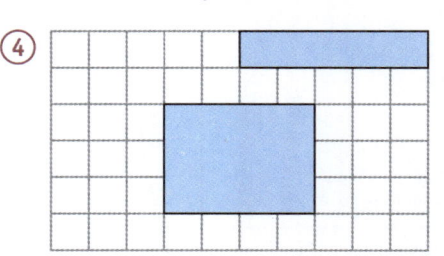

5. Area = ___ cm²

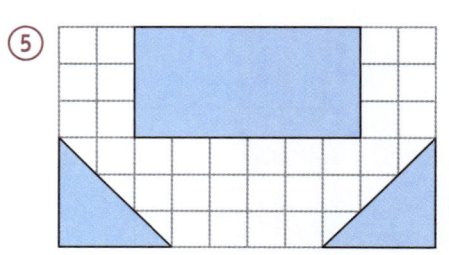

6. Area = ___ cm²

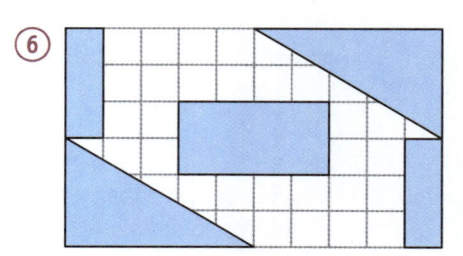

SCORE /6   0-2   3-4   5-6

NAPLAN*-style Questions

1. How much change will Alex get from $50 after buying 10 avocadoes at $1·75 each?

   $ _____

2. Which triangle has an area greater than 3 square units? 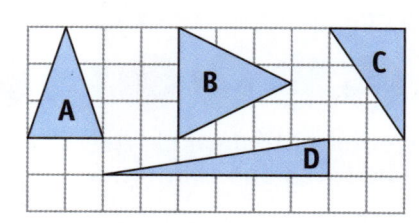
   ○ A   ○ B   ○ C   ○ D

3. Hai had a packet of jelly snakes with an equal number of red, orange, green and black snakes in it.
   Without looking, what is the chance of pulling out a red snake?
   ○ 4%   ○ 35%   ○ 25%   ○ 40%

SCORE /3   0-1   2   3

96   TARGETING MATHS HOMEWORK: YEAR 6 © PASCAL PRESS ISBN: 9781925726596

Problem of the Week

UNIT 22

AC9M6N09, AC9M6M02

Investigating Borders

"Good morning, class. This week's investigation is based on making a shape with tiles.

"We start with two tiles that will form the inside of our shape. They are joined along one side.

"Then we place extra tiles around this shape to give it a border.

"After that, find the area and perimeter of the new shape."

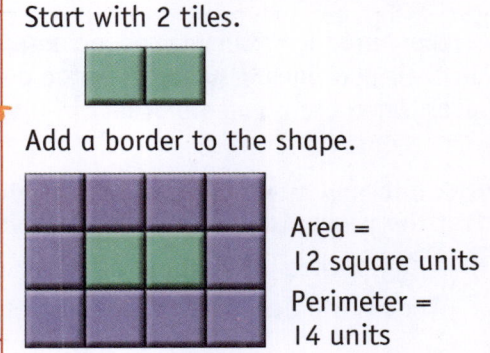

Start with 2 tiles.

Add a border to the shape.

Area = 12 square units

Perimeter = 14 units

Use the grid to investigate what different areas and perimeters you get when you use three tiles as the centre and surround them with extra tiles.

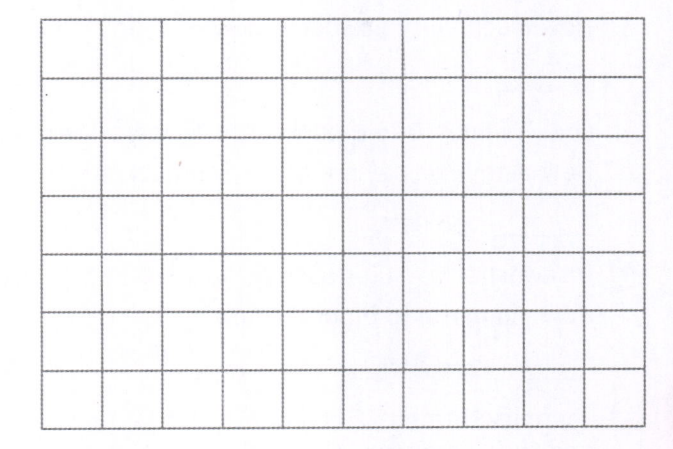

The Challenge

That was a warm-up! Repeat the process now using four tiles to make the inside of your shape. Investigate what different areas and perimeters can be made when your inside shape is surrounded by extra tiles.

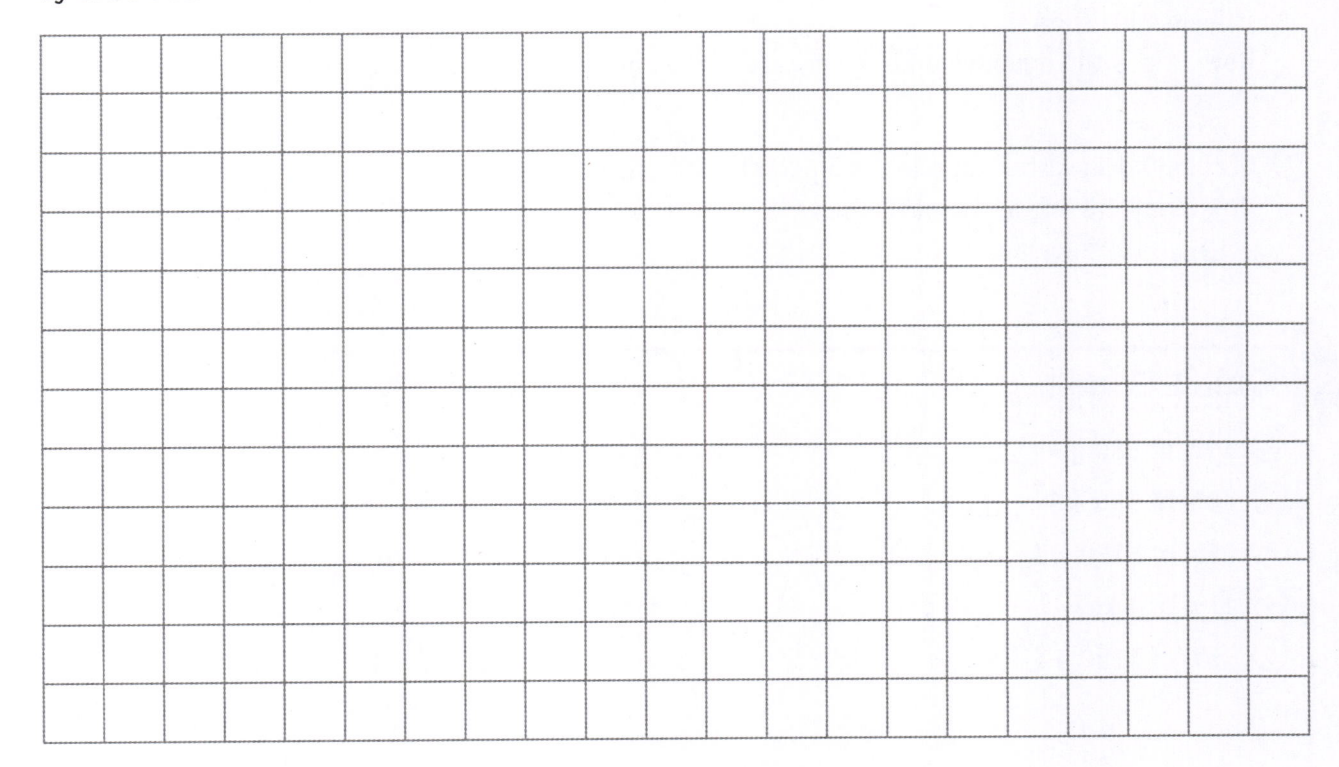

TERM 3

TARGETING MATHS HOMEWORK: YEAR 6 © PASCAL PRESS ISBN: 9781925726596

97

UNIT 23

Number & Algebra

AC9M6N07

Percentage Increases

Grocery producers sometimes increase or decrease the amount of product in their packages. Usually the price and the size of the package stay the same even when there is more or less in the package.

Work out how much more or less product is in each package after the percentage adjustments have been made.

① 750 g packets of dog biscuits have 10% fewer biscuits than before.
How much is the new mass of dog biscuits in each packet?

_____ g

② 60 g tins of curry powder have 15% less curry powder than before.
How much curry powder is now in a tin?

_____ g

③ Cookies had 10 in a packet but that has been increased by 10%.
How many cookies are there in a packet now?

_____ cookies

④ Dishwasher capsules used to have 30 in a packet but now have 20% more.
How many are in a packet now?

_____ capsules

⑤ There used to be 12 cereal biscuits in a packet, but the price has gone up and the contents of the packet has also gone up 25%.
How many cereal biscuits are there in a cereal packet now?

_____ biscuits

⑥ The length of liquorice on a liquorice pinwheel used to be 75 cm when unwound.
It is now 5% shorter.
How long is the liquorice on a liquorice pinwheel now?

_____ cm

⑦ Of the 30 dishwasher capsules in a packet, 10% have been used.
How many are left in the packet now?

_____ capsules

SCORE /7   0-3   4-5   6-7

Quick Check

① 10% of 580 g = _____ g
② 40% of $60 = $_____
③ 25% of $150 = $_____
④ 11% of 1 kg = _____ g
⑤ 35% of $150 = $_____
⑥ 20% of 750 g = _____ g
⑦ 45% of 1 kg = _____ g
⑧ 99% of $200 = $_____
⑨ 20% of 1 kg = _____ g
⑩ 20% of $1678 = $_____

SCORE /10   0-4   5-8   9-10

Number & Algebra

UNIT 23

AC9M6N02

Special Number Towers

Blocks used to make three towers:

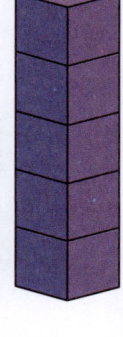

"You may use no more than 36 blocks to solve these puzzles," Mr Green told his class.

"For each puzzle, write the total number of blocks used, including the number of blocks in each tower."

He showed this picture as an example of what the class has to do for Puzzle 1.

Puzzle 1

Use a **square number** of blocks and make three towers that are all different heights and all an **odd number** of blocks high.

① The square number chosen was 9.

② The towers are ___ blocks, ___ blocks and ___ blocks high.

Now choose a different number of blocks.

③ The square number chosen was ____.

④ The towers are ____ blocks, ____ blocks and ____ blocks high.

Remember, use no more than 36 blocks.

Puzzle 2

Use a **prime number** of blocks and again make three towers that are all an **odd number** of blocks high.

⑤ The prime number chosen was ____.

⑥ The towers are ____ blocks, ____ blocks and ____ blocks high.

Now choose a different number of blocks.

⑦ The prime number chosen was ____.

⑧ The towers are ____ blocks, ____ blocks and ____ blocks high.

SCORE /8   0-3 4-6 7-8

Statistics & Probability

AC9M6ST02

Making Comparisons

The Year 5 and Year 6 students have been comparing school attendance over two years.

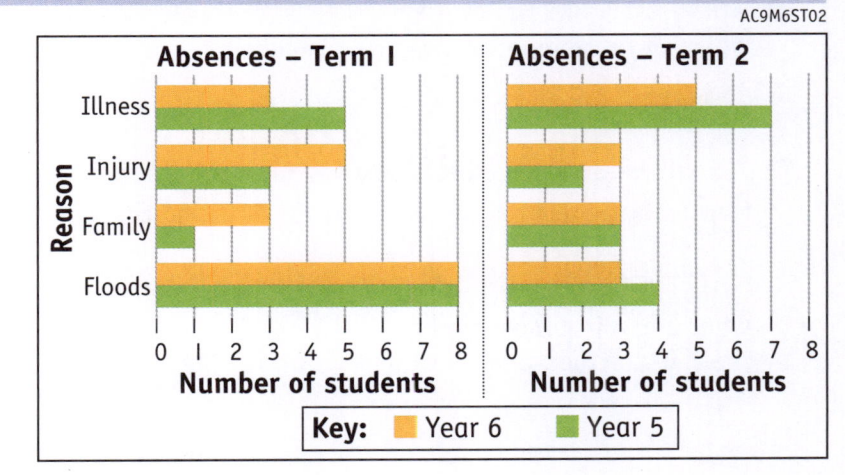

① Which year level had more absences in Term 1?

_____

② Which year level had more absences due to illness over both terms?

_____

Absences – Term 1 / **Absences – Term 2**

Reason: Illness, Injury, Family, Floods

Number of students (0–8)

Key: ■ Year 6 ■ Year 5

③ How many more absences were there in Term 1 than in Term 2? _____

④ How many school days were lost altogether? _____

⑤ Which category will look very different in Term 3? _____

⑥ Why is that? _____

SCORE /6   0-2 3-4 5-6

TERM 3

UNIT 23 — Measurement & Space

AC9M6M04

Angles in a Shape

In earlier units, we learned about angles and their size in degrees.

Angles on a straight line add to 180°.

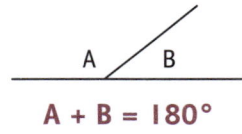

A + B = 180°

Vertically opposite angles are equal and angles at a point add to 360°.

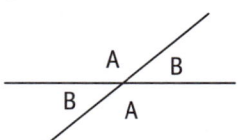

A + A + B + B = 360°

Angles of a quadrilateral add to 360°.

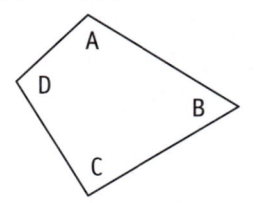

A + B + C + D = 360°

Use your knowledge of angles to work out the missing angles in this diagram.

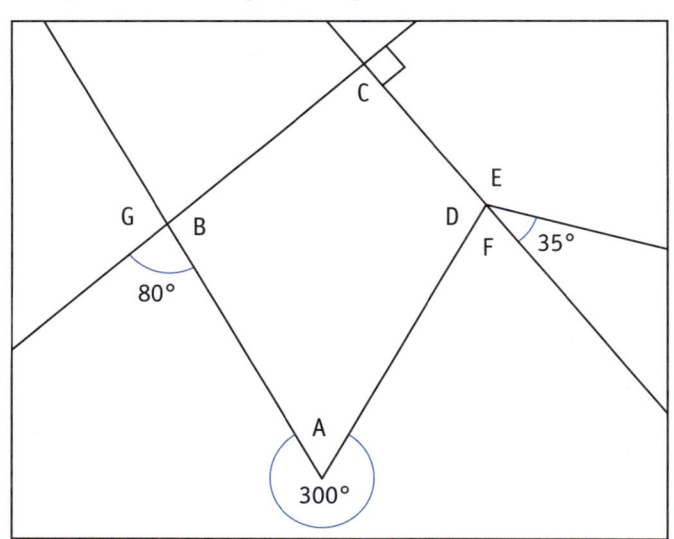

(diagram shows angles labelled A, B, C, D, E, F, G with 80°, 35°, 300° marked, and a right angle at C)

The Results

① Angle A = _____ °
② Angle B = _____ °
③ Angle C = _____ °
④ Angle D = _____ °
⑤ Angle E = _____ °
⑥ Angle F = _____ °
⑦ Angle G = _____ °

SCORE /7   0-3   4-5   6-7

NAPLAN*-style Questions

① Which of these numbers are prime numbers?
○ 41   ○ 1   ○ 39   ○ 2

② 75% of the 3500 spectators at a fun run wore the fund-raising caps. How many people did not wear the fund-raising caps?

_____ people

③ What angle is represented by the ? in the diagram?

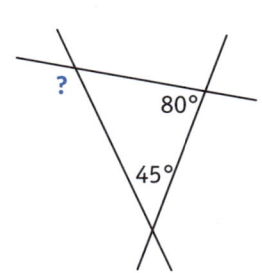

_____ °

(diagram with ?, 80°, 45°)

SCORE /3   0-1   2   3

Problem of the Week

UNIT 23

AC9M6N09

The Hexagon Puzzle

The Challenge

Arrange the numbers 1–19 in the circles so that the numbers along each side of each triangle add to the same total.

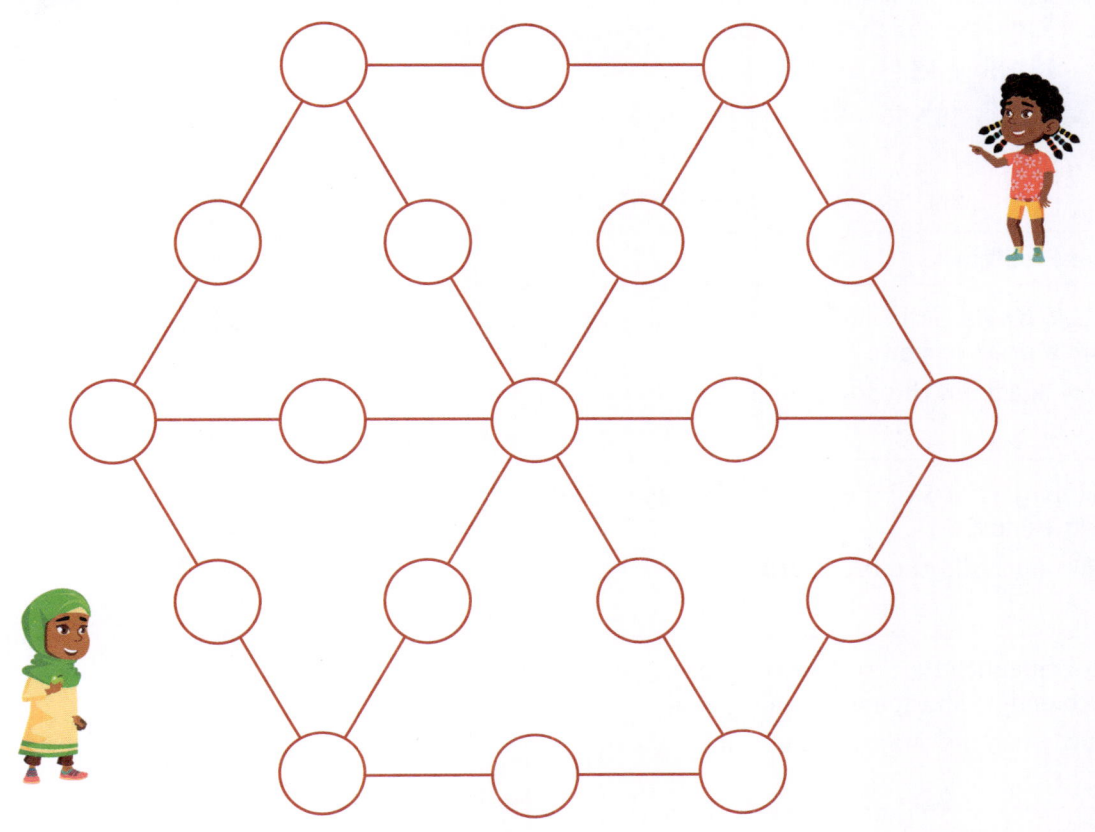

Ruby and Sara have some suggestions that will help you find the solution to this challenge.

- We made 19 small pieces of paper and wrote the numbers 1–19 on them. It meant that we never used a number more than once and that saved a lot of time.
- We found that the total along each side has to be the smallest **prime number in the 20s**.
- We put the **number 6 in the middle position** and that really helped us to find the solution.

Ruby and Sara started with the most difficult number to place, which is 19.

"What could go with 19 to make that prime number in the 20s?"

They then found that 19, 18 and 17 could be placed in sequence round the outside edge.

Working space

TARGETING MATHS HOMEWORK: YEAR 6 © PASCAL PRESS ISBN: 9781925726596

101

UNIT 24 — Number & Algebra

AC9M6A02

Word Problems with Unknowns

Answer the questions below by writing the equation that represents the problem. Then solve the equation. Here is an example.

> Min spent $165. She bought a paintbrush, a set of paints that cost $87·50 and a large canvas that cost $52. How much did the paintbrush cost?
>
> ☐ + $87·50 + $52 = $165
>
> ☐ = $165 − $87·50 − $52 = $165 − $139·50
>
> ☐ = $25·50

The Problem	The Solution
① A $24 movie ticket, a $5·50 box of popcorn and a drink came to $37. How much did the drink cost?	$24 + $5·50 + ☐ = $37
② Six burgers at $4·50 each plus six large boxes of fries cost $54. How much did the fries each cost?	
③ Alex bought 3 books at $19·50 each and a calendar. She spent $84 altogether. How much did the calendar cost?	
④ Hai spent $200 on a pair of shorts that cost $56 and four T-shirts. How much did each T-shirt cost?	
⑤ Liam made three payments of $35 towards the $200 school camp and then a fourth payment. He still has $80 left to pay. How much was his fourth payment?	

SCORE /5   0-2   3-4   5

Quick Check

① 4 at $27·50 each = $_____

② 6 at $12·39 each = $_____

③ $75 − $49·50 = $_____

④ $27·15 − $11·95 = $_____

⑤ $16·27 + $_____ = $29·50

⑥ $27·50 + $_____ = $49

⑦ $32·75 + $_____ = $189

⑧ $104 − $_____ = $65·50

⑨ $38·75 − $_____ = $15·90

⑩ $59·50 − $_____ = $27·50

SCORE /10   0-4   5-8   9-10

TERM 3

102   TARGETING MATHS HOMEWORK: YEAR 6 © PASCAL PRESS ISBN: 9781925726596

Number & Algebra

UNIT 24

AC9M6N02

Special Number Problems

Questions 1 and 2 will help you find the answers to the remaining questions.

1. List the prime numbers to 35.
   _____
   _____

2. List the square numbers to 100.
   _____
   _____

3. The single-digit square number and the single-digit composite number that add together to make 15 are
   _____ and _____.

4. The composite number greater than 90 but less than 100 which is a multiple of 7 could be
   _____ or _____.

5. List the odd composite numbers in the 20s that are not square numbers.
   _____

6. The 4th square number plus the first prime number add to
   _____.

7. The sum of the first five prime numbers is _____.

8. The difference between the fifth and sixth prime numbers is _____.

9. Two square numbers that add to a prime number in the 40s are
   _____ and _____.

10. The square number and the prime number that have a difference of 14 are
    _____ and _____.

11. The three square numbers that add to a prime number in the 20s are
    _____, _____ and _____.

12. The three prime numbers that add to a palindrome in the 30s are
    _____, _____ and _____.

A palindrome is a number that reads the same forwards as backwards, like 22 or 101.

SCORE /12   0-5   6-10   11-12

Statistics & Probability

AC9M6ST01

Making a Graph

Make a side-by-side column graph of this data.

Pets Owned by Year 4, Year 5 and Year 6 Students at Stoke Primary School

Year level	Girls	Boys
Year 4	15	12
Year 5	20	18
Year 6	16	22

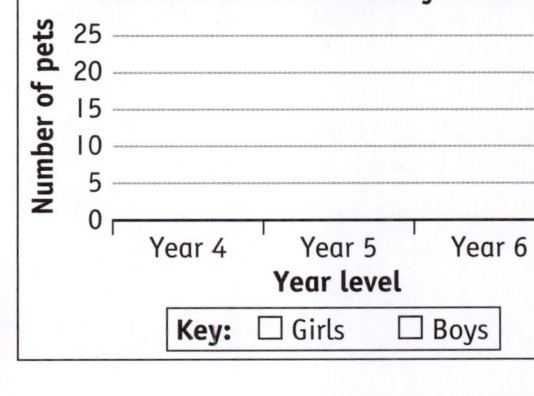

Pets Owned by Year 4, Year 5 and Year 6 Students at Stoke Primary School

Number of pets: 0, 5, 10, 15, 20, 25
Year level: Year 4, Year 5, Year 6

Key: ☐ Girls ☐ Boys

SCORE /6   0-2   3-4   5-6

TARGETING MATHS HOMEWORK: YEAR 6 © PASCAL PRESS ISBN: 9781925726596

UNIT 24 — Measurement & Space

AC9M6M03

A Train Timetable

This is part of the timetable for trains from Seaford to the City.

Station	Train A	Train B	Train C	Train D
Seaford	12:33	12:45	12:50	13:05
Merino Rocks	12:46	12:54	–	–
Goodwood	12:54	–	13:00	–
Mile End	13:03	–	13:09	–
City	13:14	13:15	13:18	13:25

1. Which is the express train?

    Train ____

2. Which train stops at all stations?

    Train ____

3. How long does the journey from Seaford to the City take on Train B?

    ____ minutes

4. How much longer does Train A take than Train D to make the journey from Seaford to the City?

    ____ minutes

5. If you had to get from Seaford to Mile End for a meeting at 1:30 pm, which train should you take?

    Train ____

6. If you wanted to admire the scenery as you travelled to the City, which train would you take?

    Train ____

7. How much longer does Train B take than Train C to make the journey from Seaford to the City?

    ____ minutes

8. How long does it take to get from Seaford to Merino Rocks on Train B?

    ____ minutes

9. How much quicker is Train C than Train A on the journey from Goodwood to the City?

    ____ minutes

10. You have a meeting in the City at 13:30 and it is a 15-minute walk from City station to the meeting. Which train should you take?

    Train ____

SCORE /10   0-4   5-8   9-10

NAPLAN*-style Questions

1. Which of these multiplications is not equal to 48 × 20?

    ○ 480 × 2
    ○ 48 × 10 × 10
    ○ 48 × 2 × 10
    ○ 6 × 8 × 2 × 10

2. Hai spent $95. He bought a T-shirt for $39.90, a cap for $27.50 and a puzzle. How much did Hai spend on the puzzle?

    $_____

3. Sara arrived at Merino Rocks station at 10:59 on her way to the City.
   At what time did she arrive at the City?

    ○ 11:29   ○ 11:30
    ○ 11:48   ○ 12:01

Station	Train A	Train B	Train C	Train D
Seaford	10:53	11:07	11:12	–
Merino Rocks	10:59	11:13	–	11:31
Goodwood	11:14	–	13:00	11:46
Mile End	11:19	11:30	–	11:51
City	11:29	–	11:48	12:01

SCORE /3   0-1   2   3

TERM 3

Problem of the Week

UNIT 24

Morning Tea Orders

Many offices near our cafe send us an order for morning tea.

Some orders do not say exactly what they want, but they say how much they would like to spend. For example, we had an order this morning: Cakes for about $100 please.

We really struggle to make up orders to match the requested amount. We think a table of values would be a big help.

I would add an extra column to show how much for 1 or 2 of everything.

Please complete the table for us.

Qty	Choc-chip muffins	Protein bars	Savoury scones	Mini-quiches	Carrot cakes
1	$3·75	$4·25	$3·25	$5·75	$3·00
2	$7·50	$8·50	$6·50	$11·50	$6·00
3					
4					
5					
6					

Use the completed table to plan two morning tea orders for $50. List the items and costs here.

Item	Quantity	Cost

Total Cost:

Item	Quantity	Cost

Total Cost:

The Challenge

Make up any morning tea you like for $100.

Item	Quantity	Cost

TERM 3

Review: Unit 17 and Unit 18

AC9M6N01, AC9M6N03, AC9M6N04, AC9M6M01, AC9M6M03

① Start with 25, subtract 30 and add 6, and the answer = ____

② Start with −26, add 15 and subtract 8, and the answer = ____

③ A square number + 6 = 70. What is the number that was squared? ____

Write the answers to these clues in 24-hour time.

From	To	24-hour time
④ am clock	pm 1:15	___:___ to ___:___ is ___ h ___ min
⑤ pm 3:45	am clock	___:___ to ___:___ is ___ h ___ min

Label the number line and place the fractions correctly on the line.

⑥ $\frac{5}{6}$ and $\frac{7}{12}$

⑦ $\frac{3}{5}$ and $\frac{4}{15}$

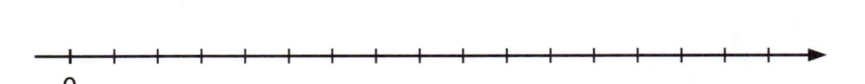

Write each decimal addition in vertical format and then work out the answer.

⑧ 1327·65 + 3·7 + 13·76

⑨ 10·7 + 0·7 + 3·765

⑩ Three 5-litre buckets of water are each $\frac{4}{5}$ full. How much water is that?

_____ litres

⑪ A 6-litre bucket of water is 75% full. How much water is in the bucket?

_____ litres

Review: Unit 19 and Unit 20

Find the lowest common denominator to add these fractions.

1. $2\frac{1}{2} + 1\frac{3}{8} =$ +   =

2. $1\frac{5}{8} + 1\frac{3}{4} =$ +   =

3. $1\frac{1}{6} + 1\frac{1}{4} =$ +   =

Complete these fraction subtractions.

4. $2\frac{3}{5} - 1\frac{3}{10} =$ −   =

5. $2\frac{5}{8} - 1\frac{3}{16} =$ −   =

6. $2\frac{5}{6} - 1\frac{1}{8} =$ −   =

7. Show how to continue this shape as a tessellating pattern. Use colour.

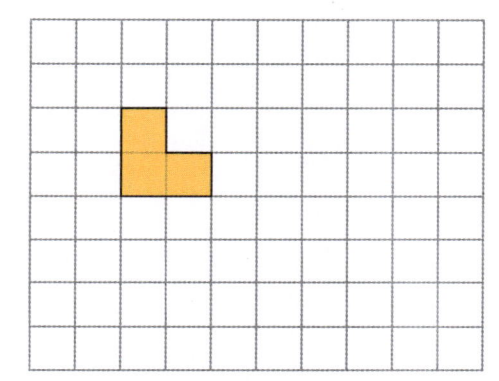

Complete these conversions and multiplications.

8. 6 × 0·5   6 × 5 ÷ 10 = _____

9. 7 × 0·3   _____

10. 16 × 0·6   _____

11. There were 20 000 spectators at the game and 80% were adults. How many under-18s were at the game?

    _____

12. Of the 20 000 spectators, 35% were under cover. How many spectators were not under cover?

    _____

13. 15% of 3 kg = _____ g

14. 11% of 50 km = _____ m

15. 26% of 1 litre = _____ mL

16. 35% of 6 m = _____ cm

Review: Unit 21 and Unit 22

① How many counters will be needed to make the 10th unit of this growing pattern?

_____ counters

First unit   Second unit   Third unit

Complete these expressions using a tree diagram.

② 27 ÷ 3 + 6 + 4 × 5

④ 64 ÷ 4 + 5 + 18 ÷ 3

③ 4 × 12 − 6 + 3 × 9

⑤ 7 × 4 − 3 + 28 ÷ 4

Complete these multiplications.

⑥ 6 × 0·4 = _____

⑧ 5 × 0·6 = _____

⑦ 13·5 × 10 = _____

⑨ 27·6 × 20 = _____

⑩ How much would it cost for 10 boxes of oranges at $12·75 per box?

$_____

⑪ Sara saved 85c every day for 100 days. How much money did Sara save?

$_____

⑫ The baker sells 1000 sliced loaves a week at $5·25 per loaf. How much does the baker get from the sales?

$_____

What are the covered and uncovered areas of these grids? Each square = 1 cm².

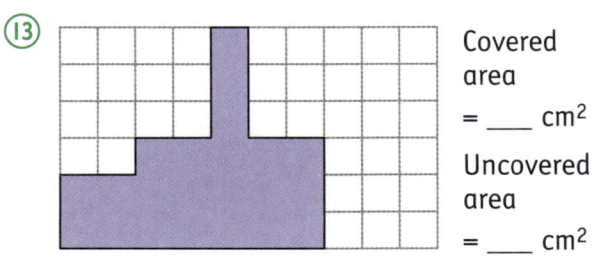

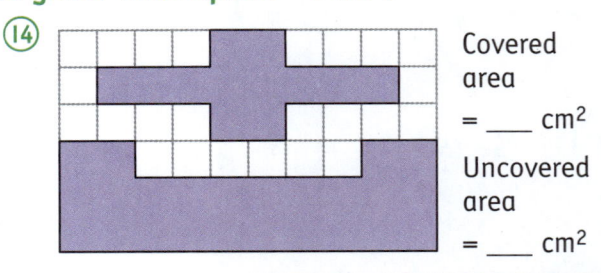

⑬ Covered area = ___ cm²
Uncovered area = ___ cm²

⑭ Covered area = ___ cm²
Uncovered area = ___ cm²

SCORE /14   0-6   7-12   13-14

108   TARGETING MATHS HOMEWORK: YEAR 6 © PASCAL PRESS ISBN: 9781925726596

Review: Unit 23 and Unit 24

AC9M6N02, AC9M6N07, AC9M6A02, AC9M6M03, AC9M6M04, AC9M6ST01

1. 25% of a 750 g packet of dog biscuits has been eaten.
   How many grams of dog biscuits are left in the packet?

   _____ g

2. 26% of a 2 L bottle of orange juice has already been drunk.
   How much orange juice is left in the bottle?

   _____ mL

3. A square number and a prime number when added together equal 26.
   What are the two numbers?

   The square number is ____ and the prime number is ____.

What are the missing angles in these diagrams?

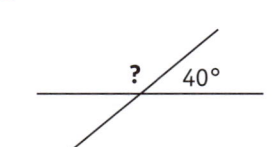

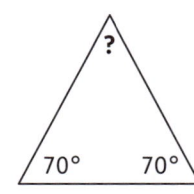

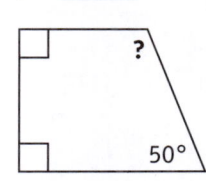

4. ? = _____°

5. ? = _____°

6. ? = _____°

What are the missing amounts in these expressions?

7. $75 − $_____ = $49·50

8. ___ × $26 + $15 = $119

9. 6 × $_____ + $5 = $95

10. $27·50 + $_____ + $15 = $55

11. List three prime numbers which, when added together, equal a square number in the 30s.

    ____, ____ and ____

12. A train leaves Seaford at 7:45 am and stops at Merino Rocks, Goodwood, Mile End and the City.
    It takes 9 minutes between each stop.
    At what time does the 7:45 am train reach the City? _____ am

Use the side-by-side column graph to answer the questions below.

13. What was the sample size for this graph?

    _____ students

14. Which year group owns the most pets?

    Year ___

15. How many more Year 6 students than Year 4 students own a pet?

    _____ students

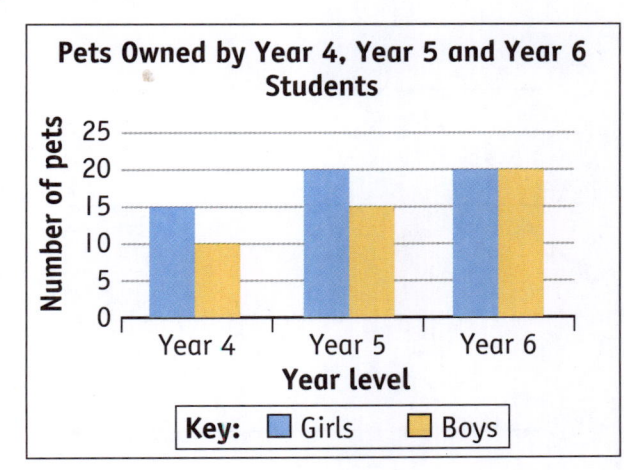

Pets Owned by Year 4, Year 5 and Year 6 Students

Key: Girls, Boys

UNIT 25

Number & Algebra

AC9M6N01

Integers on a Number Line

The following questions ask you to mark an integer on the number line as accurately as you can.

For example, show where zero fits on this line.

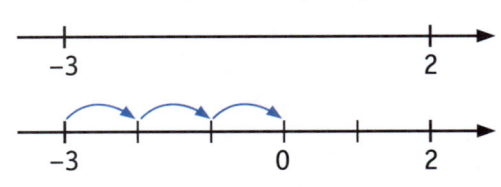

You will need to work out how many spaces to mark on the line. You can do this by counting on: −3, −2, −1, 0, 1, 2. So that's five spaces. Now you can use the line to find zero.

Complete these number line questions.

① Where will zero fit on this line? (−6 to 4)

② Where will −3 fit on this line? (−7 to 1)

③ Where will 3 fit on this line? (−1 to 9)

④ Where will 2 fit on this line? (−3 to 6)

⑤ Where will 50 fit on this line? (−50 to 100)

SCORE /5   0-2   3-4   5

Quick Check

Write the number represented by ? on these number lines.

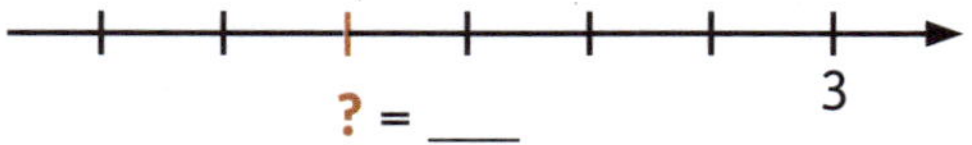

① 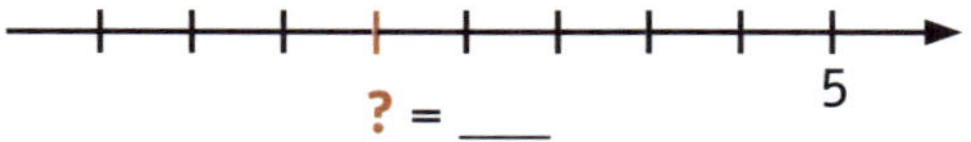 ? = ___ (line ends at 5)

② ? = ___ (line ends at 3)

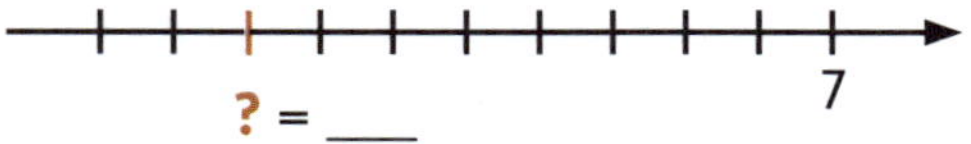

③ ? = ___ (line ends at 7)

④ ? = ___ (line ends at 12)

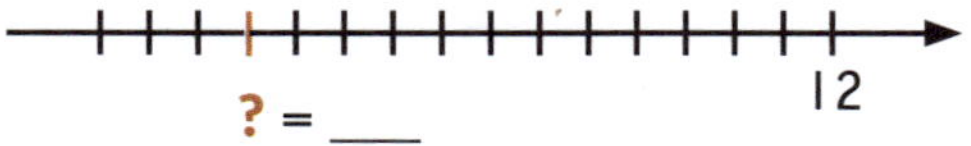

⑤ 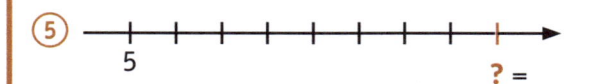 5 ... ? = ___

⑥ 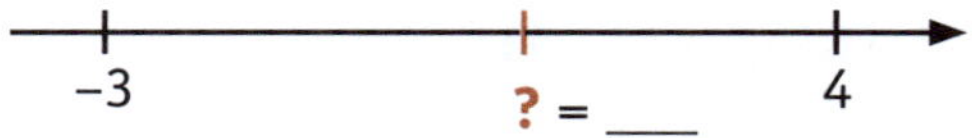 −3 ... ? = ___ ... 4

⑦ 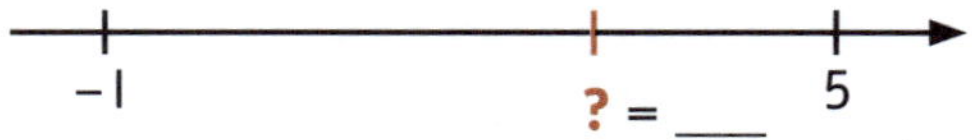 −1 ... ? = ___ ... 5

⑧ 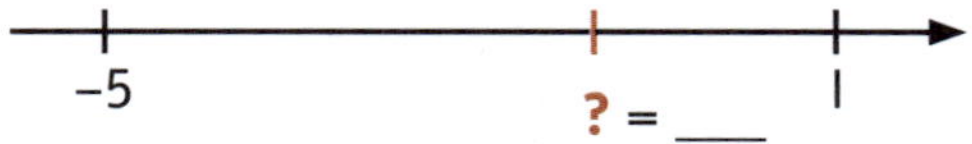 −5 ... ? = ___ ... 1

⑨ 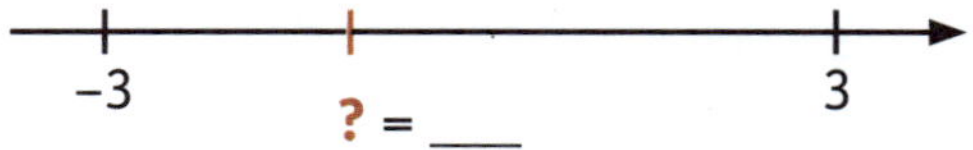 −3 ... ? = ___ ... 3

⑩ −7 ... ? = ___ ... 1

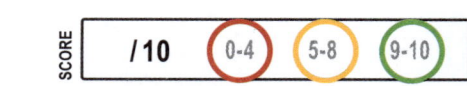

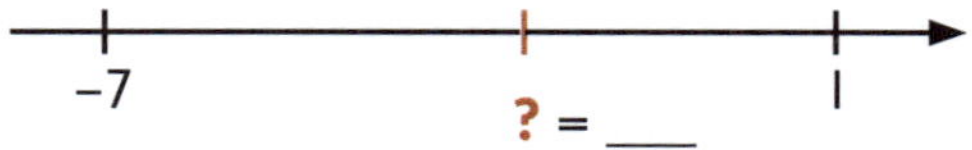

SCORE /10   0-4   5-8   9-10

Number & Algebra

Investigating Decimal Addition

"Right," said Mr Green to his class. "Here is a warm-up to get your brain thinking before we begin today's investigation."

The warm-up Mr Green gave the class was to take each decimal number he had written on the board and reverse the digits so that they had an addition that looked like this:

```
  1.3
+ 3.1
-----
```

These are the numbers that Mr Green put on the board. Follow his instructions and complete the additions.

① 2.4 +___ ___
② 3.5 +___ ___
③ 6.3 +___ ___
④ 1.7 +___ ___
⑤ 5.6 +___ ___

⑥ What type of numbers do the answers make? _____

Mr Green asked, "Do you think you will get the same results with 3-digit decimal numbers if you make two new numbers by moving the last number to the front?"

```
           34.1
Move the 1 to the front:  13.4
Move the 4 to the front: +41.3
                         -----
```

Try a few and see what happens.

⑦ 12.4 +___
⑧ 31.5 +___
⑨ 24.3 +___
⑩ 16.2 +___
⑪ 51.6 +___

⑫ What happens this time? _____

SCORE /12 (0-5) (6-10) (11-12)

Statistics & Probability

Muffin Sales

Line graphs can be used to show all kinds of data. The line graph here shows how much profit can be made by selling muffins at a fund-raiser.

Profit From Muffin Sales (Profit ($) vs Number of Muffins Sold; shown values 9 and 21 on vertical axis, 1–10 on horizontal axis)

Use the line graph to answer these questions.

① The amounts on the vertical axis are incomplete. Write the missing amounts.

② How much profit will be made if 6 muffins are sold? $____

③ How many muffins need to be sold to make a profit of $30?   ____ muffins

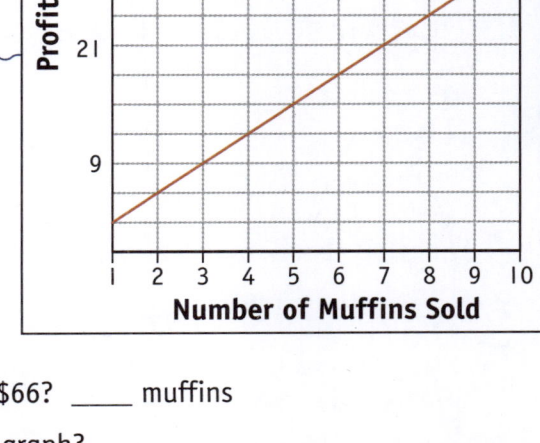

④ How many muffins need to be sold to make a profit of $66? ____ muffins

⑤ What do you notice about the shape of the line on the graph? _____

⑥ Why do you think the line makes that shape?
_____

SCORE /6 (0-2) (3-4) (5-6)

UNIT 25

Measurement & Space

AC9M6M01

Animal Mass

Draw lines to match each creature with its body mass.

	Creature	Body Mass
①	Black ant	18 kg
②	Koala	4 t
③	Elephant	6 mg
④	Hummingbird	12 kg
⑤	Border collie	20 g

Now use the clues to find the mass of food each creature eats in one day and then in 10 days.

	The Creature	The Clues	Eats per day	Eats in 10 days
⑥	Black ant	The black ant eats 30% of its own weight every day.		
⑦	Koala	The koala eats $\frac{1}{10}$ of its body weight each day.		
⑧	Elephant	The elephant eats $\frac{1}{60}$ of its body weight in a day.		
⑨	Hummingbird	A hummingbird eats its own body weight every day.		
⑩	Border collie	A working border collie needs $\frac{1}{20}$ of its body weight every day.		

SCORE /10   0-4   5-8   9-10

NAPLAN*-style Questions

① What number does **?** represent?

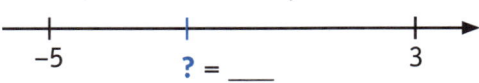

```
+------+------+------+→
-5     ?      3
```
? = _____

② Which number does not belong in the set below?

◯ 1   ◯ 6   ◯ 9   ◯ 16

③ If the oranges in one bag have a total mass of 850 g, what will the mass of 4 identical bags of oranges be?

_____ kg

SCORE /3   0-1   2   3

112   TARGETING MATHS HOMEWORK: YEAR 6 © PASCAL PRESS ISBN: 9781925726596

Problem of the Week

UNIT 25

AC9M6N02

Comparing Fractions

Min and Alex have been having fun exploring what happens when you add two special numbers.
They have used **square**, **prime** and **palindrome** numbers.
Make sure you know what each of these are before you try their questions.

Challenge 1

Using only the prime numbers up to 30, Min and Alex made this table of the additions.

① How often do two prime numbers add to a square number?

_____

② How often do two prime numbers add to a palindrome?

_____

	2	3	5	7	11	13	17	19	23	29
2	4	5	7	9	13	15	19	21	25	31
3		6	8	10	14	16	20	22	26	32
5			10	12	16	18	22	24	28	34
7				14	18	20	24	26	30	36
11					22	24	28	30	34	40
13						26	30	32	36	42
17							34	36	40	46
19								38	42	48
23									46	52
29										58

Challenge 2

**Using only square numbers, Min and Alex made this table of additions.
They left out totals that were more than 100.**

③ How often do two square numbers add to a prime number?

_____

④ How often do two square numbers add to a palindrome?

_____ What a disappointment!

	1	4	9	16	25	36	49	64	81
1	2	5	10	17	26	37	50	65	82
4		8	13	20	29	40	53	68	85
9			18	25	34	45	58	73	90
16				32	41	52	65	80	97
25					50	61	74	89	
36						72	85		
49							98		

Challenge 3

Min and Alex then made this table which is for the addition of a prime number to a square number.

⑤ How often can square numbers be made as the addition of a prime number and a square number?

_____

⑥ Which palindromes can be made from the addition of a prime number and a square number?

_____

	2	3	5	7	11	13	17	19	23	29
1	3	4	6	8	12	14	18	20	24	30
4	6	7	9	11	15	17	21	23	27	33
9	11	12	14	16	20	22	26	28	32	38
16	18	19	21	23	27	29	33	35	39	45
25	27	28	30	32	36	38	42	44	48	54
36	38	39	41	43	47	49	53	55	59	65
49	51	52	54	56	60	62	66	68	72	78
64	66	67	69	71	75	77	81	83	87	93
81	83	84	86	88	92	94	98	100	104	110

TERM 4

UNIT 26

Number & Algebra

AC9M6N03, AC9M6N05

Fractions

Recipes usually state how many serves the recipe will make. That is fine if you want to make that amount, but what if you want to make more or less than the recipe specifies?

To scale a recipe up or down, every listed ingredient has to be scaled to match.

This list of ingredients is for **6 apricot muffins**:

- $\frac{1}{4}$ cup honey
- $\frac{1}{3}$ cup mashed apricots
- $\frac{3}{8}$ cup of butter
- 2 cups sifted flour
- 2 eggs
- $2\frac{1}{2}$ teaspoons baking powder
- $\frac{3}{4}$ tablespoon apricot juice

Complete this table to show how to scale the recipe so that 3, 9, 12 or 15 muffins can be made.

	Ingredients	Quantity for:			
		3 muffins	9 muffins	12 muffins	15 muffins
①	Honey				
②	Butter				
③	Eggs				
④	Apricot juice				
⑤	Mashed apricots				
⑥	Sifted flour				
⑦	Baking powder				

SCORE /7   0-3   4-5   6-7

Quick Check

How much of each ingredient is needed to make half the recipe?

① $\frac{1}{3}$ cup of sugar ____ cup
② $1\frac{1}{4}$ cups of flour ____ cup
③ $\frac{2}{3}$ cup of currants ____ cup
④ 2 eggs ____ egg
⑤ $\frac{1}{4}$ kilogram of butter ____ kg
⑥ $\frac{5}{6}$ cup of oats ____ cup
⑦ $\frac{1}{4}$ cup of flaked almonds ____ cup

How much of each ingredient is needed to make twice as much?

⑧ $\frac{1}{3}$ cup of sugar ____ cup
⑨ $1\frac{1}{4}$ cups of flour ____ cups
⑩ $\frac{2}{3}$ cup of currants ____ cups
⑪ 2 eggs ____ eggs
⑫ $\frac{1}{4}$ kilogram of butter ____ kg
⑬ $\frac{1}{3}$ cup of oats ____ cup
⑭ $\frac{1}{4}$ cup of flaked almonds ____ cup

SCORE /14   0-6   7-12   13-14

Number & Algebra

UNIT 26

AC9M6N03

Fractions on a Number Line

The following number lines have no scale marked on them.
To mark the fractions in their correct places on the number line, you will need to choose a denominator to suit the fractions and then put the scale on the line.
Here is an example that places $\frac{1}{2}$, $\frac{1}{3}$ and $\frac{1}{6}$ on a number line.

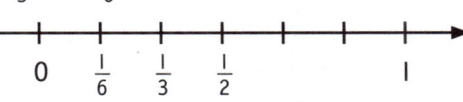

```
0   1/6  1/3  1/2        1
```

Mark the fractions in the correct places on the number line.

	Fractions	Number Line
①	$\frac{1}{4}, \frac{5}{8}, \frac{1}{2}$	0 ——— 1
②	$\frac{1}{3}, \frac{2}{9}, \frac{4}{9}$	0 ——— 1
③	$\frac{1}{2}, \frac{3}{5}, \frac{1}{10}$	0 ——— 1
④	$\frac{5}{6}, \frac{1}{4}, \frac{1}{3}$	0 ——— 1
⑤	$0.25, \frac{3}{8}, \frac{3}{4}$	0 ——— 1

SCORE /5   0-2   3-4   5

Statistics & Probability

AC9M6ST01

The Bean Experiment

Two beans were planted on the same day. Bean 1 was planted in potting mix and Bean 2 was planted in rich loam. After that, they were treated exactly the same.

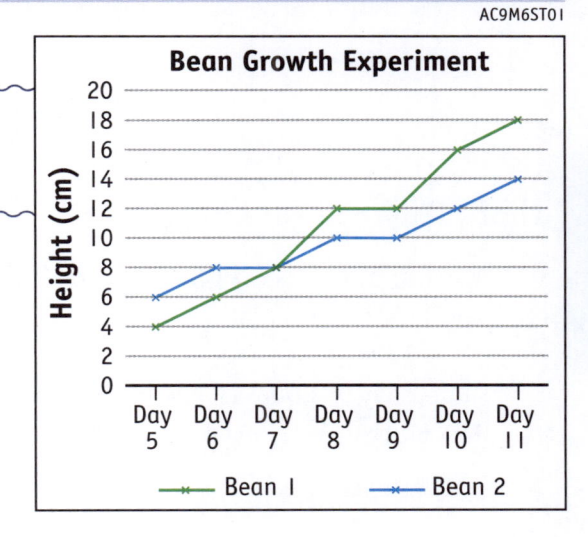

This line graph shows their progress from Day 5 to Day 11. Use it to answer the questions.

Bean Growth Experiment (line graph: Height (cm) vs Day 5–Day 11, Bean 1 and Bean 2)

① On which day were the beans the same height?
_____

② How much taller was Bean 2 than Bean 1 on Day 6?
_____

③ How many more centimetres did Bean 1 grow than Bean 2 in the 6 days?
_____

④ Between which two days did neither bean grow? _____

⑤ At this rate of growth, how much taller than Bean 2 do you think Bean 1 will be by Day 15? _____

SCORE /5   0-2   3-4   5

TERM 4

115

UNIT 26 — Measurement & Space

Congruent Faces

Two shapes are **congruent** if they are the same shape and size as one another.

These are congruent.

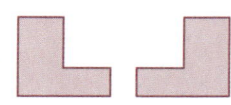

These are not congruent.

Draw the congruent faces for each of these 3D objects.
Write how many of each face there will be. The first one has been completed for you.

① **Rectangular prism** 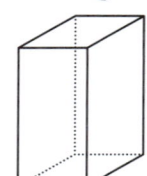
Faces: 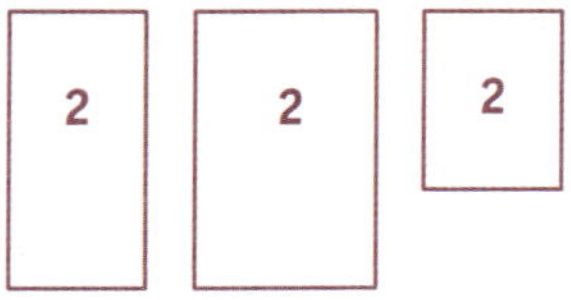 2, 2, 2

② **Triangular prism** 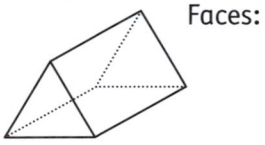
Faces:

③ **Square-based pyramid** 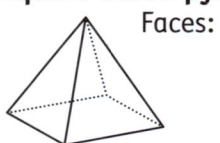
Faces:

④ **Cylinder** 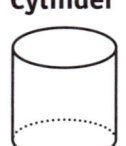
Faces:

⑤ **Octahedron** 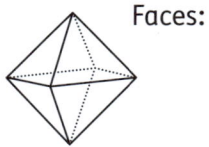
Faces:

⑥ **Pentagonal prism** 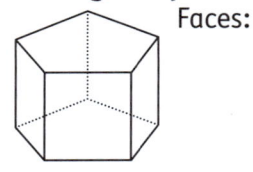
Faces:

⑦ **Pentagrammic prism**
Faces:

SCORE /7   0–3   4–5   6–7

NAPLAN*-style Questions

① Which letter marks $\frac{5}{6}$ on this number line? 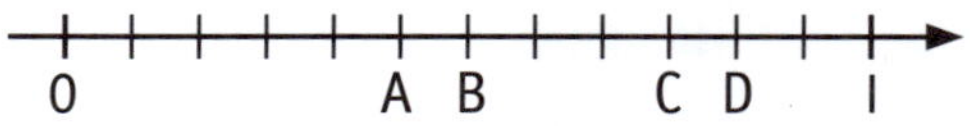
○ A   ○ B   ○ C   ○ D

0   A B   C D   1

② Three cups of flour are needed to make 8 bread rolls.
How much flour is used in each bread roll?
○ 8 cups   ○ $\frac{3}{8}$ cup   ○ $\frac{3}{4}$ cup   ○ $2\frac{2}{3}$ cup

③ Which of these 3D objects has no congruent faces?

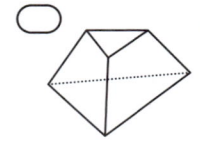

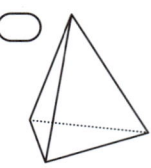

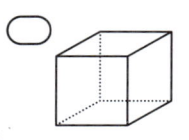

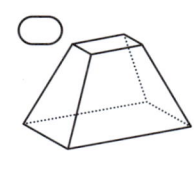

SCORE /3   0–1   2   3

Number & Algebra

UNIT 26

AC9M6N03

Fractions on a Number Line

The following number lines have no scale marked on them.
To mark the fractions in their correct places on the number line, you will need to choose a denominator to suit the fractions and then put the scale on the line.
Here is an example that places $\frac{1}{2}$, $\frac{1}{3}$ and $\frac{1}{6}$ on a number line.

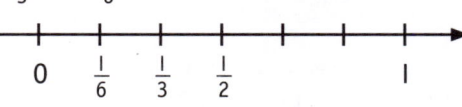

0   $\frac{1}{6}$ $\frac{1}{3}$ $\frac{1}{2}$ 1

Mark the fractions in the correct places on the number line.

	Fractions	Number Line
①	$\frac{1}{4}$, $\frac{5}{8}$, $\frac{1}{2}$	0 — 1
②	$\frac{1}{3}$, $\frac{2}{9}$, $\frac{4}{9}$	0 — 1
③	$\frac{1}{2}$, $\frac{3}{5}$, $\frac{1}{10}$	0 — 1
④	$\frac{5}{6}$, $\frac{1}{4}$, $\frac{1}{3}$	0 — 1
⑤	0.25, $\frac{3}{8}$, $\frac{3}{4}$	0 — 1

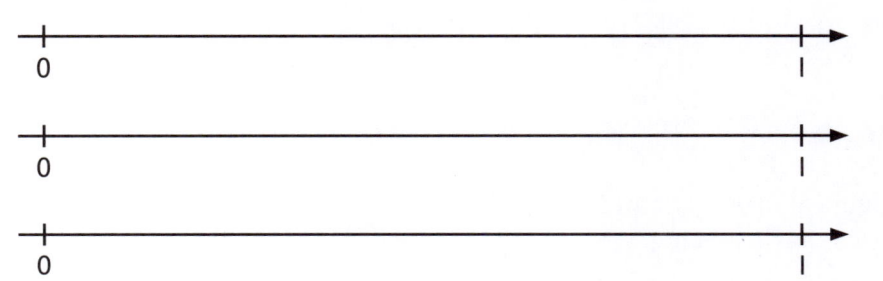

SCORE /5   0-2   3-4   5

Statistics & Probability

AC9M6ST01

The Bean Experiment

Two beans were planted on the same day. Bean 1 was planted in potting mix and Bean 2 was planted in rich loam. After that, they were treated exactly the same.

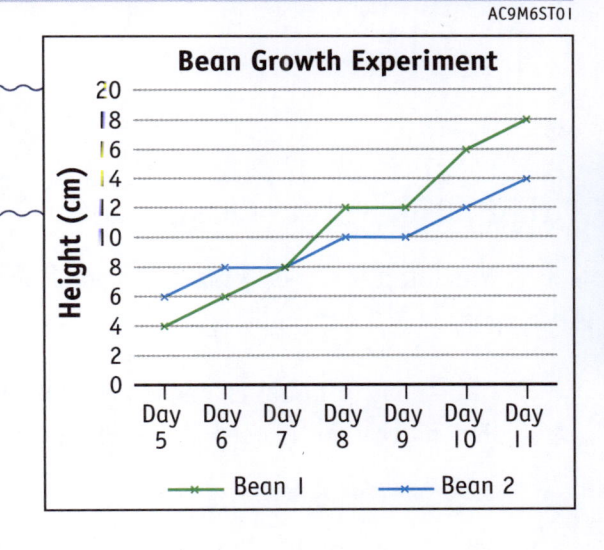

This line graph shows their progress from Day 5 to Day 11. Use it to answer the questions.

① On which day were the beans the same height?
_____

② How much taller was Bean 2 than Bean 1 on Day 6?
_____

③ How many more centimetres did Bean 1 grow than Bean 2 in the 6 days?
_____

④ Between which two days did neither bean grow? _____

⑤ At this rate of growth, how much taller than Bean 2 do you think Bean 1 will be by Day 15? _____

SCORE /5   0-2   3-4   5

TARGETING MATHS HOMEWORK: YEAR 6 © PASCAL PRESS ISBN: 9781925726596

UNIT 26 — Measurement & Space

AC9M6SP01

Congruent Faces

Two shapes are **congruent** if they are the same shape and size as one another.

These are congruent.

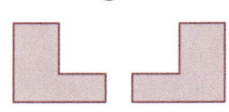

These are not congruent.

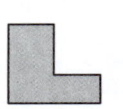

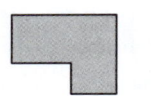

Draw the congruent faces for each of these 3D objects.
Write how many of each face there will be. The first one has been completed for you.

① **Rectangular prism** 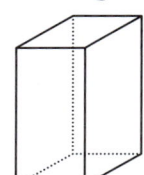
Faces: 2   2   2

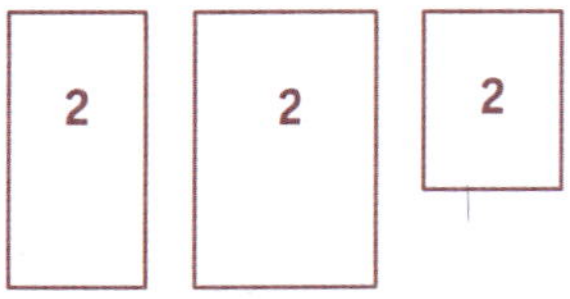

② **Triangular prism**
Faces: 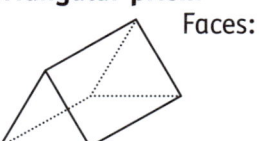

③ **Square-based pyramid** 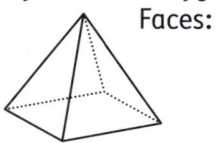
Faces:

④ **Cylinder** 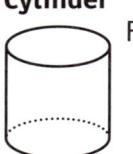
Faces:

⑤ **Octahedron** 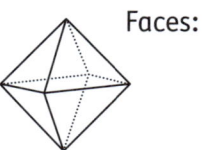
Faces:

⑥ **Pentagonal prism** 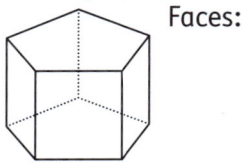
Faces:

⑦ **Pentagrammic prism** 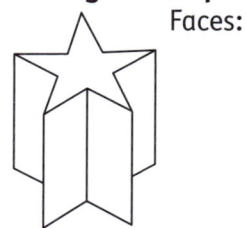
Faces:

SCORE /7   0-3   4-5   6-7

NAPLAN*-style Questions

① Which letter marks $\frac{5}{6}$ on this number line? 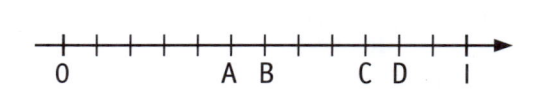
○ A   ○ B   ○ C   ○ D

② Three cups of flour are needed to make 8 bread rolls. How much flour is used in each bread roll?
○ 8 cups   ○ $\frac{3}{8}$ cup   ○ $\frac{3}{4}$ cup   ○ $2\frac{2}{3}$ cup

③ Which of these 3D objects has no congruent faces?

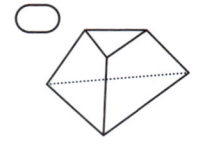

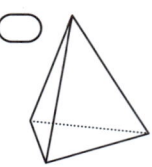

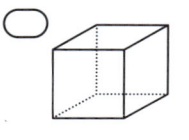

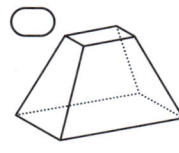

SCORE /3   0-1   2   3

TERM 4

116   TARGETING MATHS HOMEWORK: YEAR 6 © PASCAL PRESS ISBN: 9781925726596

Problem of the Week

UNIT 26

AC9M6N05, AC9M6N09

Fractions that Add to 1

We have made up this game that really helps with fractions.

- You start with the number cards 2–9 from a pack of cards.

- Shuffle them and then deal three cards to each player.
- Each player makes three fractions that have the numbers on the cards as the denominators. The numerator of each fraction must be 1 or more.
- Add the fractions.
- The player whose fraction total is closest to 1 is the winner.

Liam:
These are the cards that I was dealt. I found that I needed to find the lowest common denominator before I could work out what my numerators should be. Using 28 as my common denominator, I made these fractions:

$$\frac{1}{2} + \frac{1}{4} + \frac{2}{7} = \frac{14}{28} + \frac{7}{28} + \frac{8}{28} = \frac{29}{28}$$

① How far from 1 was Liam? _____

Elsa:
These are the cards that I was dealt. How close to 1 could I get?

_____

② Elsa could be _____ away from 1.

The Challenge

What if you were dealt these cards?

③ How close to 1 could you make the fractions that have 3, 4 and 5 as denominators?

_____

④ Who was the winner? _____

UNIT 27 — Number & Algebra

Multiplying Decimals

The order in which you multiply decimals does not change the product of those numbers. This means that you can use work-smart strategies for some decimal multiplications.

Here is an example where the actual multiplications are quite hard:

$0.5 \times 8.7 \times 4$
4.35
17.4

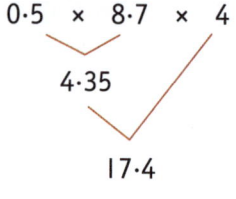

Here is the same multiplication but with the order of the numbers changed to make the multiplication easier:

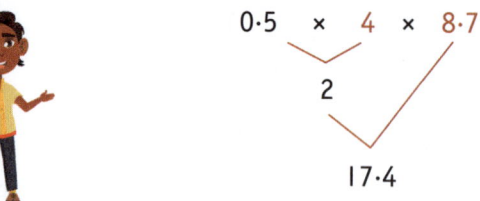

$0.5 \times 4 \times 8.7$
2
17.4

Look for work-smart strategies to solve these decimal multiplications. Rewrite them in the order that makes them easier and then work out the answer.

1. $4 \times 6.3 \times 0.25$
   Change to: _____

2. $0.2 \times 8.3 \times 5$
   Change to: _____

3. $50 \times 15.3 \times 0.4$
   Change to: _____

4. $0.4 \times 0.5 \times 6$
   Change to: _____

5. $0.02 \times 6.8 \times 50$
   Change to: _____

SCORE /5   0–2   3–4   5

Quick Check

Complete these decimal multiplications.

1. $0.3 \times 6 \times 0.5 =$ _____
2. $25 \times 3.3 \times 0.4 =$ _____
3. $0.5 \times 2.5 \times 6 =$ _____
4. $30 \times 0.8 \times 5 =$ _____
5. $0.6 \times 12 \times 0.5 =$ _____
6. $0.2 \times 67 \times 50 =$ _____
7. $0.4 \times 0.95 \times 25 =$ _____
8. $0.05 \times 6 \times 100 =$ _____
9. $3.3 \times 12 \times 0.5 =$ _____
10. $0.08 \times 500 \times 0.23 =$ _____

SCORE /10   0–4   5–8   9–10

Number & Algebra

UNIT 27

AC9M6N06, AC9M6M01

Decimal Multiplication Problems

Complete these decimal multiplication problems.

① The thickness of an exercise book is 0·022 metres.
How tall would a stack of 10 books be? _____ cm

② Coffee cans of 0·178 metres high have been stacked in a pyramid 10 cans high.
How tall is the pyramid? _____ m

③ A $5 note is 0·000 0952 metres thick.
How tall would a $5000 pile of notes be? _____ cm

④ A paperclip is 0·034 metres long.
How long would a line of 1000 paperclips laid end to end be? _____ m

⑤ A coin is 0·018 metres across.
How long will a line of 100 coins be? _____ m

⑥ If each of those 100 coins was worth 10 cents, what would the value of the coins be? $_____

SCORE /6   0-2   3-4   5-6

Statistics & Probability

AC9M6ST03

Making Comparisons

Min's brother Anh has lots of odd jobs: cleaning cars, dog-walking, baby sitting, mowing and more.

The graph shows his earnings and spending for the last 5 weeks.

Anh's Finances

Key: ■ Earned ■ Spent

① How much did Anh earn in Weeks 1 and 2?
$_____

② How much more did Anh earn than he spent in Weeks 1 and 2?
$_____

③ In which week did Anh spend more than he earned?
_____

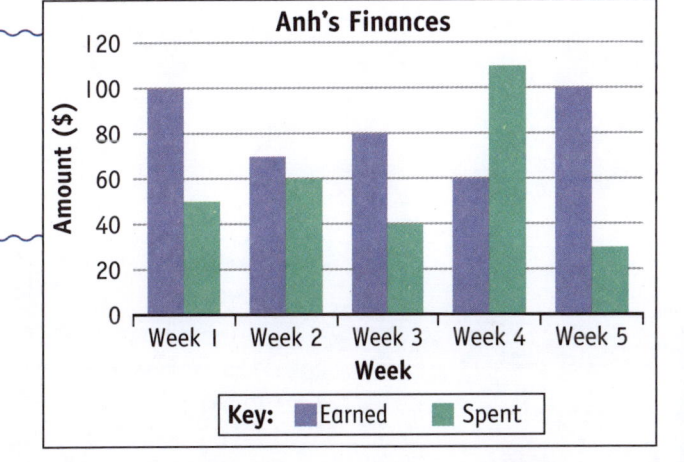

④ In which week did Anh spend the least amount of money?
_____

⑤ How much did Anh earn in the five weeks altogether?
$_____

⑥ How much more did Anh earn than he spent over the five weeks altogether?
$_____

SCORE /6   0-2   3-4   5-6

TARGETING MATHS HOMEWORK: YEAR 6 © PASCAL PRESS ISBN: 9781925726596

119

UNIT 27

Measurement & Space

AC9M6SP02

Giving Directions and Using Coordinates

We have been making up instructions for our robots to make a journey across a coordinate plane. We have to use these simple instructions:

Fwd <number> means **go forward a number of grid spaces**.
Lt means **make a quarter turn left**.
Rt means **make a quarter turn right**.

Robot A and Robot B start at position (−5, 0) with Robot A facing north and Robot B facing east. Each robot must visit all four quadrants before finishing at (5, 0) but their paths must never cross.

On the grid, draw the paths that the robots could take.
Then list the instructions (Fwd, Lt and Rt) that will send them along those paths.

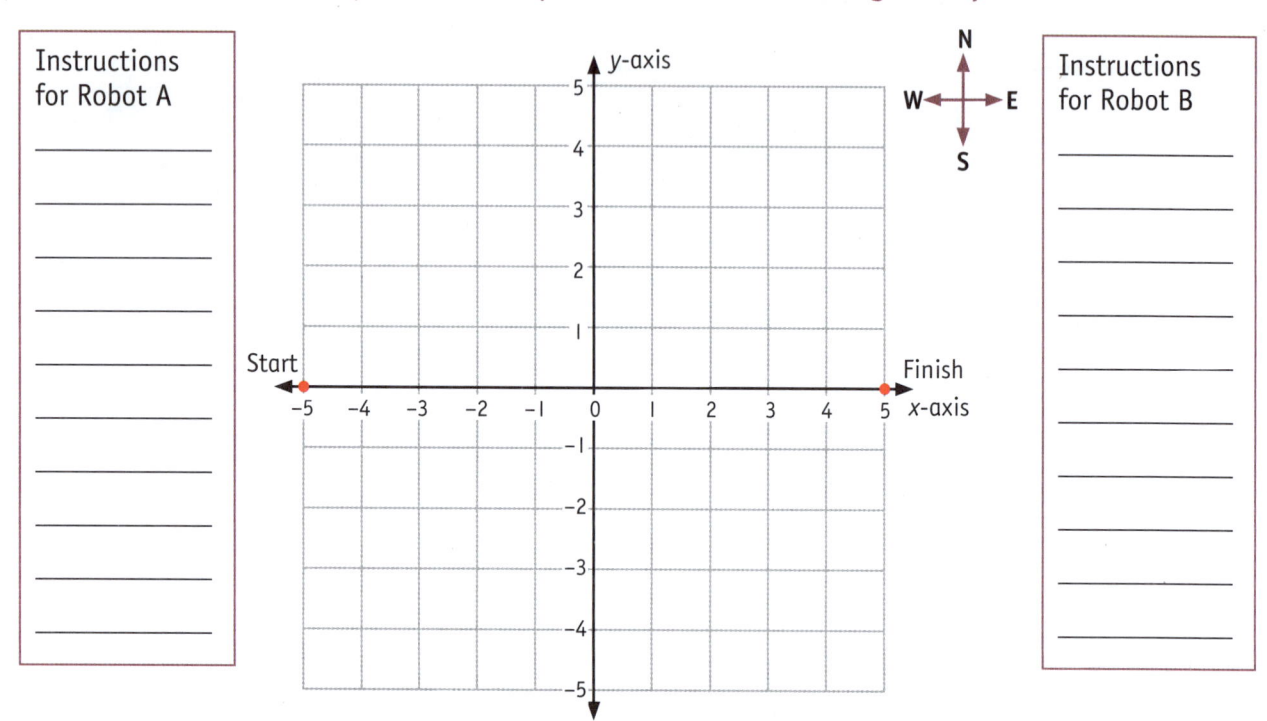

Instructions for Robot A

Instructions for Robot B

Score each sequence of instructions out of 5.   /10   0-4   5-8   9-10

NAPLAN*-style Questions

① Complete this decimal multiplication.

0·2 × 37·6 × 50 = _____

② How much change from $100 would you get after buying 100 balloons at 72 cents each?
○ $172   ○ $28   ○ $92·80   ○ $0

③ Which of these shapes has four corners with coordinates that will not have a repeated number?

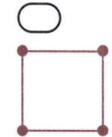

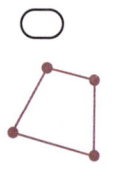

/3   0-1   2   3

Problem of the Week

UNIT 27
AC9M6N09

Dancing Robots

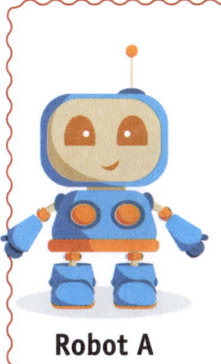

At the Junior Robotics Tournament, contestants have to make two robots perform a synchronised dance using these simple instructions:

- **Fwd** <number> means **go forward a number of grid spaces**.
- **Lt** means **make a quarter turn left**.
- **Rt** means **make a quarter turn right**.

In a **synchronised dance**, the robots always move at the same time and are always directly opposite each other vertically and horizontally.

For example, if Robot A is at (−3, 4) then Robot B has to be at (3, −4).

Robot A   **Robot B**

The Challenge

- The robots start in the positions marked below.
- Robot A faces down the grid and Robot B faces up the grid.
- Each robot must make 8 moves forward and 7 turns left or right.

**Use the grid below to draw the paths that the robots could take.
Then list the instructions (Fwd, Lt and Rt) that will send them along those paths.**

If possible, the robots should finish their synchronised dance by meeting at position (0, 0).

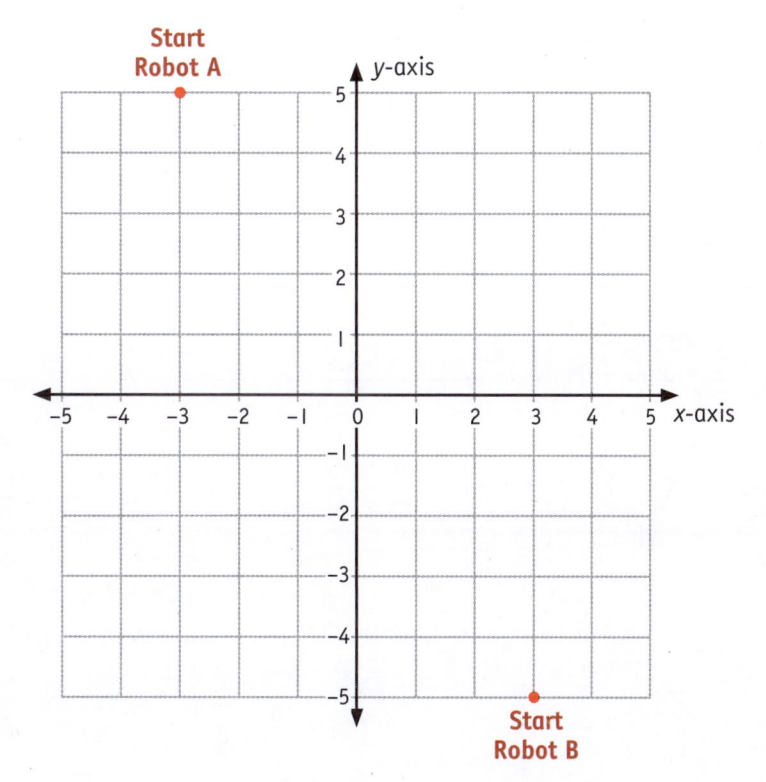

Instructions for Robot A

1. _____
2. _____
3. _____
4. _____
5. _____
6. _____
7. _____
8. _____
9. _____
10. _____
11. _____
12. _____
13. _____
14. _____
15. _____

Start Robot A at (−3, 5)

Start Robot B at (3, −5)

Instructions for Robot B

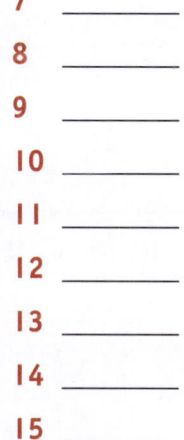

1. _____
2. _____
3. _____
4. _____
5. _____
6. _____
7. _____
8. _____
9. _____
10. _____
11. _____
12. _____
13. _____
14. _____
15. _____

TERM 4

What did your robots say to each other when they met at position (0, 0)?

_____

TARGETING MATHS HOMEWORK: YEAR 6 © PASCAL PRESS ISBN: 9781925726596

UNIT 28

Number & Algebra

AC9M6N06

Multiplying Decimals

Decimal place value can be tricky when multiplying if you do not pay attention to the decimal place.

For 2·4 × 6, the correct answer is 14·4. Yet many students give the answer 12·24. They know that 6 × 4 = 24, but the 4 in 2·4 actually means 4 tenths.

The multiplication can be written as:

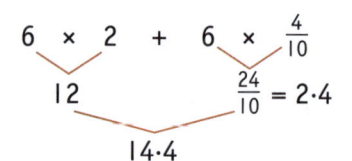

$$6 \times 2 + 6 \times \frac{4}{10}$$
$$12 \qquad \frac{24}{10} = 2\cdot4$$
$$14\cdot4$$

Rearrange the multiplications and then complete them.
Note: We suggest that you do the Quick Check questions first as a warm-up.

This is wrong!	Rearrange to make it right!
① 3·8 × 8 = 24·64 (wrong)	3 × 8 + $\frac{8}{10}$ × 8 = 24 + 6·4 = 30·4
② 23·5 × 3 = 69·15 (wrong)	
③ 15·7 × 4 = 60·28 (wrong)	
④ 32·34 × 3 = 96·102 (wrong)	
⑤ 44·92 × 2 = 88·184 (wrong)	
⑥ 23·7 × 9 = 207·63 (wrong)	
⑦ 29·64 × 8 = 145·32 (wrong)	

SCORE /7   0-3   4-5   6-7

Quick Check

Write the answers to these multiplications. Check with your calculator if you want to.

① 0·3 × 7 = _____
② 1·6 × 3 = _____
③ 0·4 × 8 = _____
④ 0·01 × 9 = _____
⑤ 0·6 × 7 = _____
⑥ 0·06 × 3 = _____
⑦ 0·73 × 2 = _____
⑧ 0·55 × 4 = _____
⑨ 0·09 × 6 = _____
⑩ 3·7 × 7 = _____

SCORE /10   0-4   5-8   9-10

Number & Algebra

UNIT 28

AC9M6N06

Number Splitting for Division

When carrying out division, number splitting can help.
For example, to divide 348 by 6, it helps to use known multiplication facts.
6 × 5 = 30 and 6 × 50 = 300
So split 348 into 300 and 48 as shown at the right.

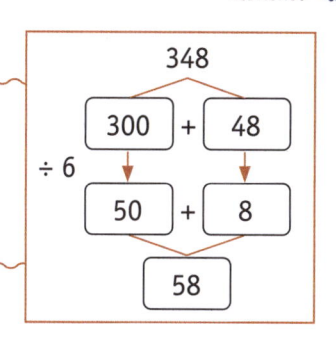

```
         348
        /   \
÷ 6   300 + 48
        ↓    ↓
       50 +  8
         \  /
          58
```

Complete these division questions using number splitting.

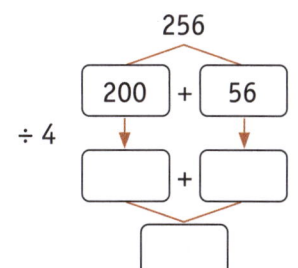

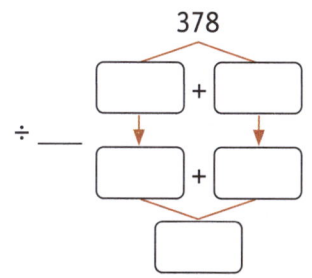

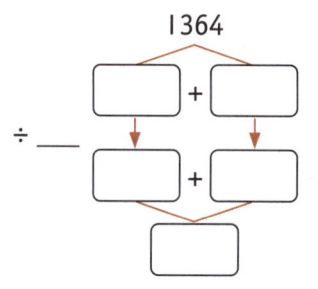

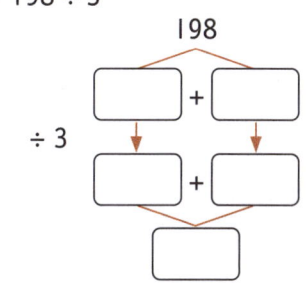

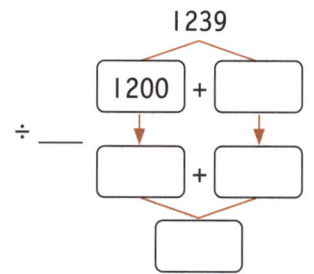

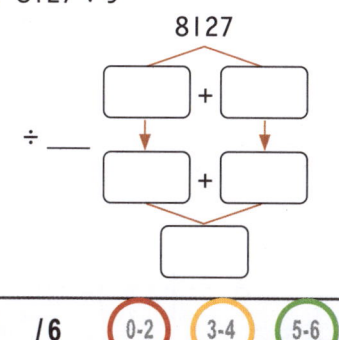

① 256 ÷ 4
  ÷ 4: 256 → 200 + 56 → □ + □ → □

② 198 ÷ 3
  ÷ 3: 198 → □ + □ → □ + □ → □

③ 378 ÷ 6
  ÷ __: 378 → □ + □ → □ + □ → □

④ 1239 ÷ 3
  ÷ __: 1239 → 1200 + □ → □ + □ → □

⑤ 1364 ÷ 4
  ÷ __: 1364 → □ + □ → □ + □ → □

⑥ 8127 ÷ 9
  ÷ __: 8127 → □ + □ → □ + □ → □

SCORE /6   0-2   3-4   5-6

Statistics & Probability

AC9M6ST03

The New Sports Colours

The Stoke Primary School has had the same sports colours for 50 years and they look very old fashioned. The students have suggested three new possibilities: teal and white, royal blue and yellow, and navy and red. So far only 25 students in the school have voted.

① Complete the first table of percentages to show how many students have voted for each colour combination so far.

② When the rest of the students vote, what do you think the results will be?
Show your thinking in the second table.
Give the reason for your predictions.

_____

_____

Colours	Per cent	Number of students
Teal and white	20%	
Royal blue and yellow	48%	
Navy blue and red	32%	

Colours	Per cent	Number of students
Teal and white		
Royal blue and yellow		
Navy blue and red		

SCORE /6   0-2   3-4   5-6

TERM 4

TARGETING MATHS HOMEWORK: YEAR 6 © PASCAL PRESS ISBN: 9781925726596

UNIT 28 — Measurement & Space

AC9M6N06, AC9M6M02

Area and Decimals

"Good morning, class. I have put this diagram and a multiplication on the board for you.

"Please check that the multiplication is correct. To do that, you only need to check the area of the large square in the diagram."

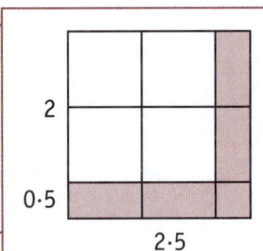

$2 \times 2.5 = 5$
$0.5 \times 2.5 = 1.25$
$\ 6.25$

Mr Green drew some more diagrams on the board. Show the multiplication of the decimals they represent.

① 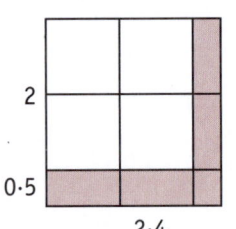 2, 0.5, 2.4

② 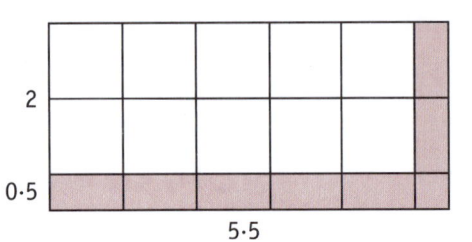 2, 0.5, 5.5

③ 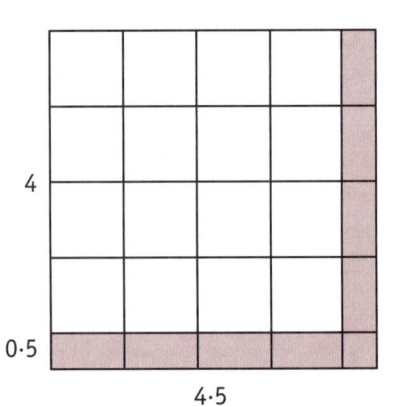 4, 0.5, 4.5

④ 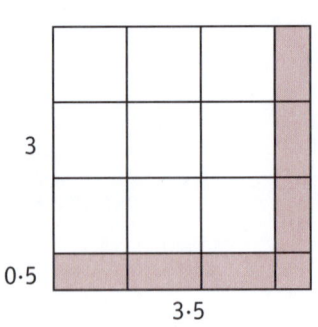 3, 0.5, 3.5

⑤ 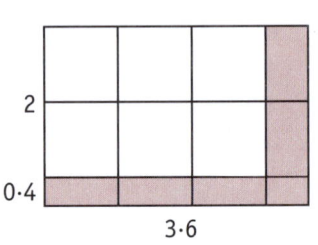 2, 0.4, 3.6

⑥ 2, 0.7, 4.3

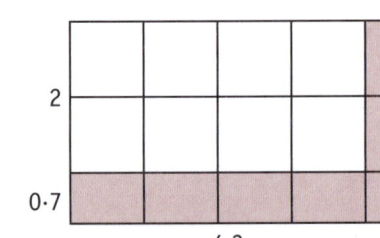

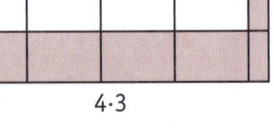

SCORE /6   0–2   3–4   5–6

NAPLAN*-style Questions

① What is the area of the grid at the right?

_____ cm²

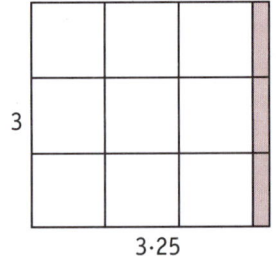

(grid labelled 3 and 3.25)

② Elsa made 8 muffins and she has 20 cherries to put on top to make identical muffins.
How many cherries should she put on each muffin?

◯ 28   ◯ 2   ◯ $2\frac{1}{2}$ ◯ $2\frac{1}{8}$

③ Only 4 out of 100 people surveyed played tennis.
What percentage of the people did not play tennis?

_____ %

SCORE /3   0–1   2   3

Problem of the Week

UNIT 28

AC9M6M02

Tiling the Patio

The tiler's new client wants a new patio in their garden made with 50 cm² pavers in three colours: grey, terracotta and white.

Starting from the outside, the client wants the first strip to be grey, 50 cm wide and going all around the patio.

The second strip should be terracotta, 50 cm wide and also go all around.

The third strip should be white, 50 cm wide and also go all around

After that, the pattern will repeat until there is a rectangle in the centre that is 3 metres by 2 metres, which will be made into a fish pond.

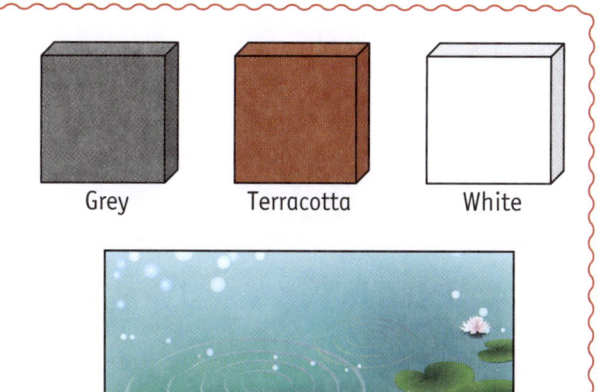

Grey   Terracotta   White

The Challenge

The tiler needs to know:
- how many grey tiles?
- how many terracotta tiles?
- how many white tiles?

Use this plan of the patio to work out how many tiles of each colour the tiler will need. Pay attention to the scale.

Scale
Each square is 1 m²

Tiles needed

Grey tiles: _____

Terracotta tiles: _____

White tiles: _____

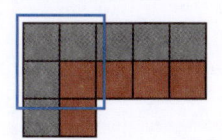

Hint: To make a start, it helps to work out how many more tiles one strip will have than the strip just inside it.

For example, in the diagram you can see how many more grey tiles than terracotta tiles there will be at each corner of a strip. There will be two more grey tiles.

TERM 4

UNIT 29 — Number & Algebra

AC9M6N06

Division and Fractions

When you find one-quarter of 36, you are dividing.
But when you divide 36 by 4, you are finding a fraction which in this case is, $\frac{1}{4}$ of 36.
It is important to link fractions and division because often the answer to a division question has a remainder which needs to be expressed as a fraction. Here is an example:

4 people shared 6 mini-pizzas fairly. How much pizza did each person get?
Is the answer 6 ÷ 4 = 1 remainder 2?
No, the question doesn't ask for a remainder. It is looking for a fraction.
Since we are dividing by 4, the remainder 2 needs to be replaced by $\frac{2}{4}$ or $\frac{1}{2}$.

Divide. Use fractions instead of remainders.

1. 10 ÷ 8 = 1 remainder 2
   which is $1\frac{2}{8}$ or $1\frac{1}{4}$

2. 12 ÷ 5 = ___ remainder ___
   which is _____

3. 15 ÷ 4 = ___ remainder ___
   which is _____

4. 17 ÷ 3 = ___ remainder ___
   which is _____

5. 21 ÷ 4 = ___ remainder ___
   which is _____

6. 39 ÷ 6 = ___ remainder ___
   which is _____

7. 47 ÷ 7 = ___ remainder ___
   which is _____

8. 52 ÷ 8 = ___ remainder ___
   which is _____

9. 26 ÷ 8 = ___ remainder ___
   which is _____

10. 102 ÷ 4 = ___ remainder ___
    which is _____

SCORE /10   0-4   5-8   9-10

Quick Check

1. 5 ÷ 4 = _____
2. 6 ÷ 5 = _____
3. 7 ÷ 3 = _____
4. 8 ÷ 5 = _____
5. 17 ÷ 6 = _____
6. 23 ÷ 4 = _____
7. 15 ÷ 3 = _____
8. 18 ÷ 8 = _____
9. 19 ÷ 4 = _____
10. 28 ÷ 3 = _____

SCORE /10   0-4   5-8   9-10

Number & Algebra

UNIT 29
AC9M6N07

Estimating with Percentages

When you see a store discount giving a percentage, you don't always need to work out the exact amount of the discount. But when you do, it is a good idea to make an estimate of the percentage discount before reaching for a calculator.

Suppose the adventure store has a 19% discount on that $68 backpack that you would really like. You know that 10% of $68 is $6·80. From that, you can work out that 20%, which is very close to 19%, is $13·60. That is close enough to help you decide whether the backpack is a bargain that you do not want to miss.
$68 − $13·60 = $54·40. A bargain!

19% discount today!

Change these percentages to known percentages to make it easy to estimate the discounts.

The Discount	Percentage Approximations
① 16% of $85	10% of $85 = $8·50 5% of $85 = $4·25 Discount Estimate = $12·75
② 24% of $90	25% of $90 = _____ Discount Estimate = _____
③ 49% of $160	____ of ____ = ____ Discount Estimate = _____
④ 18% of $180	____ of ____ = ____ Discount Estimate = _____

Remember, 5% is half of 10% and 25% is a quarter.

The Discount	Percentage Approximations
⑤ 36% of $120	____ of ____ = ____ ____ of ____ = ____ Discount Estimate = _____
⑥ 58% of $140	____ of ____ = ____ ____ of ____ = ____ Discount Estimate = _____

SCORE /6   0-2   3-4   5-6

Statistics & Probability

AC9M6ST01

Printing the School Journal

The school has a colour printer that takes 10 seconds to start and then prints 10 pages in 10 seconds. The black & white printer only takes 5 seconds to start and then prints 10 pages every 6 seconds.

Printer Speeds

(scatter plot: Time (s) vs Number of Pages Printed, Key: Colour, B & W)

① How many pages will be printed 20 seconds after starting the colour printer? ___ pages

② How many pages will be printed 20 seconds after starting the black-and-white printer? ___ pages

③ If the school journal has 15 colour pages and 25 black-and-white pages, how long will it take to print each journal?

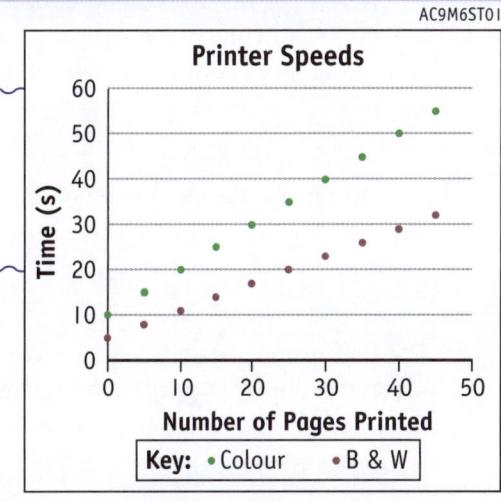

_____

SCORE /6   0-2   3-4   5-6

TARGETING MATHS HOMEWORK: YEAR 6 © PASCAL PRESS ISBN: 9781925726596

TERM 4

127

UNIT 29 Measurement & Space

Metric Unit Conversions

"Good morning, class."

"I have made these charts to help you convert between the measurements that we use in everyday life."

÷ 1000 → ÷ 1000 → ÷ 1000
milligram mg → gram g → kilogram kg → tonne t

÷ 10 → ÷ 100 → ÷ 1000
millimetre mm → centimetre cm → metre m → kilometre km

÷ 10 → ÷ 100 → ÷ 1000
millilitre mL → centilitre cL → litre L → kilolitre kL

Use Mr Green's charts to help you complete these measurement conversions.

① 156 millimetres = _____ centimetres
   = _____ metres

② 1556 metres = ___ kilometre and _____ metres or ___ . _____ kilometres

③ 1456 grams = ___ kilogram and _____ grams or ___ . _____ kilograms

④ 3365 millilitres = ___ litres and _____ millilitres or ___ . _____ litres

⑤ 1·65 metres = _____ centimetres = _____ millimetres

Now complete the conversions, using the abbreviations for the units of measure.

⑥ 1·7 t = ____ t and _____ kg or _____ kg.

⑦ 3372 m = ___ km and _____ m or ____ . _____ km.

⑧ 4450 mm = _____ cm = ___ . ____ m.

⑨ 7568 mL = _____ . ____ cL = ___ . _____ L.

⑩ 4·58 km = ___ km and _____ m or _____ m.

SCORE /10   0-4   5-8   9-10

NAPLAN*-style Questions

① Min had 9 metres of beading elastic that she used for making friendship bracelets. She shared the elastic equally with 4 friends.
How many metres of the elastic did they each have?

_____ m

② A $150 jacket has been marked with a discount of 35%. What is the new price of the jacket?

$_____

③ The line graph shows the time taken for an inkjet printer and a laser printer to print pages.
How many pages does the inkjet printer print in the time that it takes the laser printer to print 25 pages?

____ pages

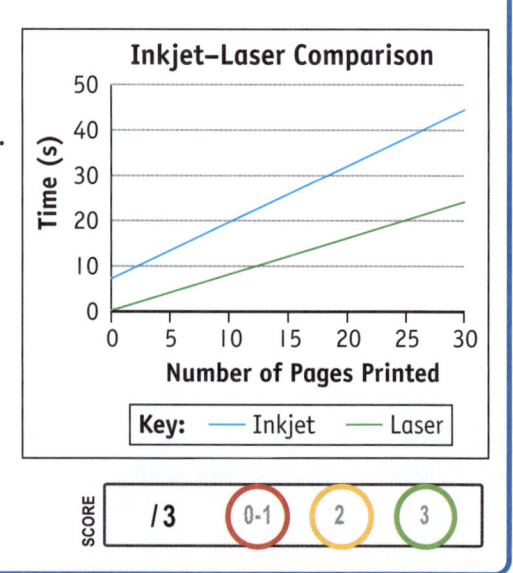

Inkjet–Laser Comparison

Key: — Inkjet — Laser

SCORE /3   0-1   2   3

Problem of the Week

Find my Number

Alex said, "My number is in the 20s."

Elsa said, "My number is in the 40s."

Hai said, "My number is in the 50s."

Tau said, "My number is in the 70s."

Liam said, "My number is in the 80s."

Ruby said, "My number is in the 90s."

Match the students to these remainder clues.

Be careful, as the remainder clues may have more than one answer and one of them is the only possible answer for one person.

Hint: For Remainder Clue 1, make a list of numbers that are two more than a multiple of 7 and check which of those numbers could be 2 more than a multiple of 3. This strategy works well for all the other clues too.

Remainder Clue 1

When divided by 7, my remainder is 2 and when divided by 3, my remainder is also 2.

____ is _____'s number.

Remainder Clue 2

When divided by 9, my remainder is 1 and when divided by 5, my remainder is also 1.

____ is _____'s number.

Remainder Clue 3

When divided by 8, my remainder is 3 but when divided by 9, my remainder is 5.

_____ is _____'s number.

Remainder Clue 4

When divided by 7, my remainder is 5 but when divided by 9, my remainder is 3.

_____ is _____'s number.

Remainder Clue 5

When divided by 9, my remainder is 1 but when divided by 5, my remainder is 2.

_____ is _____'s number.

Remainder Clue 6

When divided by 7, my remainder is 4 but when divided by 9, my remainder is 5.

_____ is _____'s number.

UNIT 30 — Number & Algebra

Multistep Number Problems

Each of these problems has a number of steps in its solution. Show each step.

① Bread rolls cost $20 for a bag of 8 rolls. Cheese slices cost $12 for 8 slices. A packet of ham costs $10 for 8 slices.
How much does it cost to make one ham-and-cheese roll?

$20 ÷ 8 = $_____ , $12 ÷ 8 = $_____ ,

$10 ÷ 8 = $_____

$_____ + $_____ + $_____ = $_____

② Four movie tickets cost $108. A bag of popcorn and a bag of jelly snakes together cost $16·60. The total cost is shared equally between 4 people.
How much does each person have to pay?

$_____ ÷ _____ = $_____ ,

$_____ ÷ _____ = $_____

$_____ + $_____ = $_____

③ The dinner bill was $280 for meals and $50 for soft drinks. The bill was split equally between 6 diners.
How much did each diner pay?

_____

_____

_____

④ Sara bought a coat for $140, a pair of boots for $100 and a sweatshirt for $60.
When she got to the checkout, she discovered that there was a 25% off everything sale.
How much did Sara pay?
Hint: Add the amounts before dividing!

_____

_____

_____

⑤ 4 people shared 6 share plates at the Mexican restaurant at $24 a plate. They also shared a bottle of sparkling water at $8·20. They gave a 10% tip.
How much did each person have to pay if they split the bill evenly?

_____

_____

_____

_____

_____

SCORE /5   0-2   3-4   5

Quick Check

Give the cost per item.

① 4 movie tickets cost $108.
1 movie ticket costs $_____.

② 8 oranges cost $6.
1 orange costs $_____.

③ 7 pizzas cost $87·50.
1 pizza costs $_____.

④ 6 notebooks cost $7·80.
1 notebook costs $_____.

⑤ 8 fruit smoothies cost $28.
1 fruit smoothie costs $_____.

Give the amount of the discount.

⑥ 15% off $95
$_____

⑦ 25% off $120
$_____

⑧ 51% off $85
$_____

⑨ 20% off $170
$_____

⑩ 26% off $126
$_____

SCORE /10   0-4   5-8   9-10

Number & Algebra

UNIT 30

AC9M6N07, AC9M6N08

Percentage Skill Builder

You know how to find 1%, 10%, 25% and 50%.
Here are some extra practice questions to help you build fluency, flexibility and accuracy with percentages.

To find 26% of $120:
Think 25% which is a quarter of $120 or $30.
Then find 1% which is $1·20.
Add the two together and the answer is **$31·20**.

Make estimates and then use known percentages to work out the actual answers.

1. 11% of $97

    Estimate: $_____

    _____% of $_____ = $_____

    _____% of $_____ = $_____

    $_____ + $_____ = $_____

2. 21% of $16

    Estimate: $_____

    _____% of $_____ = $_____

    _____% of $_____ = $_____

    $_____ + $_____ = $_____

3. 24% of $25

    Estimate: $_____

    _____

    _____

    _____

4. 9% of $48

    Estimate: $_____

    _____

    _____

    _____

5. 51% of $160

    Estimate: $_____

    _____

    _____

    _____

SCORE /5   0-2   3-4   5

Statistics & Probability

AC9M6ST02

Survey Results

100 students were surveyed about new flavours for muesli bars: pineapple chunk, banana & pistachio, choc chip & macadamia, and cherry & hazelnut. The pie graph shows the results of the survey.

Muesli Bar Survey Results

Key
- 🟩 _____
- 🟨 _____
- 🟪 _____
- 🟧 _____

Solve the clues and complete the key of the pie chart with the flavours and the number of votes each flavour received.

Clues
- Twice as many people voted for pineapple chunk as voted for choc chip & macadamia.
- Cherry & hazelnut was the second most popular.

SCORE /4   0-1   2-3   4

TERM 4

131

UNIT 30 — Measurement & Space

AC9M6M03

The Year 1 Timetable

Start times	Mon.	Tue.	Wed.	Thu.	Fri.
9:00	Literacy	Literacy	Science	Maths	Literacy
9:30	Literacy	Literacy	Maths	Maths	Literacy
10:45	Break	Break	Break	Break	Break
11:00	Maths	Maths	Literacy	Literacy	Maths
12:00	HASS	Maths	Literacy	Literacy	Maths
12:45	Break	Break	Break	Break	Break
1:30	Health & PE	Science	HASS	Dance	Health & PE
2:15	Art	Music	Health & PE	Library	Art
3:00	End of school day				

How much time do Year 1 students spend each week on each subject?

1. Literacy: ___ h ____ min
2. Maths: ___ h ____ min
3. Science: ___ h ____ min
4. Art: ___ h ____ min
5. HASS: ___ h ____ min
6. Music: ___ h ____ min
7. Dance: ___ h ____ min
8. Health & PE: ___ h ____ min
9. Library: ___ h ____ min

10. How much break time do the Year 1s get each day? ___ h ____ min

SCORE /10   0-4   5-8   9-10

TERM 4 — NAPLAN*-style Questions

1. Min stopped swimming 60% of the way through her 500-metre trial because she had muscle cramps.
   How far through her swim did she get before she had to stop?

   _____ metres

2. Four movie tickets cost $96.
   How much were the tickets each?

   $_____

3. Alex plays Micro Worlds on Saturdays. He starts playing at 9:45 am and plays for $2\frac{1}{2}$ hours.
   At what time does Alex stop playing Micro Worlds?

   _____ am/pm

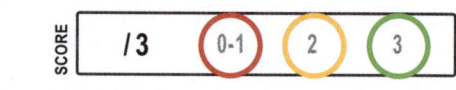

SCORE /3   0-1   2   3

Problem of the Week

UNIT 30

AC9M6N09, AC9M6M03

The Busy Week

"Please don't tell the students in my class, but I really do not enjoy making the weekly timetable.

"The week is so full that I find it hard to fit everything in and make time to have a class meeting or to give students time to finish off all their tasks.

"These are the constraints that I have to work with.

"Each week I must fit in:
- 300 minutes of Maths
- 500 minutes of Literacy
- 120 minutes of Health and PE
- 180 minutes of Science
- 180 minutes of HASS.

"I then have to plan time for Technology, Art and Music."

Design a timetable for Mr Green's class.

Of course, you know that nobody wants to do the same subject all day.
Subjects need to be spread across the week for best effect.

Start times	Mon.	Tue.	Wed.	Thu.	Fri.
8:30					
10:50	Break				
11:15					
1:00	Break				
1:45					
3:15	End of School Day				

Note: You may need to break a session into two parts.
When you do, make sure that the start time for the second part is marked on your timetable.

UNIT 31 — Number & Algebra

AC9M6N04, AC9M6N05

Number Patterns

Continue these decimal number patterns and write the rule used to make the pattern.

① 0, 0·125, 0·25, _____, _____, _____.   The rule is _____.

② 0·004, 0·008, 0·012, _____, _____, _____.   The rule is _____.

③ 0·002, 0·007, 0·012, _____, _____, _____.   The rule is _____.

④ 0·055, 0·066, 0·077, _____, _____, _____.   The rule is _____.

⑤ 1·06, 1·04, 1·02, _____, _____, _____.   The rule is _____.

⑥ 1·4, 1·25, 1·1, _____, _____, _____.   The rule is _____.

Continue these fraction number patterns, always writing the fraction in its simplest form. Then write the rule used to make the pattern.

For example, $\frac{2}{4}$ should be written as $\frac{1}{2}$ and $\frac{15}{12}$ should be written as $1\frac{1}{4}$.

⑦ 0, $\frac{1}{6}$, $\frac{1}{3}$, ____, ____, ____, ____.   The rule is _____.

⑧ 0, $\frac{1}{8}$, $\frac{1}{4}$, ____, ____, ____, ____.   The rule is _____.

⑨ $\frac{1}{2}$, $\frac{3}{5}$, $\frac{7}{10}$, ____, ____, ____, ____.   The rule is _____.

⑩ $\frac{2}{3}$, $\frac{3}{4}$, $\frac{5}{6}$, ____, ____, ____, ____.   The rule is _____.

⑪ $1\frac{1}{12}$, $\frac{11}{12}$, $\frac{3}{4}$, ____, ____, ____, ____.   The rule is _____.

⑫ 4, $3\frac{5}{8}$, $3\frac{1}{4}$, ____, ____, ____, ____.   The rule is _____.

SCORE /12   0-5   6-10   11-12

Quick Check

Write the number that is $\frac{5}{1000}$ more than each of these decimals.

① 0·006 _____

② 0·019 _____

③ 0·97 _____

④ 0·3 _____

⑤ 0·4783 _____

Write in simplest form the fraction that is $\frac{1}{12}$ greater than each of these fractions.

⑥ $\frac{1}{4}$ _____

⑦ $\frac{2}{3}$ _____

⑧ $\frac{5}{6}$ _____

⑨ $\frac{23}{12}$ _____

⑩ $\frac{7}{6}$ _____

SCORE /10   0-4   5-8   9-10

Number & Algebra

UNIT 31

AC9M6N07, AC9M6N08

Estimation Strategies

For each of these questions:
- make a reasonable estimate of the answer
- check with a calculator.

For example, to find 52% of 180, you know that 50% is half. You also know what half of $180 is.

So, a reasonable estimate of 52% of 180 is 90.

This key sequence: [1] [8] [0] [×] [5] [2] [%] [=]

produces the result 93·64, which is quite close to the estimate of 90.

Follow Liam's method for making a reasonable estimate of these percentage amounts. Extend the method to multiplications and divisions.
After making your estimate, use your calculator to check how close you were.

	Amount	Estimate	Calculator check
①	26% of $160		
②	21% of $140		
③	19 × 47		

	Amount	Estimate	Calculator check
④	49 × 68		
⑤	154 ÷ 7		
⑥	192 ÷ 8		

SCORE /6   0-2   3-4   5-6

Statistics & Probability

AC9M6P02

Percentage Chance

Write the numbers 10, 11, 12, 13, 14, 15, 16, 17, 18 and 19 onto small pieces of paper and place them in a paper bag.

① If you removed one piece of paper from the bag, what are the chances that the number would be odd, even, prime or square?

Record your answers as percentages in the table.

② If you were to take out one piece of paper then put it back in the bag and repeat the process 10 times, what are the chances that the numbers will be odd, even, prime or square?

Record your answers as percentages in the table.

	Chance as a Percentage			
	Odd	Even	Prime	Square
Calculate: Remove 1 piece of paper				
Calculate: Remove 1 piece of paper and replace it (10 times)				
Experiment: Remove 1 piece of paper				
Experiment: Remove 1 piece of paper and replace it (10 times)				

③ Now try the experiment. Draw up your own table to record the numbers you take out. Add the percentage of each type of number to the table.

④ Why do the actual results not match the expected probabilities?

_____

SCORE /4   0-1   2-3   4

TERM 4

UNIT 31

Measurement & Space

AC9M6M04

Angles

Use your protractor to construct and label these angles.

① Construct an angle of 60° and label both angles made.

② Construct an angle of 100° and label both angles made.

③ Construct a pair of vertically opposite acute angles and show their sizes.

④ Construct a pair of vertically opposite obtuse angles and show their sizes.

⑤ Construct four angles at a point: one of 60°, one of 180° and two of equal size. Show their sizes.

⑥ Construct four angles at a point, each a different size, and show their sizes.

SCORE /6   0-3   4-5   6

NAPLAN*-style Questions

① Which of these is the best estimate for 52% of $90?
  ○ $50   ○ $45   ○ $48   ○ $142

② Elsa has an apple with her school lunch once a week. Today is a school day. What is the percentage chance that Elsa will have an apple for lunch today?
  _____ %

③ What is the size of angle A in this isosceles triangle?
  ○ 90°   ○ 180°   ○ 45°   ○ 55°

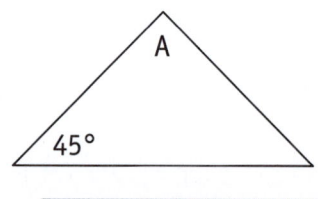

  (triangle with angle A at top, 45° at bottom left)

SCORE /3   0-1   2   3

TERM 4

136 TARGETING MATHS HOMEWORK: YEAR 6 © PASCAL PRESS ISBN: 9781925726596

Problem of the Week

What Is my Number?

Challenge 1
Tau chose the number 35 and made up these clues.
- If you add 5, you can divide my number by 8.
- If you subtract 2, you can divide my number by 3.
- My number is more than 20.

Are Tau's clues correct? _____

Challenge 2
Ruby chose a number and made up these clues.
- Add 4 to my number and you can divide by 5.
- Add 3 to my number and you can divide by 4.
- My number is between 30 and 50.

What is Ruby's number? _____

Challenge 3
Sara chose a number and made up these clues.
- Divide me by 3 and there is a remainder of 1.
- Divide me by 4 and there is a remainder of 1.
- Divide me by 5 and there is a remainder of 1.

What might Sara's number be? _____

Challenge 4
Choose a number and make up three division clues.

_____
_____
_____

What might your number be? _____

UNIT 32 — Number & Algebra

Function Machines

In Unit 7, you learned about function machines and function rules using whole numbers. In this unit, we will include decimal numbers.

In the list of inputs and outputs at the right, you can see that the output is always: **input + 0·5**.

That is why we write **+ 0·5** as the function rule.

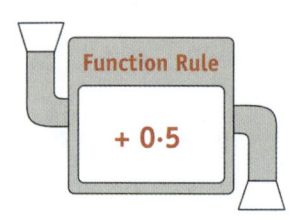

Function Rule: **+ 0·5**

Input	Output
6	6·5
6·5	7
7	7·5

Write the function rules for these function machines.

①
Input	Output
0·8	1·05
1·05	1·3
3·7	3·95

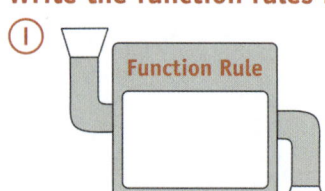

②
Input	Output
1·67	1·675
1·75	1·755
3·855	3·86

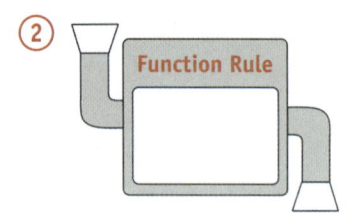

③
Input	Output
2·75	5·5
3·05	6·1
4·37	8·74

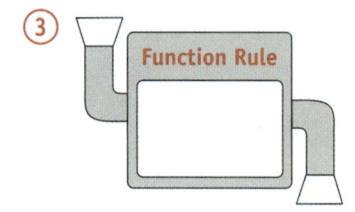

④
Input	Output
9·2	8·95
12	11·75
15·5	15·25

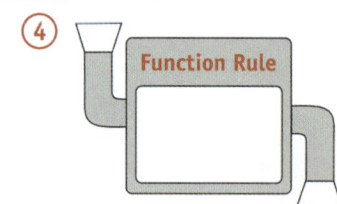

⑤
Input	Output
3·75	3·2
4·8	4·25
6·3	5·75

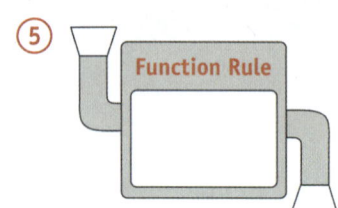

⑥
Input	Output
39	13
64·8	21·6
73·2	24·4

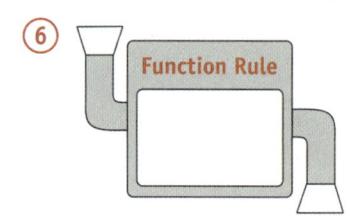

SCORE /6   0-2   3-4   5-6

Quick Check

Complete these input–output sequences.

①
Input	6·7	8·4	5·2	
Output	7·2		5·7	6·55

②
Input	3·7		7·95	8·3
Output	3·85	4·75		8·45

③
Input	3·07		6·3	7·95
Output	2·77	4·02		7·65

④
Input	6·3	7·08	8·34	9
Output	6·29		8·33	

⑤
Input	1·75	2·6	6·48	
Output	3·5		8·23	6·75

⑥
Input	0·6	3·05	4·8	
Output	1·2		5·4	10·4

⑦
Input	7·05	8	7·25	
Output	7		7·2	11·04

SCORE /7   0-3   4-5   6-7

Number & Algebra

UNIT 32

AC9M6A02

Number Sentences

Here are some word problems about a marble tournament in which every competitor starts with 15 marbles and plays 5 rounds. Write the correct number sentence for each word problem. Remember to use the correct order of operations in your number sentences.

① Alex won 6 marbles in the first round and then won 4 marbles in each of the next 3 rounds. He lost 2 marbles in the last round.

How many marbles did Alex finish with? _____

② Hai won 2 marbles in each of his first 2 rounds and then won 4 marbles in each of his next 2 rounds before losing 8 marbles in the last round.

How many marbles did Hai finish with? _____

③ Liam lost 3 marbles in his first round, 4 in the second round and then won 5 in each of the remaining rounds.

How many marbles did Liam finish with? _____

④ Elsa won 6 marbles, lost 5 and then won 4 marbles in each of her last rounds.

How many marbles did Elsa finish with? _____

⑤ Tau was on a winning streak. He won 4 marbles in each of his first 2 rounds and 3 in the next 2 rounds before losing 6 marbles in his last round.

How many marbles did Tau finish with? _____

SCORE /5   0-2   3-4   5

Statistics & Probability

AC9M6ST01

Reading Data

Ruby and Sara have both read 60 pages of the same graphic novel. The graph shows the number of pages that they each read on Monday, Tuesday and Wednesday nights.

① How many more pages did Sara read than Ruby on Monday night?

_____

② On which night were the most pages altogether read?

_____

③ How many pages altogether were read on Tuesday?

_____

④ How many fewer pages did Ruby read on Wednesday than Sara?

_____

⑤ What fraction of the total number of pages was read on Tuesday night?

Sara read _____ of the Tuesday pages.

Ruby read _____ of the Tuesday pages.

SCORE /5   0-2   3-4   5

TERM 4

139

UNIT 32 Measurement & Space

Area

Min cut her 8 cm by 8 cm square into 3 rectangles, all different.
One rectangle has an area of 16 cm² and one has an area of 30 cm².
One of the rectangles has long sides of 8 cm.

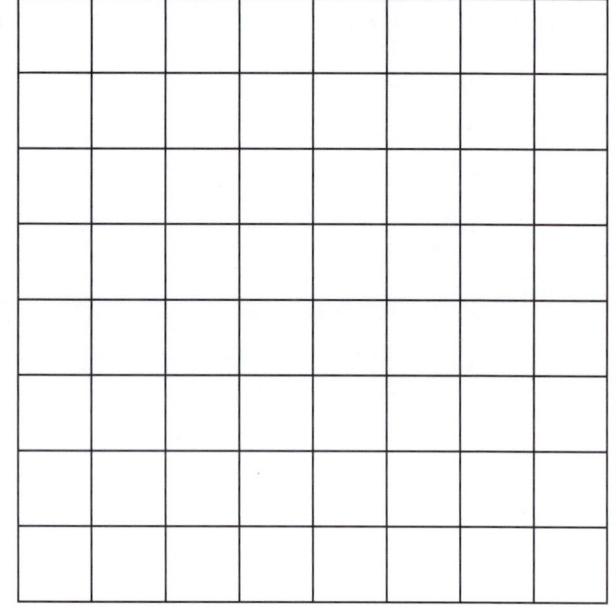

① Use the grid to show how Min cut her rectangles. (3 points)

② What is the perimeter of each rectangle?

A _____

B _____

C _____

③ What is the area of the each rectangle? (3 points)

A _____

B _____

C _____

SCORE /9   0-4   5-7   8-9

NAPLAN*-style Questions

① Movie tickets cost $24 for an adult and $12 for a child.
A family of 6 paid $108 for their tickets.
How many adults tickets were purchased?

____ adult tickets

② What is the value of A on this number line?

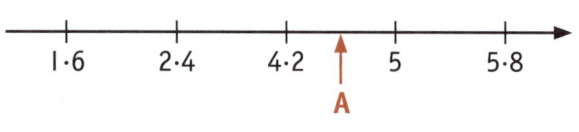

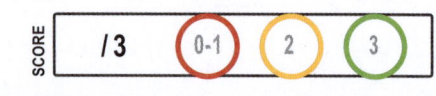

1·6   2·4   4·2   ↑   5   5·8
              A

○ 4·3   ○ 4·4   ○ 4·5   ○ 4·6   ○ 4·7

③ What is the area of this shape?

○ 12 cm²
○ 10 cm²
○ 16 cm²
○ 24 cm²

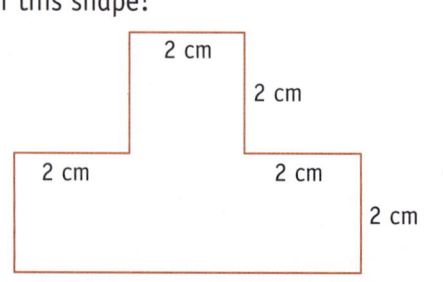

2 cm, 2 cm, 2 cm, 2 cm, 2 cm

SCORE /3   0-1   2   3

Problem of the Week

UNIT 32

AC9M6N09

An Area Puzzle

Alex cut his 9 cm by 9 cm square into 3 identical rectangles.

Then he overlapped one of them to make this letter H.

The area of Alex's letter H is 69 cm².

The First Challenge

① What is the area of the middle bar of the H? _____

② What is the length of line A? _____

③ What is the length of line B? _____

④ What is the area of the hidden part of the strip? _____

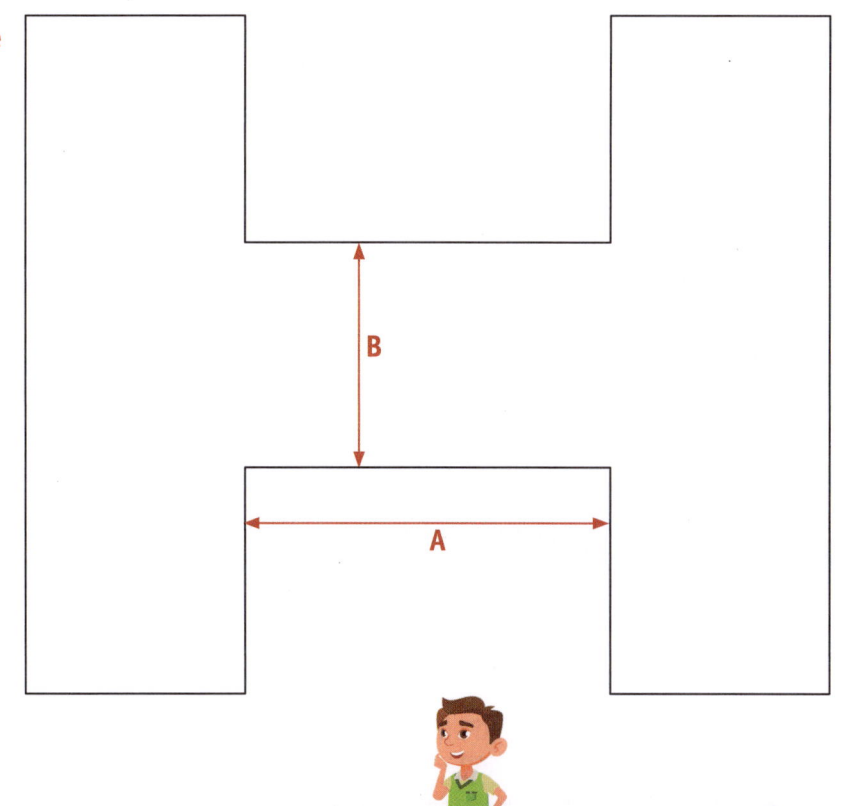

The Second Challenge

**Use this grid to make a puzzle of your own.
Write three questions that allow people to solve your puzzle.**

Suggestion: You might want to cut up some grid paper to make your puzzle and test your questions.

Write your questions here.

- _____

- _____

- _____

TERM 4

TARGETING MATHS HOMEWORK: YEAR 6 © PASCAL PRESS ISBN: 9781925726596

Review: Unit 25 and Unit 26

AC9M6N01, AC9M6N03, AC9M6N05, AC9M6M01, AC9M6SP01, AC9M6ST01

Place the given number on these number lines.

① Place 4 on this line.

```
+----------------+----------------+--->
0                6
```

② Place 0 on this line.

```
+----------------+----------------+--->
-3               5
```

This line graph shows the time taken to ice and decorate cupcakes.

③ How many cupcakes can be iced and decorated in $4\frac{1}{2}$ minutes?

_____ cupcakes

④ How long will it take to ice and decorate 7 cupcakes?

_____ minutes

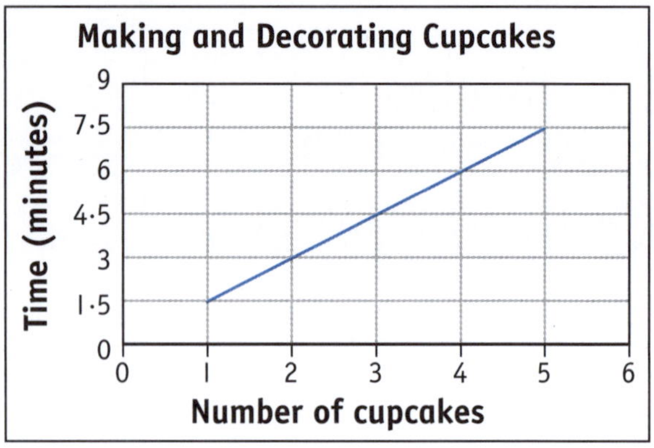

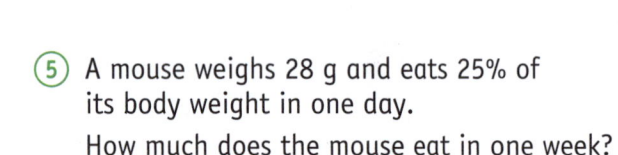

⑤ A mouse weighs 28 g and eats 25% of its body weight in one day.
How much does the mouse eat in one week?

_____ g

Making and Decorating Cupcakes

(graph: Time (minutes) vs Number of cupcakes)

What would half of each of these quantities be?

⑥ Half of $\frac{1}{2}$ cup is _____.

⑦ Half of $\frac{1}{3}$ cup is _____.

⑧ Half of $1\frac{1}{2}$ cups is _____.

⑨ Half of $\frac{1}{4}$ cup is _____.

⑩ Half of 3 cups is _____.

⑪ Half of $5\frac{1}{2}$ cups is _____.

Mark the fractions in the correct places on the number line.

⑫ $\frac{1}{2}, \frac{2}{3}, \frac{2}{6}$

```
+---------------------------------+--->
0                                 1
```

⑬ $\frac{5}{8}, \frac{3}{4}, \frac{1}{2}$

```
+---------------------------------+--->
0                                 1
```

Draw the congruent faces for each of these 3D objects. Write how many of each face there will be.

⑭

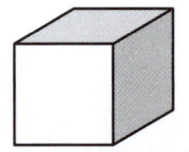

⑮

SCORE /15   0-7   8-13   14-15

142   TARGETING MATHS HOMEWORK: YEAR 6 © PASCAL PRESS ISBN: 9781925726596

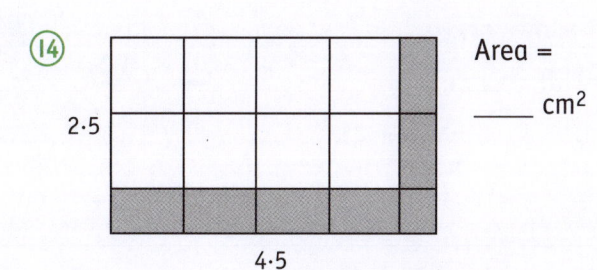

Review: Unit 27 and Unit 28

AC9M6N06, AC9M6A02, AC9M6M01, AC9M6M02, AC9M6ST03

Use work–smart strategies to reorder and multiply these decimals.

① $0.5 \times 3.6 \times 6$

Change to: _____

② $6 \times 3.5 \times 0.2$

Change to: _____

③ The thickness of a piece of cardboard is 0·0022 metres. Cardboard comes in packets of 100 sheets.

How thick is one packet?

_____ m

The graph shows Liam's earnings and spendings in dollars for five weeks.

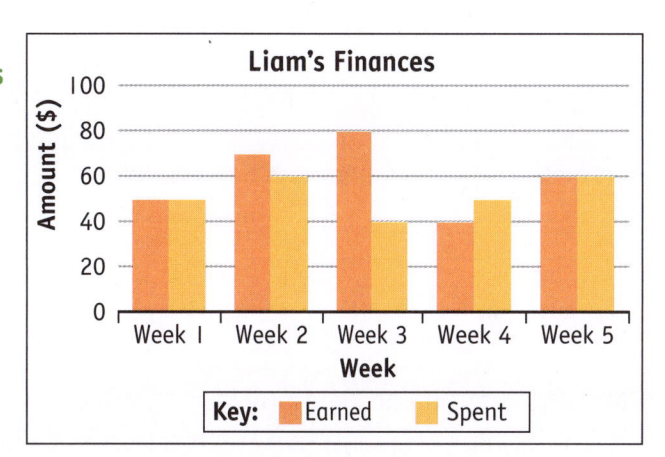

④ How much did Liam earn in the 5 weeks?

$_____

⑤ How much more did Liam earn than he spent in that time?

$_____

⑥ In which weeks did Liam spend the most?

_____

Write the answer to these multiplications. Then check with your calculator.
If your answer was wrong, write the correct answer and explain where you went wrong.

⑦ $0.4 \times 8 =$ ____   Check: _____

⑨ $0.7 \times 6 =$ ____   Check: _____

⑧ $0.07 \times 3 =$ ____   Check: _____

⑩ $0.09 \times 5 =$ ____   Check: _____

Use number splitting to complete these divisions.

⑪ $287 \div 7$

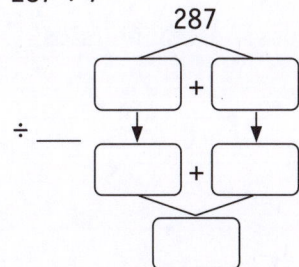

⑫ $1625 \div 5$

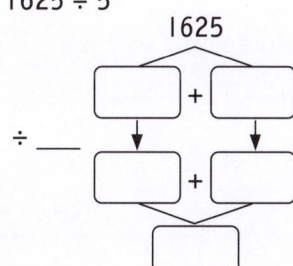

Find the area of these rectangles.

⑬ 2·5 by 3·5   Area = ____ cm²

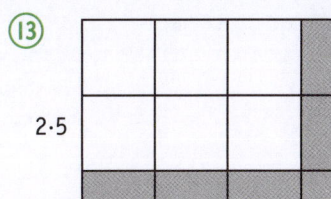

⑭ 2·5 by 4·5   Area = ____ cm²

Review: Unit 29 and Unit 30

AC9M6N06, AC9M6N07, AC9M6N08, AC9M6M01, AC9M6ST02

Give the answers to these divisions as fractions instead of remainders.

① 12 ÷ 5 = _____ ② 9 ÷ 4 = _____ ③ 17 ÷ 6 = _____

Use smart strategies to work out these percentages.

④ 21% of $56

____% of $____ = $_____

____% of $____ = $_____

$_____ + $_____ = $_____

⑤ 26% of $78

____% of $____ = $_____

____% of $____ = $_____

$_____ + $_____ = $_____

⑥ 52% of $76

____% of $____ = $_____

____% of $____ = $_____

$_____ + $_____ = $_____

⑦ 73% of $48

____% of $____ = $_____

____% of $____ = $_____

$_____ + $_____ = $_____

Complete these measurement conversions

⑧ 750 mm = _____ cm = _____ m

⑨ 1356 mL = _____ cL = _____ L

⑩ 4565 mm = _____ cm = _____ m

Solve these multistep word problems. Show each step.

⑪ Five movie tickets cost $75 and five icy-poles cost $30.
How much did each of the five people have to pay?

_____

⑫ There was a 25% off special at the art shop, so Hai bought 3 paintbrushes at $12 each, two sketchbooks at $16 each and a box of acrylic paints for $68.
When the discount was taken off, how much did Hai spend?

_____

This pie graph shows the results of a survey of the colour of cars that pass the school gates between 9:00 am and 10:00 am.

There were 48 cars recorded in that time. The pie graph shows the percentage of each colour.

Write the number of cars of each colour that were recorded in the survey.

⑬ Blue cars: ____

⑭ Red cars: ____

⑮ Silver cars: ____

⑯ Yellow cars: ____

⑰ White cars: ____

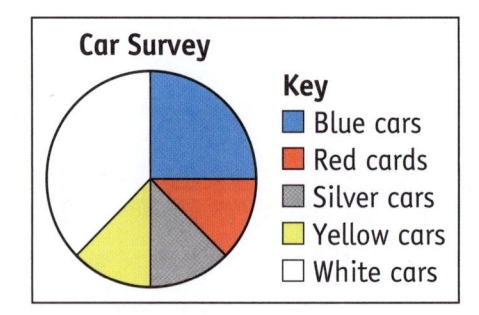

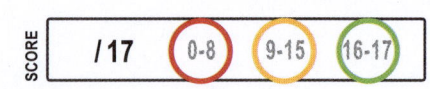

Car Survey

Key
- Blue cars
- Red cards
- Silver cars
- Yellow cars
- White cars

Review: Unit 31 and Unit 32

AC9M6N04, AC9M6N05, AC9M6N07, AC9M6N08, AC9M6A02, AC9M6A03, AC9M6ST01

Continue these decimal number patterns and write the pattern rule.

① 0·13, 0·25, 0·37, _____, _____, _____.   The pattern rule is _____.

② 0·96, 0·91, 0·86, _____, _____, _____.   The pattern rule is _____.

Estimate these percentage discounts and then check with your calculator.

	Amount	Estimate	Calculator Check
③	16% of $86		
④	26% of $118		

Construct angles to match the descriptions.

⑤ Draw a pair of vertically opposite acute angles of 70°.

⑥ Draw three angles at a point where two of the angles are 80° and 130°.

Write the size of the third angle: _____.

Write the function rules for these function machines.

⑦ Function Rule

Input	Output
7·6	8·2
3·59	4·19
2·8	3·4

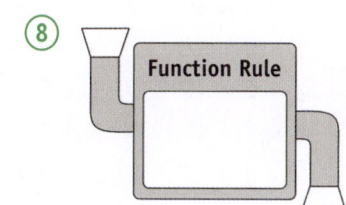

⑧ Function Rule

Input	Output
9·75	9·62
1·08	0·95
8·76	8·63

Write the correct number sentence and answer for this word problem.

⑨ Elsa started with 12 marbles in the first round. She won 2 marbles in each of the first two rounds. Then she lost 6 marbles in the next round but won 4 marbles and 3 marbles in the last two rounds. How many marbles did Elsa finish with?

_____

Tau and Ruby made a chart of the number of pages they read over the weekend.

⑩ On which day did they read the least number of pages?

Tau on _____

Ruby on _____

⑪ How many pages did they each read altogether?

Tau read ____ pages.

Ruby read ____ pages.

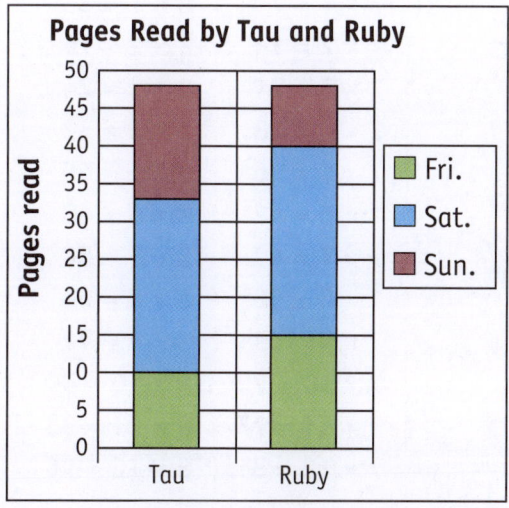

SCORE /11   0-5   6-9   10-11

★ QUICK MATHS FACTS ★

Measurement

Length
1 km = 1000 m
1 m = 100 cm
1 cm = 10 mm

Area
1 m^2 = 10 000 cm^2
1 hectare = 10 000 m^2
1 km^2 = 1 000 000 m^2

Capacity
1 L = 1000 mL

Mass
1 t = 1000 kg
1 kg = 1000 g

Fractions, decimals and percentages

$\frac{1}{100}$ = 0·01 = 1%
$\frac{25}{100}$ = 0·25 = 25%
$\frac{50}{100}$ = 0·5 = 50%
$\frac{75}{100}$ = 0·75 = 75%
$\frac{100}{100}$ = 1 = 100%

Place value

Ones	1
Tens	12
Hundreds	123
Thousands	1234
Ten thousands	12 345
Hundred thousands	123 456
Millions	1 234 567
Ten millions	12 345 678
Hundred millions	123 456 789

Time

60 s = 1 min
60 min = 1 h
1440 min = 1 day
24 h = 1 day
7 days = 1 week
365 days = 1 year
52 weeks = 1 year
12 months = 1 year

✸ Multiplication tables ✸

1 × 1 = 1	2 × 1 = 2	3 × 1 = 3	4 × 1 = 4	5 × 1 = 5	6 × 1 = 6
1 × 2 = 2	2 × 2 = 4	3 × 2 = 6	4 × 2 = 8	5 × 2 = 10	6 × 2 = 12
1 × 3 = 3	2 × 3 = 6	3 × 3 = 9	4 × 3 = 12	5 × 3 = 15	6 × 3 = 18
1 × 4 = 4	2 × 4 = 8	3 × 4 = 12	4 × 4 = 16	5 × 4 = 20	6 × 4 = 24
1 × 5 = 5	2 × 5 = 10	3 × 5 = 15	4 × 5 = 20	5 × 5 = 25	6 × 5 = 30
1 × 6 = 6	2 × 6 = 12	3 × 6 = 18	4 × 6 = 24	5 × 6 = 30	6 × 6 = 36
1 × 7 = 7	2 × 7 = 14	3 × 7 = 21	4 × 7 = 28	5 × 7 = 35	6 × 7 = 42
1 × 8 = 8	2 × 8 = 16	3 × 8 = 24	4 × 8 = 32	5 × 8 = 40	6 × 8 = 48
1 × 9 = 9	2 × 9 = 18	3 × 9 = 27	4 × 9 = 36	5 × 9 = 45	6 × 9 = 54
1 × 10 = 10	2 × 10 = 20	3 × 10 = 30	4 × 10 = 40	5 × 10 = 50	6 × 10 = 60
1 × 11 = 11	2 × 11 = 22	3 × 11 = 33	4 × 11 = 44	5 × 11 = 55	6 × 11 = 66
1 × 12 = 12	2 × 12 = 24	3 × 12 = 36	4 × 12 = 48	5 × 12 = 60	6 × 12 = 72

7 × 1 = 7	8 × 1 = 8	9 × 1 = 9	10 × 1 = 10	11 × 1 = 11	12 × 1 = 12
7 × 2 = 14	8 × 2 = 16	9 × 2 = 18	10 × 2 = 20	11 × 2 = 22	12 × 2 = 24
7 × 3 = 21	8 × 3 = 24	9 × 3 = 27	10 × 3 = 30	11 × 3 = 33	12 × 3 = 36
7 × 4 = 28	8 × 4 = 32	9 × 4 = 36	10 × 4 = 40	11 × 4 = 44	12 × 4 = 48
7 × 5 = 35	8 × 5 = 40	9 × 5 = 45	10 × 5 = 50	11 × 5 = 55	12 × 5 = 60
7 × 6 = 42	8 × 6 = 48	9 × 6 = 54	10 × 6 = 60	11 × 6 = 66	12 × 6 = 72
7 × 7 = 49	8 × 7 = 56	9 × 7 = 63	10 × 7 = 70	11 × 7 = 77	12 × 7 = 84
7 × 8 = 56	8 × 8 = 64	9 × 8 = 72	10 × 8 = 80	11 × 8 = 88	12 × 8 = 96
7 × 9 = 63	8 × 9 = 72	9 × 9 = 81	10 × 9 = 90	11 × 9 = 99	12 × 9 = 108
7 × 10 = 70	8 × 10 = 80	9 × 10 = 90	10 × 10 = 100	11 × 10 = 110	12 × 10 = 120
7 × 11 = 77	8 × 11 = 88	9 × 11 = 99	10 × 11 = 110	11 × 11 = 121	12 × 11 = 132
7 × 12 = 84	8 × 12 = 96	9 × 12 = 108	10 × 12 = 120	11 × 12 = 132	12 × 12 = 144

Days in the month

Thirty days have September, April, June and November.
All the rest have thirty-one, except February alone...
which has twenty-eight days clear, and twenty-nine each leap year.

Answers - Homework Year 6

TERM 1

UNIT 1 NUMBER & ALGEBRA

Integers
1 –3 and 3
2 –5 and 2
3 –1 and 5
4 –2 and 5
5 0 and 2
6 –1 and 4
7 –4 and 2

Quick Check
1 –1, 0, 1, 2, 3
2 –3, –2, –1, 0, 1
3 –2, –1, 0, 1, 2
4 –2, –1, 0, 1, 2
5 –6, –5, –4, –3, –2
6 0, 1, 2, 3, 4
7 –5, –4, –3, –2, –1
8 –3, –2, –1, 0, 1
9 –1 0, 1, 2, 3
10 –4, –3, –2, –1, 0

Growing Patterns

	Sequence								10th	Total
1	1	3	6	10	15	21	28	36	45	55	220
2	1	2	4	7	11	16	22	29	37	46	175
3	1	3	2	4	3	5	4	6	5	7	40
4	2	4	3	6	5	10	9	18	17	34	108
5	1	3	5	7	9	11	13	15	17	19	100

UNIT 1 STATISTICS & PROBABILITY

Speed Trials Results
1 8
2 4
3 At 3:45 with 12 people
4 8
5 49

UNIT 1 MEASUREMENT & SPACE

Metric Conversions

	km	m	cm	mm
1	4	4000	400 000	4 000 000
2	15	15 000	1 500 000	15 000 000
3	1½	1500	150 000	1 500 000
4	5	5000	500 000	5 000 000
5	1·8	1800	180 000	1 800 000
6	7·5	7500	750 000	7 500 000

UNIT 1 NAPLAN*-STYLE QUESTIONS
1 –4
2 55
3 4350 mm

UNIT 1 PROBLEM OF THE WEEK

Number Patterns

	1	2	3	4	5	6	7	8	9	10
Ruby	3	5	7	9	11	13	15	17	19	21
Sara	4	7	10	13	16	19	22	25	28	31
Min	5	9	13	17	21	25	29	33	37	41

1 The smallest number is 13.

Extending the sequences

	11	12	13	14	15	16	17	18	19	20
Ruby	23	25	27	29	31	33	35	37	39	41
Sara	34	37	40	43	46	49	52	55	58	61
Min	45	49	53	57	61	65	69	73	77	81

2 All the patterns use the numbers 13, 25, and 37. These numbers form a sequence that increases by 12 each time and, surprise, the numbers 3, 4 and 5 add to 12.

UNIT 2 NUMBER & ALGEBRA

Negative Numbers
1 –4 + 6 = 2
2 3 – 8 = –5
3 –5 + 10 = 5
4 2 – –2 = 4.
The difference is 4.
5 3 – –6 = 9.
The difference is 9.

Quick Check
1 2
2 –4
3 –1
4 2
5 0
6 6
7 6
8 4
9 7
10 8

Finding Prime Numbers
2, 3, 5, 7, 11, 13, 17, 19, 23, 29, 31, 37, 41, 43, 47, 53, 59, 61, 67, 71, 73, 79, 83, 89, 97.

UNIT 2 STATISTICS & PROBABILITY

Probability
1 50% (marked on number line between 0% and 100%)
2 0% (marked at left end)
3 Open-ended
4 About 15% 
5 Open-ended

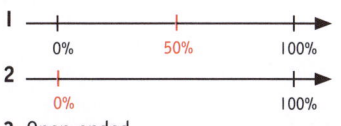

UNIT 2 MEASUREMENT & SPACE

The Cartesian Plane
Questions 1–4 are open-ended, but a typical answer might be:

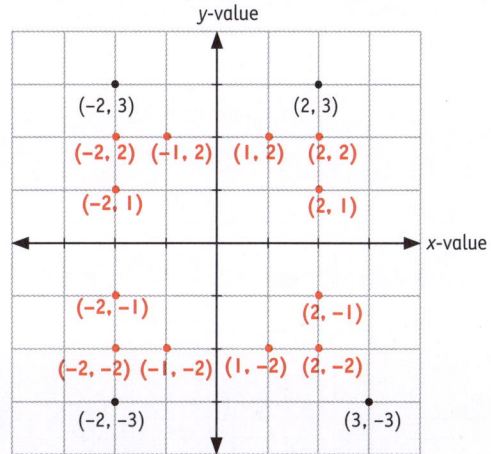

Coordinates shown: (–2, 3), (2, 3), (–2, 2), (–1, 2), (1, 2), (2, 2), (–2, 1), (2, 1), (–2, –1), (2, –1), (–2, –2), (–1, –2), (1, –2), (2, –2), (–2, –3), (3, –3)

Score 1 point for each correct coordinate.

UNIT 2 NAPLAN*-STYLE QUESTIONS
1 You will spin a prime number.
2 3, 2 and 11.
3 15

UNIT 2 PROBLEM OF THE WEEK

Closest to Zero
1 Sara
2 Elsa
3 6
4 5 of hearts and diamonds, 4 of hearts and diamonds and 3 of hearts
OR 5 of spades and clubs, 4 of spades and clubs and 3 of spades
5 Open-ended

UNIT 3 NUMBER & ALGEBRA

Fractions

1. $\frac{3}{5} = \frac{6}{10}$, $\frac{2}{10} = \frac{2}{10}$, $\frac{1}{2} = \frac{5}{10}$
   $\frac{2}{10}, \frac{5}{10}, \frac{6}{10}$

2. $\frac{7}{12} = \frac{7}{12}$, $\frac{5}{6} = \frac{10}{12}$, $\frac{1}{3} = \frac{4}{12}$
   $\frac{4}{12}, \frac{7}{12}, \frac{10}{12}$

3. $\frac{5}{8} = \frac{10}{16}$, $\frac{1}{2} = \frac{8}{16}$, $\frac{9}{16} = \frac{9}{16}$
   $\frac{8}{16}, \frac{9}{16}, \frac{10}{16}$

4. $\frac{9}{14} = \frac{9}{14}$, $\frac{3}{7} = \frac{6}{14}$, $\frac{1}{2} = \frac{7}{14}$
   $\frac{6}{14}, \frac{7}{14}, \frac{9}{14}$

5. $\frac{2}{3} = \frac{8}{12}$, $\frac{3}{4} = \frac{9}{12}$, $\frac{7}{12} = \frac{7}{12}$
   $\frac{7}{12}, \frac{8}{12}, \frac{9}{12}$

Quick Check

1. $\frac{9}{12}$
2. $\frac{4}{12}$
3. $\frac{4}{12}$
4. $\frac{4}{12}$
5. $\frac{8}{12}$
6. $\frac{9}{18}$
7. $\frac{12}{18}$
8. $\frac{15}{18}$
9. $\frac{30}{18}$
10. $\frac{8}{18}$

Decimal Addition

1. 36.5 + 104.35 + 27.35 = 168.2
2. 180.6 + 39.75 + 2.05 = 222.4
3. 18.75 + 206.05 + 3.37 = 228.17
4. 19.007 + 2.38 + 20.06 = 41.447
5. 6.5 + 13.005 + 27.63 = 47.135
6. 12.37 + 6.008 + 3.96 = 22.338

UNIT 3 STATISTICS & PROBABILITY

Comparing Data Displays

1. 50
2. 11
3. Soccer
4. Graph
5. Open-ended

UNIT 3 MEASUREMENT & SPACE

Area of a Rectangle

1. 4 × 8 = 32 cm²
2. 7 × 9 = 63 cm²
3. 13 × 5 = 65 cm²
4. 4 × 7 = 28 m²
5. 9 × 8 = 72 m²
6. 12 × 13 = 156 m²
7. 3 × 4 = 12 km²
8. 15 × 20 = 300 km²

UNIT 3 NAPLAN*-STYLE QUESTIONS

1. $1953
2. $\frac{5}{16}$
3. 17.825

UNIT 3 PROBLEM OF THE WEEK

Investigating Shapes with the Same Perimeter

Height	1	2	3	4	5	6	7	8	9
Width	9	8	7	6	5	4	3	2	1
Perimeter	20	20	20	20	20	20	20	20	20
Area	9	16	21	24	25	24	21	16	9

Height	1	2	3	4	5	6	7
Width	7	6	5	4	3	2	1
Perimeter	16	16	16	16	16	16	16
Area	7	12	15	16	15	12	7

The student might notice that the area is largest when the sides are the same length.

UNIT 4 NUMBER & ALGEBRA

Multiplying and Dividing Decimals

		H	T	O	.	Tths	Hths	Thths
1	3.7			3	.	7		
2	3.7 × 10		3	7	.			
3	3.7 ÷ 10			0	.	3	7	
4	13.06		1	3	.	0	6	
5	13.06 × 10	1	3	0	.	6		
6	13.06 ÷ 10			1	.	3	0	6
7	4.6			4	.	6		
8	4.6 × 100	4	6	0	.	0		
9	4.6 ÷ 100			0	.	0	4	6
10	0.012 × 100			1	.	2		

Quick Check

1. 65
2. 1.75
3. 275
4. 3.675
5. 10.673
6. 23.6
7. 375
8. 0.146
9. 10.875
10. 37.65

Fraction and Division

1. 12 ÷ 4 = 3, 3 × 3 = 9
2. 30 ÷ 3 = 10, 10 × 2 = 20
3. 20 ÷ 5 = 4, 4 × 3 = 12
4. 40 ÷ 8 = 5, 5 × 5 = 25
5. 27 ÷ 9 = 3, 3 × 4 = 12
6. 50 ÷ 10 = 5, 5 × 7 = 35

UNIT 4 STATISTICS & PROBABILITY

After-school Activities Survey

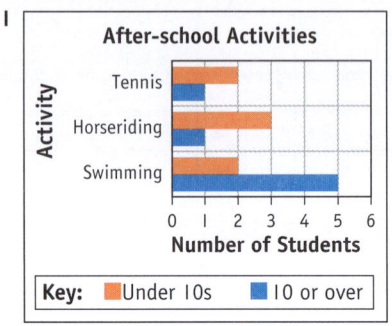

1. [Bar graph: After-school Activities, showing Tennis, Horseriding, Swimming by Under 10s and 10 or over]
2. 7
3. Tennis and Swimming
4. 7 students did swimming.
5. Horseriding

UNIT 4 MEASUREMENT & SPACE

Timetables

1. 6:45
2. 1 hour
3. Donald Duck
4. $1\frac{1}{2}$ hours
5. Open-ended

UNIT 4 NAPLAN*-STYLE QUESTIONS

1. 3656.5
2. $15
3. $5

UNIT 4 PROBLEM OF THE WEEK

Holiday Savings

	Week 1		Week 2	
	$ Saved	$ Short by	$ Saved	$ Short by
Hai	60	140	90	110
Liam	12	188	72	128
Elsa	30	170	96	104

UNIT 5 NUMBER & ALGEBRA

Division by Decimals, Fractions and Percentages

1. $12
2. $\frac{4}{10}$ of $160
   $\frac{1}{10}$ of $160 = $16
   4 × $16 = $64
3. 40% of $150
   10% of $150 = $15
   4 × $15 = $60
4. 0.2 × $80
   0.2 × 10 = 2
   2 × $8 = $16
5. 75% of $60
   50% of $60 = $30
   25% of $60 = $15
   $30 + $15 = $45
6. 11% of $100
   10% of $100 = $10
   1% of $100 = $1
   $10 + $1 = $11
7. $\frac{7}{10}$ of $140
   $\frac{1}{10}$ of $140 = $14
   7 × $14 = $98

Quick Check

| 1 $5 | 3 $30 | 5 $3·60 | 7 $36 | 9 $40 |
| 2 $18 | 4 $24 | 6 $11 | 8 $7·20 | 10 $32 |

Making Approximations

1. 0·5 + 0·45 is about 1 because 0·5 is half and 0·45 is close to half
2. 4% of $102 is about $4 because 4% of $100 = $4
3. 0·21 × $70 is about $14 because 0·21 is about $\frac{2}{10}$ and $\frac{2}{10}$ of $70 = $14
4. 33% of $90 is about $30 because 33% is about $\frac{1}{3}$ and $90 ÷ 3 = $30
5. $\frac{7}{8}$ of $82 is about $70 because $82 is about $80 and $\frac{7}{8}$ of $80 = $70
6. 0·25 × $81 is about $20 because 0·25 is $\frac{1}{4}$ and $\frac{1}{4}$ of $80 = $20

UNIT 5 STATISTICS & PROBABILITY

Interpreting Graphs

1. Open-ended, but we chose School C as the graph had more pink than any other!
2. School B
3. The scale
4. School B may be a country school.
5. Open-ended, but School C could be in a built-up area with high-rise apartments.

UNIT 5 MEASUREMENT & SPACE

Cross-sections

| 1 G | 2 C | 3 E | 4 D | 5 A | 6 F | 7 B |

UNIT 5 NAPLAN*-STYLE QUESTIONS

1. 88%
2. $30
3. (triangle)

UNIT 5 PROBLEM OF THE WEEK

Drawing Cross-sections

This Problem of the Week is completely open-ended.

UNIT 6 NUMBER & ALGEBRA

Fractions of a Price

| 1 $3 | 3 $5·60 | 5 $20 |
| 2 $15·50 | 4 $28·80 | 6 $25 |

Quick Check

| 1 $6·50 | 3 $4·50 | 5 $2 | 7 $9·25 | 9 $12·50 |
| 2 $37·50 | 4 $2·60 | 6 $6 | 8 $9 | 10 $24 |

Order of Operations

1. 3 × 8 ÷ (4 + 2)
  = 24 ÷ 6
  = 4
2. 20 ÷ 5 × (3 + 5)
  = 4 × 8
  = 32
3. (5 + 7) ÷ (10 − 4)
  = 12 ÷ 6
  = 2
4. (30 − 12) ÷ (12 − 3)
  = 18 ÷ 9
  = 2
5. 5 × 6 + 16 ÷ 2
  = 30 + 8
  = 38
6. 18 ÷ 3 + 21 ÷ 7
  = 6 + 3
  = 9

UNIT 6 STATISTICS & PROBABILITY

Toss Two Coins

1. Open-ended
2. Open-ended
3. The result should be similar to:

Outcome	2H	HT	2T
Frequency	2	4	2

UNIT 6 MEASUREMENT & SPACE

Tessellation

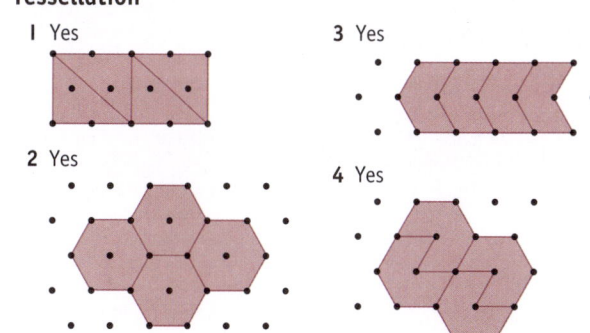

1. Yes
2. Yes
3. Yes
4. Yes

UNIT 6 NAPLAN*-STYLE QUESTIONS

1. $4·50
2. 21
3. The square and the hexagon

UNIT 6 PROBLEM OF THE WEEK

Patterns with Two Shapes

This relies on pairing the shapes as follows.

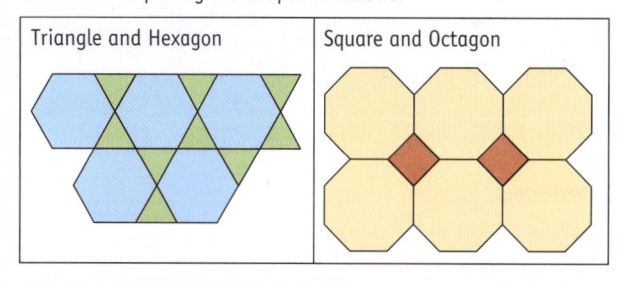

Triangle and Hexagon

Square and Octagon

UNIT 7 NUMBER & ALGEBRA

Patterns and Pattern Rules

| 1 Double or × 2 | 3 − 2 | 5 ÷ 4 |
| 2 × 3 | 4 ÷ 2 | 6 − 6 |

Quick Check

1. In: 34 Out: 16
2. In: 6 Out: 48
3. In: 9 Out: 10
4. In: 48 Out: 27
5. In: 22 Out: 21
6. Out: 45, 36
7. In: 33 Out: 4
8. In: 87 Out: 56

Square Numbers

The results will be 4 × 4 = 16, 5 × 5 = 25, 6 × 6 = 36, 7 × 7 = 49, 8 × 8 = 64, 9 × 9 = 81, 10 × 10 = 100 and 1 × 1 = 1.
Score 1 point for each new square number and 2 points for spotting that 1 is also a square number.

UNIT 7 STATISTICS & PROBABILITY

Total of 2 Dice

1.

+	1	2	3	4	5	6
1	2	3	4	5	6	7
2	3	4	5	6	7	8
3	4	5	6	7	8	9
4	5	6	7	8	9	10
5	6	7	8	9	10	11
6	7	8	9	10	11	12

2. 7
3. 2 and 12
4. 18 in 36 or 50%

UNIT 7 MEASUREMENT & SPACE

Problem Solving with Angles

1. 270°
2. 135°
3. 60°
4. 75°
5. 60°
6. 66°

UNIT 7 NAPLAN*-STYLE QUESTIONS
1 $+\frac{4}{10}$ 2 6   3 110°

UNIT 7 PROBLEM OF THE WEEK
Pavers for my Patio
The square number must be a multiple of 3, so 9 or 36. Only 36 pavers can be made into a rectangle (4 × 9) with an even number on one side and an odd number on the other.
As Mr Green wants a rectangular patio that is a minimum of 3 pavers wide, the possible patio sizes are 1 × 18, 3 × 12 or 4 × 9 but not 6 × 6.

Extra Challenge
With 4 packets, there would be 48 pavers and they could make rectangles 1 × 48, 2 × 24, 3 × 16, 4 × 12 and 6 × 8.
The choice for Mr Green will be open-ended.

UNIT 8 NUMBER & ALGEBRA
On a Budget
1 $140   2 $47   3 $125

4	Week 1	Week 2	Week 3	Week 4	Week 5
Item 1	Movies	Footy	Movies	Tuck shop	Movies
Item 2	Junk food	Tuck shop	Junk food		Tuck shop
$ Saved	$27	$20	$27	$15	$36
$ Spent	$20	$27	$20	$32	$11

5 This allows Min to save $125 at her current level of spending.
6 Min will have reached her $500 target exactly by the end of Week 5.

Quick Check
1 $27   2 $20   3 $74

Unit Cost Problems
1 70c each or 65c each
2 11c each or 10c each
3 $1·20 each or $1·15 each
4 90c each or $1·02 each
5 $1·20 each or 90c each

UNIT 8 STATISTICS & PROBABILITY
Make a Spinner
1–5
6 15%

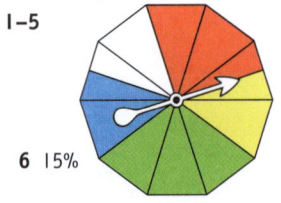

UNIT 8 MEASUREMENT & SPACE
Translation of a Shape
1 A (−6, −2)   4 D (−2, −6)   7 B (1, 7)
2 B (−3, 4)   5 See diagram   8 C (6, 1)
3 C (2, −2)   6 A (−2, 1)   9 D (2, −3)

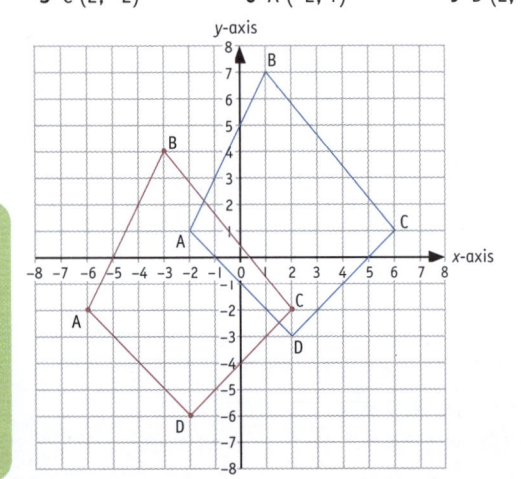

UNIT 8 NAPLAN*-STYLE QUESTIONS
1 $1·30   2 12 weeks   3 (−1, −3)

UNIT 8 PROBLEM OF THE WEEK
Holiday Destination
Open-ended

TERM 1 REVIEW

Review: Unit 1 and Unit 2
1 −1 and 2
2 −6 and 1
3 9
4 4
5 7
6 3, 9, 4, 12, 5, 15, 6, 18, 7, 21
7 4, 7, 5, 8, 6, 9, 7, 10, 8, 11
8 1500
9 500 000
10 2, 5, 7, 13
11 100%
12 50%
13 A = (1, 2)
14 B = (3, 1)
15 C = (1, −3)
16 D = (−2, −2)
17 E = (−3, 2)

Review: Unit 3 and Unit 4
1 12
2 10
3 8
4 6
5 8
6 9
7 37·05
  36·007
  8·01
  71·067
8 105·26
  3·7
  80·05
  189·01
9 6 × 6 = 36 m²
10 3 × 12 = 36 cm²
11 7 × 8 = 56 cm²
12 3·5 × 8 = 28 mm²
13 36
14 4705
15 9·56
16 0·3675
17 $27
18 $24
19 $40
20 $40
21 31
22 3
23 Swimming

Review: Unit 5 and Unit 6
1 $12
2 $32
3 $21·60
4 $27
5 $12·50
6 $60
7 1 because $\frac{3}{10}$ is about $\frac{1}{4}$
8 $32 because 39% is about 40%
9 Lemon
10 Pineapple
11 Tomato
12 $10·80
13 $28
14 $7·20

15
16 4 × 6 ÷ (3 + 3)
   = 24 ÷ 6
   = 4
17 27 ÷ 3 + 6 × 8
   = 9 + 48
   = 57

Review: Unit 7 and Unit 8
1 + 3
2 × 4
3 Input: 3, 5, 12
  Output: 10, 16, 37
4 Input: 26, 61, 111
  Output: 13, 48, 98
5 5
6 121
7 80°
8 50°
9 $60
10 $60 − $21 = $39
11 6 for $4·68
12–15
16 30%

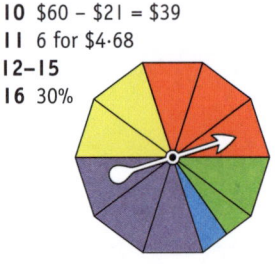

TERM 2

UNIT 9 NUMBER & ALGEBRA
Integers in the Context of Money
1–4 Ruby's balances are $55, −$45, $20, $55
5–8 Sara's balances are $170, $45, $0, −$60
9–12 Min's balances are $120, $95, −$30, $20
13 Ruby

Quick Check

1 –$50	3 –$20	5 –$100	7 –$25	9 –$25
2 –$15	4 –$100	6 $2	8 –$5	10 $75

Prime Factors

There are other ways to break the numbers into their factors, but the prime factors will still be the same.

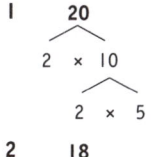

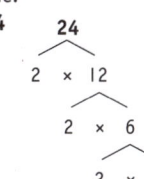

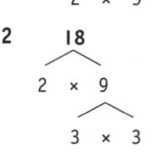

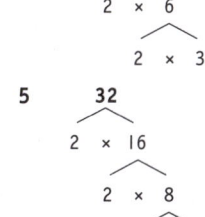

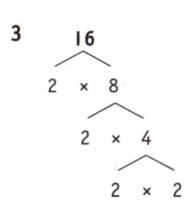

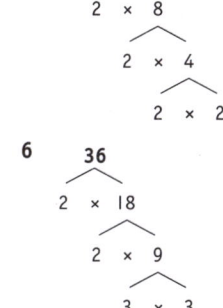

1 20
2 × 10
2 × 5

2 18
2 × 9
3 × 3

3 16
2 × 8
2 × 4
2 × 2

4 24
2 × 12
2 × 6
2 × 3

5 32
2 × 16
2 × 8
2 × 4
2 × 2

6 36
2 × 18
2 × 9
3 × 3

UNIT 9 STATISTICS & PROBABILITY

What Is the Litter?

Sample answers:
Have you ever dropped litter?
Are the bins close to where the litter is dropped?
Do people drop food scraps on the ground?
Are there many drink cartons or bottles in the litter?
What litter could be recycled?

UNIT 9 MEASUREMENT & SPACE

The Cartesian Plane

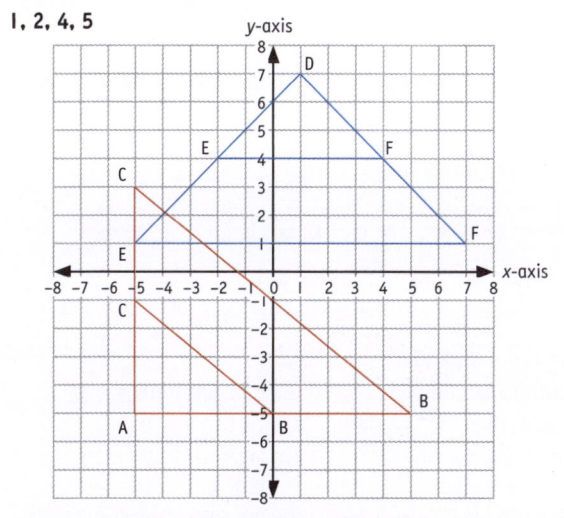

1, 2, 4, 5

3 B is now at (5, –5) and C is now at (–5, 3).
6 E is now at (–5, 1) and F is now at (7, 1).
7–8 Open-ended

UNIT 9 NAPLAN*-STYLE QUESTIONS

1 second floor
2 9
3 A = (–1, 5) and B = (5, 0)

UNIT 9 PROBLEM OF THE WEEK

Draw Me a House

Note: Window positions will vary.
Top right corners:
- Window 1 is at (–3, 2).
- Window 2 is at (3, 2).
- Window 3 is at (–3, –2).
- Window 4 is at (3, –2).

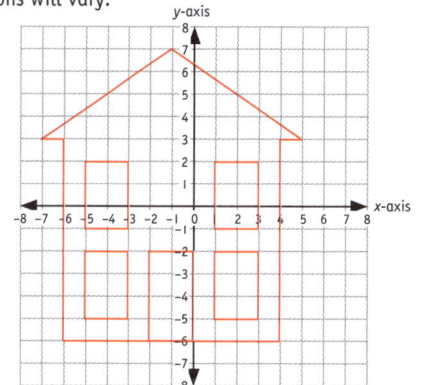

UNIT 10 NUMBER & ALGEBRA

Estimating and Rounding

1 Estimate: 37 + 27 = 64
Check: 64·044
2 Estimate: 28 – 18 = 10
Check: 10·513
3 Estimate: 18 + 18 = 36
Check: 35·902
4 Estimate: 40 + 28 = 68
Check: 67·598
5 Estimate: 57 – 28 = 29
Check: 28·918
6 Estimate: 74 – 37 = 37
Check: 37·567
7 Estimate: 39 + 28 = 67
Check: 67·374
8 Estimate: 57 – 18 = 39
Check: 39·354
9 Estimate: 57 + 102 = 159
Check: 158·582

Quick Check

1 38	3 47	5 18	7 13	9 109
2 38	4 33	6 28	8 54	10 201

Which Fraction Is the Larger?

1 $\frac{4}{10}$ or $\frac{5}{10}$, $\frac{1}{2} > \frac{2}{5}$
2 $\frac{8}{12}$ or $\frac{9}{12}$, $\frac{3}{4} > \frac{2}{3}$
3 $\frac{16}{24}$ or $\frac{15}{24}$, $\frac{2}{3} > \frac{5}{8}$
4 $\frac{10}{15}$ or $\frac{9}{15}$, $\frac{3}{5} < \frac{2}{3}$
5 $\frac{15}{18}$ or $\frac{14}{18}$, $\frac{7}{9} < \frac{5}{6}$
6 $\frac{15}{35}$ or $\frac{14}{35}$, $\frac{2}{5} < \frac{3}{7}$

UNIT 10 STATISTICS & PROBABILITY

Fake Data

1 Jan. 2020 – Feb. 2021
2 Feb. 2021 – Mar. 2022
3 Mar. to Dec. is 1 year and 9 months, 8 months more than the other timespans.
4 You think the timespans are the same.
5 12-month periods or same length periods.

UNIT 10 MEASUREMENT & SPACE

Right Prisms

1 congruent
2 similar
3 congruent
4 congruent
5 similar
6 congruent

UNIT 10 NAPLAN*-STYLE QUESTIONS

1 $\frac{5}{8}$
2 19
3 $\frac{5}{10}$

UNIT 10 PROBLEM OF THE WEEK

Matching Pairs

Sample answers. Other answers are possible.

	Numbers on the Board	Round and add or subtract
1	3·655 and 6·499	4 + 6 = 10
2	5·077 and 4·998	5 + 5 = 10
3	6·456 and 16·013	16 – 6 = 10
4	14·785 and 5·409	15 – 5 = 10
5	12·756 and 3·042	13 – 3 = 10
6	2·789 + 6·632	3 + 7 = 10

Extra Challenge: Open-ended

UNIT 11 NUMBER & ALGEBRA

Adding Fractions

1. $\frac{1}{4} + \frac{2}{4} = \frac{3}{4}$
2. $\frac{2}{9} + \frac{6}{9} = \frac{8}{9}$
3. $\frac{12}{16} + \frac{5}{16} = \frac{17}{16} = 1\frac{1}{16}$
4. $\frac{6}{10} + \frac{4}{10} = \frac{10}{10} = 1$
5. $\frac{9}{15} + \frac{8}{15} = \frac{17}{15} = 1\frac{2}{15}$
6. $\frac{9}{24} + \frac{7}{24} = \frac{16}{24} = \frac{2}{3}$
7. $\frac{3}{6} + \frac{4}{6} = \frac{7}{6} = 1\frac{1}{6}$
8. $\frac{9}{21} + \frac{7}{21} = \frac{16}{21}$
9. $\frac{16}{40} + \frac{25}{40} = \frac{41}{40} = 1\frac{1}{40}$
10. $\frac{15}{18} + \frac{14}{18} = \frac{29}{18} = 1\frac{11}{18}$
11. $\frac{12}{15} + \frac{10}{15} = \frac{22}{15} = 1\frac{7}{15}$
12. $\frac{20}{24} + \frac{15}{24} = \frac{35}{24} = 1\frac{11}{24}$

Quick Check

1. 6
2. 20
3. 6
4. 14
5. 16
6. 40
7. 42
8. 60
9. 36
10. 100

Fraction Sequences

	A	B	C	D	E	F
1	$\frac{1}{4}$	$\frac{3}{4}$	$1\frac{1}{4}$	$1\frac{3}{4}$	$2\frac{1}{4}$	$2\frac{3}{4}$
2	$\frac{1}{3}$	$\frac{2}{3}$	1	$1\frac{1}{3}$	$1\frac{2}{3}$	2
3	$\frac{1}{2}$	$1\frac{1}{4}$	2	$2\frac{3}{4}$	$3\frac{1}{2}$	$4\frac{1}{4}$

4. $1, 1\frac{1}{6}, 1\frac{2}{6}$
5. $3\frac{1}{4}, 3\frac{1}{8}, 3$
6. $1\frac{9}{10}, 1\frac{7}{10}, 1\frac{5}{10}$
7. $2, 1\frac{1}{3}, \frac{2}{3}$

UNIT 11 STATISTICS & PROBABILITY

A Colour Spinner

1. 20%
2. Yes
3. 1 in 5 chance
4.

	Red	Yellow	Blue	Green	Black
Percentage	20%	10%	30%	0%	40%

5. 20 + 10 + 30 + 0 + 40 = 100%

UNIT 11 MEASUREMENT & SPACE

Measurement Units

1. 3 m
2. 14·35 m
3. 2 m
4. 12·45 m

UNIT 11 NAPLAN*-STYLE QUESTIONS

1. $\frac{4}{5}$
2. $6\frac{2}{6}$
3. 3 m

UNIT 11 PROBLEM OF THE WEEK

Sequences of Fractions

Ruby made up Sequence 1.
Elsa made up Sequence 2.
Tau made up Sequence 3.
Liam made up Sequence 4.

UNIT 12 NUMBER & ALGEBRA

Multiplying Decimal Numbers

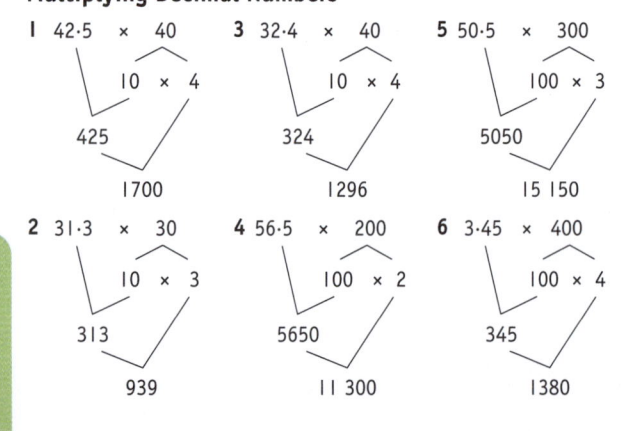

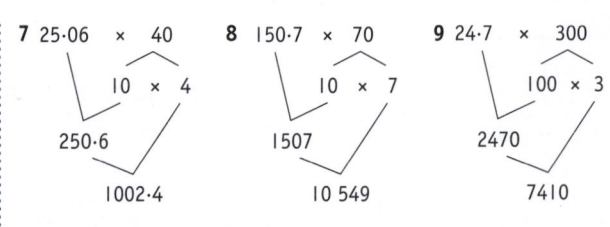

1. 42·5 × 40 → 10 × 4 → 425 → 1700
2. 31·3 × 30 → 10 × 3 → 313 → 939
3. 32·4 × 40 → 10 × 4 → 324 → 1296
4. 56·5 × 200 → 100 × 2 → 5650 → 11 300
5. 50·5 × 300 → 100 × 3 → 5050 → 15 150
6. 3·45 × 400 → 100 × 4 → 345 → 1380
7. 25·06 × 40 → 10 × 4 → 250·6 → 1002·4
8. 150·7 × 70 → 10 × 7 → 1507 → 10 549
9. 24·7 × 300 → 100 × 3 → 2470 → 7410

Quick Check

1. 70
2. 189
3. 1520
4. 2560
5. 1800
6. 686
7. 252
8. 696
9. 3535
10. 4444

Dividing Decimal Numbers

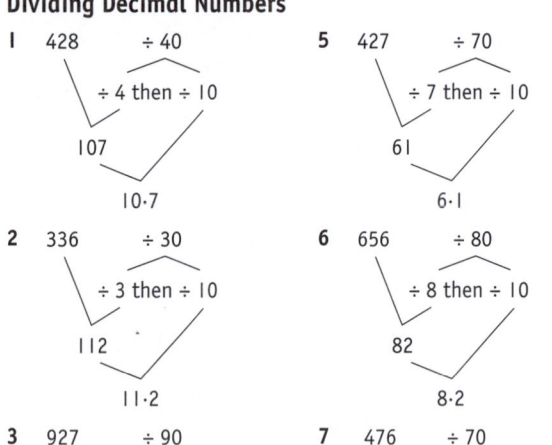

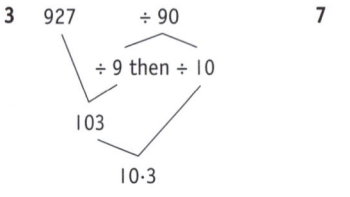

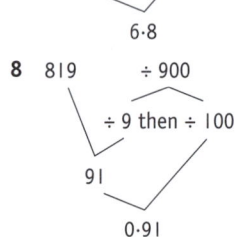

1. 428 ÷ 40 → ÷ 4 then ÷ 10 → 107 → 10·7
2. 336 ÷ 30 → ÷ 3 then ÷ 10 → 112 → 11·2
3. 927 ÷ 90 → ÷ 9 then ÷ 10 → 103 → 10·3
4. 378 ÷ 60 → ÷ 6 then ÷ 10 → 63 → 6·3
5. 427 ÷ 70 → ÷ 7 then ÷ 10 → 61 → 6·1
6. 656 ÷ 80 → ÷ 8 then ÷ 10 → 82 → 8·2
7. 476 ÷ 70 → ÷ 7 then ÷ 10 → 68 → 6·8
8. 819 ÷ 900 → ÷ 9 then ÷ 100 → 91 → 0·91

UNIT 12 STATISTICS & PROBABILITY

Rainfall Record

1. 5 mm
2. 60 mm
3. 135 mm
4. 100 mm

UNIT 12 MEASUREMENT & SPACE

Converting Metric Units

1. 900 g or 0·9 kg
2. 900 mL or 0·9 L
3. 1500 g or 1·5 kg
4. 0·25 kg or 250 g
5. 0·75 kg or 750 g

UNIT 12 NAPLAN*-STYLE QUESTIONS

1. $52·50
2. $24·20
3. 3000 ÷ 250

UNIT 12 PROBLEM OF THE WEEK

Shopping for Camp

0·875 kg of flour
10·5 kg of sausages
2·8 kg of tomatoes
14 L of orange juice
Note: orange juice comes in 750 mL bottles so 19 bottles are needed.

Second Challenge

Flour $3·50
Sausages $149·60
Tomatoes $19·60
Orange juice $123·50
Total cost $296·20

UNIT 13 NUMBER & ALGEBRA

Percentage Discounts

1. $23·40
2. $18
3. $20·80
4. $1332
5. $3·60 each

Quick Check

1. $6·50
2. $6
3. $15
4. 60c
5. $3·74
6. $245
7. $18
8. $44
9. $105
10. $60

Fractions, Decimals and Percentages

	Percentage to find	Calculator with a % key	Calculator without a % key
2	42% of 74	7 4 × 4 2 % = (31·08)	7 4 × 0 · 4 2 = (31·08)
3	17% of 1300	1 3 0 0 × 1 7 % = (221)	1 3 0 0 × 0 · 1 7 = (221)
4	58% of 4250	4 2 5 0 × 5 8 % = (2465)	4 2 5 0 × 0 · 5 8 = (2465)
5	73% of 247	2 4 7 × 7 3 % = (180·31)	2 4 7 × 0 · 7 3 = (180·31)

UNIT 13 STATISTICS & PROBABILITY
A Graph of Exercise Times
1. 190
2. 0 to 45
3. 16–25
4. Short and long exercise times are unpopular.
5. 30 students

UNIT 13 MEASUREMENT & SPACE
Translation of a Shape
1. Quadrant 1: A = (3, 2), B = (6, 2) C = (7, 6) and D = (2, 7).
2.
3. Quadrant 2: A = (−5, 2), B = (−2, 2) C = (−1, 6) and D = (−6, 7).
4. Quadrant 3: A = (−5, −6), B = (−2, −6) C = (−1, −2) and D = (−6, −1).
5. Quadrant 4: A = (5, −6), B = (2, −6) C = (1, −2) and D = (6, −1).

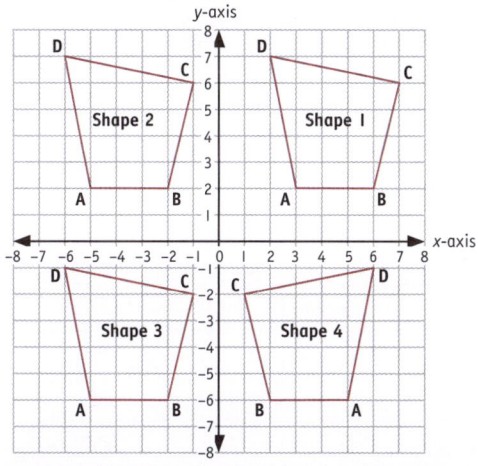

UNIT 13 NAPLAN*-STYLE QUESTIONS
1. $111.25
2. 0.45
3. (−2, 2)

UNIT 13 PROBLEM OF THE WEEK
Best Buy

	Shop 1	Shop 2	Shop 3	Shop 4
Anorak	$33.75	$40.50	$16.20	$15.00
Shorts	$16.25	$6.50	$32.50	$19.00
Thongs	$12.15	$7.29	$7.29	$16.20
T-Shirt	$10.00	$8.00	$8.80	$10.00
Total	$72.15	$62.29	$64.79	$60.20

	From Shop	Amount saved
Anorak	Shop 2	$40.50
Shorts	Shop 3	$32.50
Thongs	Shop 4	$16.20
T-Shirt	Shop 1 or 4	$10.00
	Total	$99.20

UNIT 14 NUMBER & ALGEBRA
Numerical Equations
Note that other answers are possible.
1. 6 + 3 × 7 = 5 × 5 + 2 = 5 × 4 + 7
2. 6 + 3 × 7 = 4 × 7 − 1 = 4 × 8 − 5
3. 8 × 3 + 6 = 7 × 4 + 2 = 7 × 3 + 9
4. 8 × 3 − 4 = 6 × 3 + 2 = 6 × 2 + 8
5. 5 × 9 + 3 = 9 × 5 + 3 = 9 × 4 + 12
6. 7 × 9 + 6 = 8 × 9 − 3 = 8 × 10 − 11
7. 4 + 6 × 7 = 8 × 5 + 6 = 8 × 4 + 14
8. 4 × 7 + 3 = 24 ÷ 1 + 7 = 24 ÷ 2 + 19
9. 8 + 6 × 3 = 10 × 3 − 4 = 10 × 4 − 14
10. 36 ÷ 9 + 4 = 24 ÷ 6 + 4 = 24 ÷ 4 + 2

Quick Check
1. 36 3. 9 5. 8 7. 24 9. 7
2. 59 4. 4 6. 6 8. 8 10. 7

Sticky Word Problems

1	6 × 8 + 8 + 3 × 6	48 + 8 + 18 = 74	Min had 74 stickers.
2	48 − (48 ÷ 3) − 11	48 − 16 − 11 = 21	Alex has 21 stickers left.
3	6 × 12 ÷ 4	72 ÷ 4 = 18	Liam put 18 stickers on each page.
4	6 + 2 × 12 + 3 × 8 + 3	6 + 24 + 24 + 3 = 57	Elsa had 57 stickers altogether.
5	$60 − 3 × $3.50 − 6 × $2.75	$60 − $10.50 − $16.50 = $33	Tau has $33 left.

UNIT 14 STATISTICS & PROBABILITY
Weather Predictions
Open-ended

UNIT 14 MEASUREMENT & SPACE
Angles
1. 40° 3. 68° 5. 110° 7. 130°
2. 75° 4. 55° 6. 75° 8. 90°

UNIT 14 NAPLAN*-STYLE QUESTIONS
1. 5
2. 3 × 12 + 6 + 4 × 8
3. 125°

UNIT 14 PROBLEM OF THE WEEK
Make the Number 30
The winner was Hai with an expression that equals 30.
Challenge: Johnny's expression was (4 + 4 − 6) × 5 × 3 = 30!
Extra Challenge: Ann's expression was (2 × 7 + 1) × (8 − 6) = 30!

UNIT 15 NUMBER & ALGEBRA
Number Sequences
1. 1.75, 2.0, 2.25, 2.5, 2.75, 3.
   The rule is + 0.25.
2. 15, 3, 30, 6, 60, 12, 120, 24
   The rule is ÷ 5 and then × 10.
3. 6, 24, 12, 48, 24, 96, 48
   The rule is × 4 and then ÷ 2.
4. 0.075, 0.08, 0.085, 0.09, 0.095, 0.1
   The rule is + 0.005.
5. $\frac{1}{2}$, $1\frac{2}{3}$, $2\frac{1}{3}$, 3, $3\frac{2}{3}$, $4\frac{1}{3}$, 5
   The rule is + $\frac{2}{3}$.
6. $\frac{3}{5}$, $1\frac{1}{5}$, $1\frac{4}{5}$, $2\frac{2}{5}$, 3, $3\frac{3}{5}$, $4\frac{1}{5}$
   The rule is + $\frac{3}{5}$.
7. $\frac{1}{2}$, $\frac{7}{8}$, $1\frac{1}{4}$, $1\frac{5}{8}$, 2, $2\frac{3}{8}$, $2\frac{3}{4}$
   The rule is + $\frac{3}{8}$.
8. $\frac{1}{3}$, $\frac{3}{4}$, $1\frac{1}{6}$, $1\frac{7}{12}$, 2, $2\frac{5}{12}$, $2\frac{5}{6}$
   The rule is + $\frac{5}{12}$.

Quick Check

1. $\frac{9}{10}$, 1
2. 0·92, 0·96
3. 6, 12
4. $3\frac{1}{8}$, 3
5. 9·25, 9
6. 11·025, 11
7. 42, 54
8. 16, 32
9. 84, 105
10. 28, 33

Subtracting Fractions

1. $\frac{4}{6} - \frac{3}{6} = \frac{1}{6}$
2. $\frac{15}{20} - \frac{8}{20} = \frac{7}{20}$
3. $\frac{25}{30} - \frac{24}{30} = \frac{1}{30}$
4. $\frac{9}{30} - \frac{5}{30} = \frac{4}{30} = \frac{2}{15}$
5. $\frac{10}{15} - \frac{9}{15} = \frac{1}{15}$
6. $\frac{15}{21} - \frac{14}{21} = \frac{1}{21}$
7. $\frac{9}{24} - \frac{8}{24} = \frac{1}{24}$
8. $\frac{6}{10} - \frac{5}{10} = \frac{1}{10}$
9. $\frac{14}{18} - \frac{12}{18} = \frac{2}{18} = \frac{1}{9}$
10. $\frac{21}{28} - \frac{20}{28} = \frac{1}{28}$

UNIT 15 STATISTICS & PROBABILITY

Clown Dress-up Day

1. Open-ended

2–5 1 point for correctly entered items.

		Hats	Red noses	Baggy pants	Big shoes
2	Hats	6	5		
3	Red noses				
4	Baggy pants	3	8	8	
5	Big shoes		10		9
6	Total	9	23	8	9

UNIT 15 MEASUREMENT & SPACE

Area

1. 5 m
2. 4 m
3. 4 m
4. 2 m
5. 20 m²
6. 8 m²
7. 28 m²
8. 35 m²
9. $2448

UNIT 15 NAPLAN*-STYLE QUESTIONS

1. 2·475 m
2. $\frac{1}{24}$
3. 24 m²

UNIT 15 PROBLEM OF THE WEEK

House Plans

Tiles (m²)	
Hall	10
Kitchen/Dining	35
Laundry/Bathroom	10
Ensuite	9
Total	64

Carpet (m²)	
Family/Lounge	30
Bedrooms	50
Study	15
Walk-in Robe	2
Total	97

Pavers (m²)	
Outdoor	39
Pathway	66
Total	105

The last part is open-ended.

UNIT 16 NUMBER & ALGEBRA

Prime, Composite and Square Numbers

1. 24 is not a square number.
2. 5 is not a composite number.
3. 23 is not a multiple of 3.
4. 27 is not a prime number.
5. 62 is not a multiple of 8.

Spotting Patterns

	The Square Number	The Difference
	$1^2 = 1$	
6	$2^2 = 4$	3
7	$3^2 = 9$	5
8	$4^2 = 16$	7
9	$5^2 = 25$	9
10	$6^2 = 36$	11

	The Square Number	The Difference
	$6^2 = 36$	
11	$7^2 = 49$	13
12	$8^2 = 64$	15
13	$9^2 = 81$	17
14	$10^2 = 100$	19
15	$11^2 = 121$	21

16. The difference between two square numbers is odd.

Quick Check

1. 25
2. 36
3. 121
4. 81
5. 144
6. 5
7. 4
8. 17
9. 36
10. 23

Measuring Temperatures

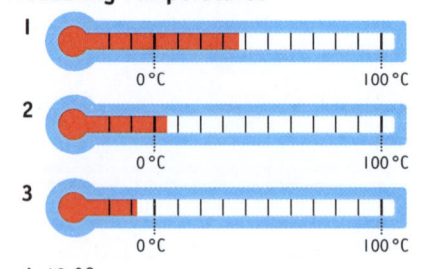

4. 13 °C
5. 16 °C

UNIT 16 STATISTICS & PROBABILITY

Probability

	The chance	As a fraction	As a decimal	As a percentage
1	1 in 8	$\frac{1}{8}$	0·125	12·5%
2	25 in 100	$\frac{1}{4}$	0·25	25%
3	2 in 5	$\frac{2}{5}$	0·4	40%
4	6 in 8	$\frac{6}{8}$	0·75	75%
5	37 in 50	$\frac{37}{50}$	0·74	74%

UNIT 16 MEASUREMENT & SPACE

Angles of a Polygon

1. 124°
2. 100°
3. 117°
4. 105°
5. 94°
6. pentagon
7. 540°

UNIT 16 NAPLAN*-STYLE QUESTIONS

1. 40, because 1, 2, 4, 5, 8 10, 20 and 40 are all factors of 40.
2. 140 °C
3.

UNIT 16 PROBLEM OF THE WEEK

A Numbers Game

Min: 263. Alex: 349 and 439.

Extra Challenge

Square Number: 9
Prime Numbers: 53, 59, 359, 593 and 953
Score: 30

TERM 2 REVIEW

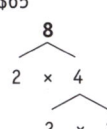

Review: Unit 9 and Unit 10

1. −$50
2. −$25
3. $110
4. $65
5. 8 → 2 × 4 → 2 × 2
6. 28 → 2 × 14 → 2 × 7
7. 42 → 2 × 21 → 3 × 7
8. A is at (−3, 4)
9. B is at (4, 1)
10. C is at (1, −4)
11. D is at (−5, −2)
12. 37
13. 50
14. 37
15. Estimate 75, Actual 75·834
16. Estimate 88, Actual 83·603
17. $\frac{10}{12}$ or $\frac{9}{12}$, $\frac{5}{6} > \frac{9}{12}$
18. $\frac{12}{16}$ or $\frac{13}{16}$, $\frac{3}{4} < \frac{13}{16}$
19. $\frac{9}{15}$ or $\frac{11}{15}$, $\frac{3}{5} < \frac{11}{15}$

Review: Unit 11 and Unit 12

1. $\frac{15}{20} + \frac{12}{20} = 1\frac{7}{20}$
2. $\frac{5}{16} + \frac{12}{16} = 1\frac{1}{16}$
3. $\frac{3}{9} + \frac{6}{9} = 1$
4. $\frac{6}{30} + \frac{15}{30} = \frac{21}{30} = \frac{7}{10}$
5. 1, $1\frac{1}{6}$, $1\frac{1}{3}$
6. $1\frac{2}{3}$, 2, $2\frac{1}{3}$
7. $1\frac{1}{4}$, $1\frac{5}{8}$, 2
8. $\frac{5}{9}$, $\frac{2}{3}$, $\frac{7}{9}$
9. ||

10.

	Red	White	Yellow	Green	Blue
Percentage	20%	20%	20%	30%	10%

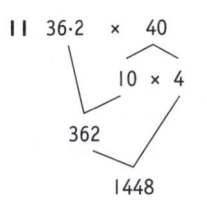

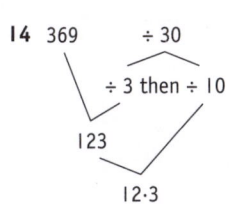

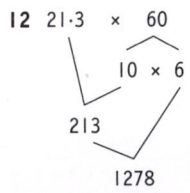

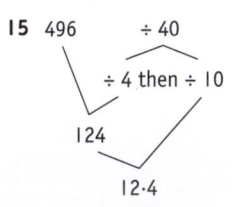

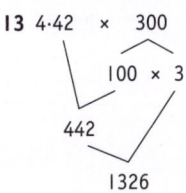

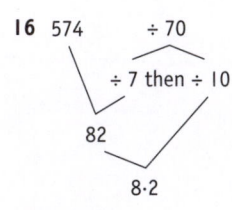

11. 36·2 × 40 → 10 × 4 → 362 → 1448
12. 21·3 × 60 → 10 × 6 → 213 → 1278
13. 4·42 × 300 → 100 × 3 → 442 → 1326
14. 369 ÷ 30 → ÷ 3 then ÷ 10 → 123 → 12·3
15. 496 ÷ 40 → ÷ 4 then ÷ 10 → 124 → 12·4
16. 574 ÷ 70 → ÷ 7 then ÷ 10 → 82 → 8·2
17. 425 g
18. 1950 mL

Review: Unit 13 and Unit 14

1. $27
2. $12·25
3. $93·15
4. $31·32
5. $580·80
6. $17·28
7. 60
8. 30 to 75
9. 46–55
10. 5 × 5 + 2, 5 × 4 + 7
11. 6 × 6 − 2, 6 × 7 − 8
12. 56 ÷ 7 + 7, 56 ÷ 8 + 8
13. 56 ÷ 7 + 5, 56 ÷ 8 + 6
14. $52·90
15. $159
16. 11

Review: Unit 15 and Unit 16

1. 1·65, 1·9, 2·15, 2·4, 2·65, 2·9
 The rule is + 0·25
2. $\frac{7}{16}$, $\frac{9}{16}$, $\frac{11}{16}$, $\frac{13}{16}$, $\frac{15}{16}$, $1\frac{1}{16}$
 The rule is + $\frac{2}{16}$
3. $1\frac{1}{4}$, $1\frac{1}{2}$
4. 15, 14·7
5. $\frac{9}{12} - \frac{6}{12} = \frac{3}{12} = \frac{1}{4}$
6. $\frac{7}{12} - \frac{2}{12} = \frac{5}{12}$
7. 8 m
8. 32 m²
9. 64, 1, 16, 121
10. 7, 11, 2

11–14. (thermometer diagrams)

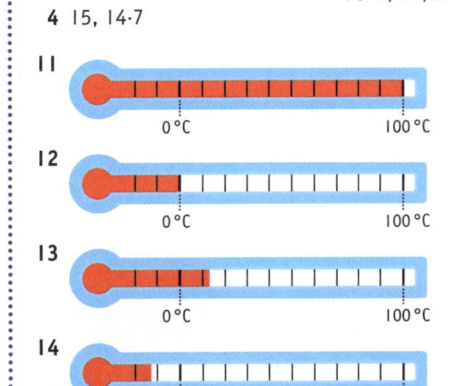

15. 25 %
16. 12·5 %
17. 5 %
18. 1 %

TERM 3

UNIT 17 NUMBER & ALGEBRA

Integer Addition and Subtraction

Products	Insect Spray Out	Insect Spray In	Rose Spray Out	Rose Spray In	Ant Dust Out	Ant Dust In	Slug Bait Out	Slug Bait In	Snail Pellets Out	Snail Pellets In
In Stock		100		100		100		100		100
Mon.	15	85	26	74	39	61	6	94	24	76
Tue.	46	39	16	58	18	43	15	79	12	64
Wed.	35	4	18	40	24	19	22	57	28	36
Thu.	49	−45	17	23	13	6	26	31	37	−1
Fri.	12	−57	24	−1	21	−15	14	17	25	−26
Reorder Quantity	157		101		115		83		126	

Quick Check

1. 2
2. −6
3. 3
4. −15
5. −9
6. −12
7. −48
8. 4
9. −86
10. −17

Solving Equations with Square Numbers

1. 4² + 6 = 22 or 4 × 4 + 6 = 22
2. 3² + 4 = 13 or 3 × 3 + 4 = 13
3. 7² + 4 = 53 or 7 × 7 + 4 = 53
4. 8² − 3 = 61 or 8 × 8 − 3 = 61
5. 5² + 11 = 36 or 5 × 5 + 11 = 6 × 6

UNIT 17 STATISTICS & PROBABILITY

Pizza Toppings

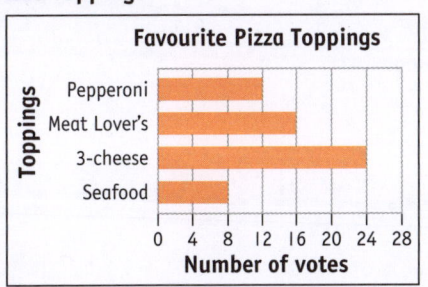

Favourite Pizza Toppings (bar graph: Pepperoni, Meat Lover's, 3-cheese, Seafood vs Number of votes 0–28)

4. 16
5. 16

UNIT 17 MEASUREMENT & SPACE

Time

1. 06:20 to 19:40 is 13 h 20 min
2. 18:55 to 07:30 is 12 h 35 min
3. 04:35 to 16:15 is 11 h 40 min
4. 22:20 to 01:15 is 2 h 55 min
5. 13:45
6. 16:25
7. 22:00
8. 09:45
9. 15:45

UNIT 17 NAPLAN*-STYLE QUESTIONS

1. 16
2. $55
3. 2 h 45 min

UNIT 17 PROBLEM OF THE WEEK

The Gardener's Daily Schedule

Challenge 1

Activity List	
Activity	**Duration**
Break 1	15
Break 2	45
Lawn 1	90
Lawn 2	30
Weed 1	30
Weed 2	30
Tree-lop	45
Seedlings	60
Tidy up	15

Challenge 2
Open-ended, but possibly similar to:

Gardener's Timetable			
Activity	**Duration**	**Start**	**Finish**
Weed 1	30	9:00	9:30
Lawn 2	30	9:30	10:00
Break 1	15	10:00	10:15
Seedlings	60	10:15	11:15
Lawn 1	90	11:15	12:45
Break 2	45	12:45	1:30
Weed 2	30	1:30	2:00
Tree-Lop	45	2:00	2:45
Tidy Up	15	2:45	3:00

UNIT 18 NUMBER & ALGEBRA

Fractions

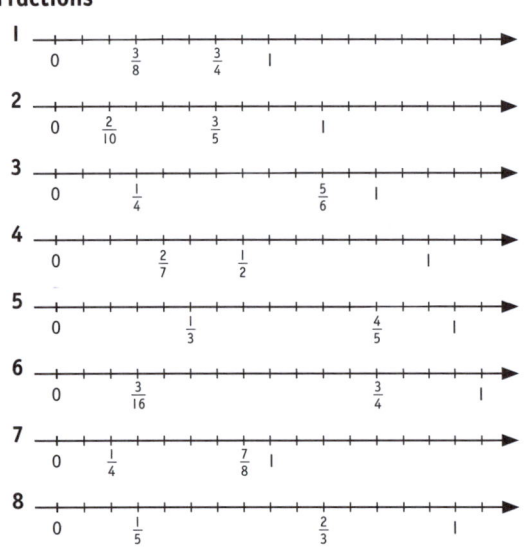

1. number line with $\frac{3}{8}$, $\frac{3}{4}$
2. number line with $\frac{2}{10}$, $\frac{3}{5}$
3. number line with $\frac{1}{4}$, $\frac{5}{6}$
4. number line with $\frac{2}{7}$, $\frac{1}{2}$
5. number line with $\frac{1}{3}$, $\frac{4}{5}$
6. number line with $\frac{3}{16}$, $\frac{3}{4}$
7. number line with $\frac{1}{4}$, $\frac{7}{8}$
8. number line with $\frac{1}{5}$, $\frac{2}{3}$

Quick Check

1. 40
2. 30
3. 9
4. 24
5. 30
6. 12
7. 35
8. 24
9. 36
10. 24

Decimal Additions

1. 13·05 + 6·45 + 4·3 = 23·80
2. 6·83 + 12·06 + 3·756 = 22·646
3. 14·36 + 127·65 + 1·06 = 143·07
4. 37·6 + 12·08 + 31·76 = 81·44
5. 33·39 + 12·65 + 126·12 = 172·16
6. 13·455 + 7·51 + 4·035 = 25·000

UNIT 18 STATISTICS & PROBABILITY

The Family Journey

1. 10:15 am
2. 3:00 pm
3. 40 km
4. 120 km
5. 0–40 km and 200–240 km
6. Open-ended, but expect 'driving in a city'.

UNIT 18 MEASUREMENT & SPACE

The Water Bucket Relay

Team 1 carried 28·5 L of water.
Team 2 carried 28·57 L of water.
Team 3 carried 20 L of water.
Team 2 won the relay by 70 mL.

UNIT 18 NAPLAN*-STYLE QUESTIONS

1. $\frac{1}{3}$
2. $23·70
3. 1·7 L

UNIT 18 PROBLEM OF THE WEEK

Decimal Target

	Alex	Hai	Liam	Min
Start	1·00	1·00	1·00	1·00
Throw 1	−0·22	−0·62	−0·53	−0·31
Throw 2	−0·43	−0·45	−0·26	−0·42
Throw 3	−0·4	−0·13	0·10	−0·55
Throw 4	0·1	0·20	−0·30	0·3
Finish	0·05	0·00	0·01	0·02

Hai won the game.

UNIT 19 NUMBER & ALGEBRA

Addition of Mixed Fractions

1. $2\frac{3}{4} + 1\frac{3}{8} = 3 + \frac{6}{8} + \frac{3}{8} = 3 + 1\frac{1}{8} = 4\frac{1}{8}$
2. $1\frac{5}{6} + 2\frac{5}{12} = 3 + \frac{10}{12} + \frac{5}{12} = 3 + \frac{15}{12} = 4\frac{3}{12} = 4\frac{1}{4}$
3. $2\frac{2}{3} + 1\frac{5}{6} = 3 + \frac{4}{6} + \frac{5}{6} = 4\frac{3}{6} = 4\frac{1}{2}$
4. $4\frac{1}{2} + 3\frac{1}{3} = 7 + \frac{3}{6} + \frac{2}{6} = 7\frac{5}{6}$
5. $3\frac{3}{12} + 1\frac{1}{3} = 4 + \frac{3}{12} + \frac{4}{12} = 4\frac{7}{12}$
6. $1\frac{5}{8} + 2\frac{3}{24} = 3 + \frac{15}{24} + \frac{3}{24} = 3\frac{18}{24} = 3\frac{3}{4}$
7. $3\frac{1}{6} + 2\frac{1}{5} = 5 + \frac{5}{30} + \frac{6}{30} = 5\frac{11}{30}$
8. $5\frac{5}{12} + 2\frac{1}{9} = 7 + \frac{15}{36} + \frac{4}{36} = 7\frac{19}{36}$

Quick Check

1. $1\frac{3}{4}$
2. $4\frac{1}{3}$
3. $5\frac{7}{10}$
4. $2\frac{7}{10}$
5. $5\frac{5}{8}$
6. $4\frac{5}{18}$
7. $3\frac{1}{4}$
8. $5\frac{1}{30}$
9. $3\frac{5}{24}$
10. $3\frac{11}{14}$

Subtraction of Mixed Fractions

1. $2\frac{1}{2} - 1\frac{1}{4} = \frac{10}{4} - \frac{5}{4} = \frac{5}{4} = 1\frac{1}{4}$
2. $2\frac{3}{5} - 1\frac{7}{10} = \frac{26}{10} - \frac{17}{10} = \frac{9}{10}$
3. $4\frac{3}{4} - 2\frac{1}{2} = \frac{19}{4} - \frac{10}{4} = \frac{9}{4} = 2\frac{1}{4}$
4. $3\frac{3}{10} - 2\frac{3}{5} = \frac{33}{10} - \frac{26}{10} = \frac{7}{10}$
5. $2\frac{4}{5} - 1\frac{1}{2} = \frac{28}{10} - \frac{15}{10} = \frac{13}{10} = 1\frac{3}{10}$

UNIT 19 STATISTICS & PROBABILITY

Measuring Chance Events

1. 50% even chance
2. 100% certain
3. 0% impossible (depending on location)
4. Open-ended
5. Open-ended

UNIT 19 MEASUREMENT & SPACE
Tessellations with a Shape

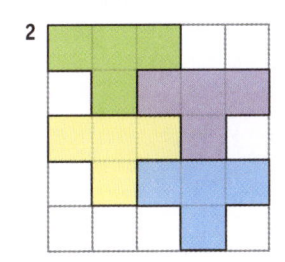

UNIT 19 NAPLAN*-STYLE QUESTIONS
1 $1\frac{7}{8}$ 2 40%   3

UNIT 19 PROBLEM OF THE WEEK
A Chance Experiment
Predict
The chance of taking out a 3 is 10%.
In the second experiment, it is the same chance, 10%.

The Experiment
The rest of the challenge is open-ended.

UNIT 20 NUMBER & ALGEBRA
Multiplication by a Decimal
1 8 × 0·5 =   8 × 5 ÷ 10 = 40 ÷ 10   = 4
2 10 × 0·4 =   10 × 4 ÷ 10 = 40 ÷ 10   = 4
3 9 × 0·3 =   9 × 3 ÷ 10 = 27 ÷ 10   = 2·7
4 15 × 0·2 =   15 × 2 ÷ 10 = 30 ÷ 10   = 3
5 27 × 0·3 =   27 × 3 ÷ 10 = 81 ÷ 10   = 8·1
6 165 × 0·2 = 165 × 2 ÷ 10 = 330 ÷ 10 = 33
7 122 × 0·6 = 122 × 6 ÷ 10 = 732 ÷ 10 = 73·2
8 125 × 0·8 = 125 × 8 ÷ 10 = 1000 ÷ 10 = 100

Quick Check
1 2·6   3 2   5 4·2   7 5·6   9 3·9
2 4·2   4 8·4   6 7·2   8 10   10 7·6

Percentage Problems
1 1·4 L   4 72
2 32 wrong answers   5 $507·50
3 $2·09   6 3 L

UNIT 20 STATISTICS & PROBABILITY
Stadium Statistics
1 14 000 spectators.
2 4200 away-team supporters.
3 1680 were under 16 away-team supporters.
4 2940 were under 16 home-team supporters.
5 4340 more home-team supporters.
6 1260 more home-team supporters.

UNIT 20 MEASUREMENT & SPACE
Measurement Percentages
1 3 km = 3000 m, 10% of 3000 m = 300 m
2 8 m = 800 cm, 15% of 800 cm = 120 cm
3 4 L = 4000 mL, 70% of 4000 mL = 2800 mL
4 2 kg = 2000 g, 15% of 2000 g = 300 g
5 3 m = 300 cm, 11% of 300 cm = 33 cm
6 1 kg = 1000 g, 26% of 1000 g = 260 g
7 3 tonnes = 3000 kg, 21% of 3000 kg = 630 kg

UNIT 20 NAPLAN*-STYLE QUESTIONS
1 19·35
2 292·5 km
3 18 000 were not under cover.

UNIT 20 PROBLEM OF THE WEEK
Fraction and Percentage Clues
Elsa: Liam:
White 40   White 13
Red 2   Red 28
Purple 1   Purple 18
Blue 11   Blue 13
Yellow 6   Yellow 8

The Challenge
Open-ended

UNIT 21 NUMBER & ALGEBRA
Growing Patterns

1	1 1 + 3 1 + 3 + 3	1 + (Unit − 1) × 3	The 10th unit will use 28 counters.
2	2 2 + 2 2 + 2 + 2	Unit × 2	The 10th unit will use 20 counters.
3	3 3 + 3 3 + 3 + 3	Unit × 3	The 10th unit will use 30 counters.

Quick Check
1 19   3 34   5 37   7 27   9 87
2 23   4 27   6 40   8 89   10 232

Order of Operations Revisited
1 6 × 3 ÷ 2 + (3 + 9)   4 6 + (12 − 7) × 4 + 3
  = 18 ÷ 2 + 12   = 6 + 5 × 4 + 3
  = 9 + 12   = 6 + 20 + 3
  = 21   = 29
2 3 × 7 + (6 − 4) × 10   5 36 ÷ 9 + 48 ÷ 8
  = 21 + 2 × 10   = 4 + 6
  = 21 + 20   = 10
  = 41   6 31 × 4 − 24 ÷ 6 × 3
3 28 ÷ 4 + 27 ÷ 9   = 124 − 24 + 18
  = 7 + 3   = 118
  = 10

UNIT 21 STATISTICS & PROBABILITY
Sara's Socks
Sara needs to take out 4 socks. The last one must match one of the first 3 if those were all different.

UNIT 21 MEASUREMENT & SPACE
Transformations
1 Although this question is open-ended as to where on the grid the shapes are drawn, our example shows what is required when listing the coordinates.

Shape 1
(0, 8)
(0, 6)
(2, 6)
Shape 2
(0, 6)
(0, 3)
(2, 3)
(2, 5)
Shape 3
(0, 0)
(1, 2)
(2, 2)
(3, 0)

2 Open-ended
3 Open-ended

UNIT 21 NAPLAN*-STYLE QUESTIONS
1 46
2 4 × 6 + 5 × 8 = 64
3 21 counters

UNIT 21 PROBLEM OF THE WEEK
Figurate Numbers

1. 1, 3, 6, 10, 15, 21, 28, 36, 45, 55.
2. Square numbers
3. 1, 4, 9, 16, 25, 36, 49, 64, 81, 100.
4. They are made by adding odd numbers.
5. Hexagons
6. 1, 6, 15, 28, 45.
7. The hexagonal numbers all occur in the list of triangular numbers.

UNIT 22 NUMBER & ALGEBRA
Multiplying Decimals

1. 23·4 × 4 = 93·6
2. 23·5 × 4 = 93·6 + 0·1 × 4 = 94
3. 33·5 × 4 = 94 + 10 × 4 = 134
4. 33·6 × 4 = 134 + 0·1 × 4 = 134·4
5. 43·6 × 4 = 134·4 + 10 × 4 = 174·4
6. 38·4 × 6 = 230·4
7. 38·5 × 6 = 230·4 + 0·1 × 6 = 231
8. 28·5 × 6 = 231 − 10 × 6 = 171
9. 48·5 × 6 = 231 + 10 × 6 = 291
10. 48·7 × 6 = 291 + 0·2 × 6 = 292·2

Quick Check

1. 162·4, 163·1, 233·1
2. 153·2, 145·2, 225·2
3. 93·5, 94, 144
4. 109·2, 109·8, 139·8
5. 118·4, 118, 78

Multiplying Money Amounts

1. $125
2. $375
3. $175
4. $3860
5. $13 750

UNIT 22 STATISTICS & PROBABILITY
10 Counters in the Bag

1. 0%
2. 50%
3. 80%
4. 100%
5. 80%

UNIT 22 MEASUREMENT & SPACE
Hidden Areas

1. 36 cm²
2. 42 cm²
3. 24 cm²
4. 43 cm²
5. 33 cm²
6. 31 cm²

UNIT 22 NAPLAN*-STYLE QUESTIONS

1. $32·50
2. B
3. 25%

UNIT 22 PROBLEM OF THE WEEK
Investigating Borders

Note: To find the area it is sufficient to count the blocks, but for the perimeter, it is the outside edge of the new shape that must be measured rather than counting the number of blocks used to make the edge.

With three tiles as the centre, the possibilities are:

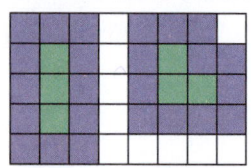

The areas are both 15 cm² and the perimeters are both 16 cm.
With four tiles as the centre, the possibilities are:

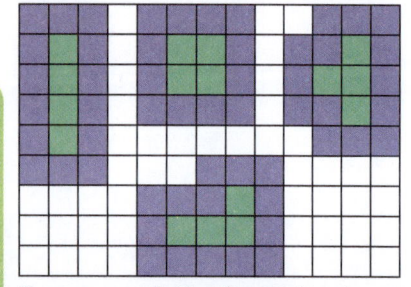

The areas are all 18 cm² apart from the square shape whose area is 16 cm².
The perimeters are all 18 cm apart from the square shape whose perimeter is 16 cm.

UNIT 23 NUMBER & ALGEBRA
Percentage Increases

1. 675 g
2. 51 g
3. 11 cookies
4. 36 capsules
5. 15 biscuits
6. 71·25 cm
7. 27

Quick Check

1. 58 g
2. $24
3. $37·50
4. 110 g
5. $52·50
6. 150 g
7. 450 g
8. $198
9. 200 g
10. $335·60

Special Number Towers
Puzzle 1

1. The square number chosen was 9.
2. The towers are 1 block, 3 blocks and 5 blocks high.
3. The square number chosen was 25.
4. The towers are 5 blocks, 9 blocks and 11 blocks high. (Other answers are possible.)

Puzzle 2 (Sample answers)

5. The prime number chosen was 11.
6. The towers are 1 block, 3 blocks and 7 blocks high.
7. The prime number chosen was 13.
8. The towers are 1 block, 5 blocks and 7 blocks high.

There are many more possible answers to Puzzle 2.

UNIT 23 STATISTICS & PROBABILITY
Making Comparisons

1. Year 6
2. Year 5
3. 6
4. 66
5. Floods
6. Term 3 is not in the rainy season.

UNIT 23 MEASUREMENT & SPACE
Angles in a Shape

1. Angle A = 60°
2. Angle B = 100°
3. Angle C = 90°
4. Angle D = 110°
5. Angle E = 145°
6. Angle F = 70°
7. Angle G = 100°

UNIT 23 NAPLAN*-STYLE QUESTIONS

1. 41, 2
2. 875
3. 125°

UNIT 23 PROBLEM OF THE WEEK
The Hexagon Puzzle

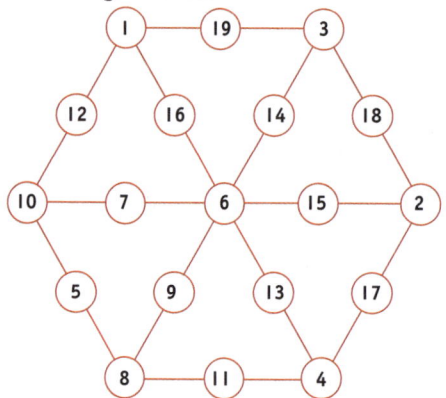

UNIT 24 NUMBER & ALGEBRA
Word Problems with Unknowns

1. $24 + $5·50 + ☐ = $37; ☐ = $7·50
2. 6 × $4·50 + 6 × ☐ = $54; ☐ = $4·50
3. 3 × $19·50 + ☐ = $84; ☐ = $25·50
4. 4 × ☐ + $56 = $200; ☐ = $36
5. 3 × $35 + ☐ + $80 = $200; ☐ = $15

Quick Check

1. $110
2. $74·34
3. $25·50
4. $15·20
5. $13·23
6. $21·50
7. $156·25
8. $38·50
9. $22·85
10. $32

158

TARGETING MATHS HOMEWORK: YEAR 6 © PASCAL PRESS ISBN: 9781925726596

Special Number Problems

1. 2, 3, 5, 7, 11, 13, 17, 19, 23, 29, 31
   1, 4, 9, 16, 25, 36, 49, 64, 81, 100
2. 9 and 6
3. 91 or 98
4. 21, 27
5. 21, 22, 24, 26, 27, 28
6. 18
7. 28
8. 2
9. 16 and 25
10. 11 and 25 or 2 and 16
11. 4, 9 and 16
12. 3, 11 and 19 or 3, 13 and 17 or 3, 7 and 23 or 5, 11 and 17

UNIT 24 STATISTICS & PROBABILITY

Making a Graph

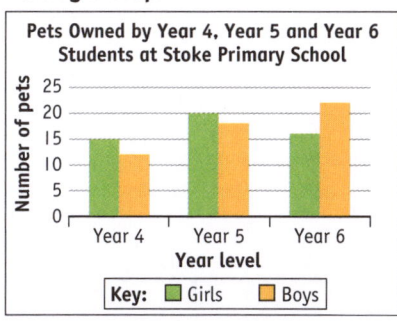

Pets Owned by Year 4, Year 5 and Year 6 Students at Stoke Primary School
(Bar graph showing Girls and Boys across Year 4, Year 5, Year 6)

UNIT 24 MEASUREMENT & SPACE

A Train Timetable

1. Train D
2. Train A
3. 30 minutes
4. 21 minutes
5. Train C
6. Train A
7. 2 minutes
8. 9 minutes
9. 2 minutes
10. Train A or B

UNIT 24 NAPLAN*-STYLE QUESTIONS

1. 48 × 10 × 10
2. $27·60
3. 11:29

UNIT 24 PROBLEM OF THE WEEK

Morning Tea Orders

The completed table with row totals is:

Qty	Choc-chip Muffins	Protein bars	Savoury scones	Mini-quiches	Carrot cakes	Total
1	$3·75	$4·25	$3·25	$5·75	$3·00	$20·00
2	$7·50	$8·50	$6·50	$11·50	$6·00	$40·00
3	$11·25	$12·75	$9·75	$17·25	$9·00	$60·00
4	$15·00	$17·00	$13·00	$23·00	$12·00	$80·00
5	$18·75	$21·25	$16·25	$28·75	$15·00	$100·00
6	$22·50	$25·50	$19·50	$34·50	$18·00	$120·00

One way to make up a $50 order would be to use the row that adds to $60 and then remove two items that add to $10. This would be a Protein bar and Mini-quiche.

A second choice might be to select from one row only to make the total cost = $50.

Item	Qty	Cost
Choc-muffin	3	$11·25
Protein bars	2	$8·50
Savoury scones	3	$9·75
Mini-quiches	2	$11·50
Carrot cakes	3	$9·00
Total cost:		$50·00

Items	Qty	Cost
Choc-muffin	4	$15·00
Mini-quiches	4	$23·00
Carrot cakes	4	$12·00
Total cost:		$50·00

The Challenge

Open-ended.
The row of 5 items would bring the total cost to $100 very easily.

TERM 3 REVIEW

Review: Unit 17 and Unit 18

1. 1
2. –19
3. 8
4. 7:15 – 13:15 = 6 h
5. 15:45 – 09:30 = 17 h 45 min
6. Number line from 0 to 1 with $\frac{7}{12}$ and $\frac{5}{6}$ marked
7. Number line from 0 to 1 with $\frac{4}{15}$ and $\frac{3}{5}$ marked
8. 1327·65
   3·7
   + 13·76
   1345·11
9. 10·7
   0·7
   + 3·765
   15·165
10. 12 litres
11. 4·5 litres

Review: Unit 19 and Unit 20

1. $3\frac{4}{8} + \frac{3}{8} = 3\frac{7}{8}$
2. $2\frac{5}{8} + \frac{6}{8} = 3\frac{3}{8}$
3. $2\frac{2}{12} + \frac{3}{12} = 2\frac{5}{12}$
4. $1\frac{6}{10} - \frac{3}{10} = 1\frac{3}{10}$
5. $1\frac{10}{16} - \frac{3}{16} = 1\frac{7}{16}$
6. $1\frac{20}{24} - \frac{3}{24} = 1\frac{17}{24}$
7. There are many possibilities and here are three: (grid diagram)
8. 6 × 0·5 = 6 × 5 ÷ 10 = 3
9. 7 × 0·3 = 7 × 3 ÷ 10 = 2·1
10. 16 × 0·6 = 16 × 6 ÷ 10 = 9·6
11. 4000
12. 13 000
13. 450 g
14. 5500 m
15. 260 mL
16. 210 cm

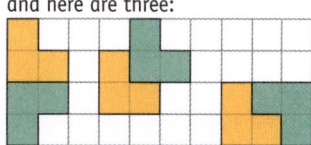

Review: Unit 20 and Unit 21

1. 1 + (10 – 1) × 4 = 37
2. 27 ÷ 3 + 6 + 4 × 5
   = 9 + 6 + 20
   = 35
3. 4 × 12 – 6 + 3 × 9
   = 48 – 6 + 27
   = 69
4. 64 ÷ 4 + 5 + 18 ÷ 3
   = 16 + 5 + 6
   = 27
5. 7 × 4 – 3 + 28 ÷ 4
   = 28 – 3 + 7
   = 32
6. 6 × 0·4 = 2·4
7. 13·5 × 10 = 135
8. 5 × 0·6 = 3
9. 27·6 × 20 = 552
10. $127·50
11. $85
12. $5250
13. Covered area = 22 cm², uncovered area = 38 cm²
14. Covered area = 36 cm², uncovered area = 24 cm²

Review: Unit 23 and Unit 24

1. 562·5 g
2. 1480 mL
3. The square number is 9 and the prime number is 17.
4. 140°
5. 40°
6. 130°
7. $25·50
8. 4
9. $15
10. $12·50
11. 2, 11, 23, but 2, 17, 17 is acceptable.
12. 8:21 am
13. 100 students
14. Year 6
15. 15 students

TERM 4

UNIT 25 NUMBER & ALGEBRA
Integers on a Number Line
1. number line from −6 to 4, marker at 0
2. number line from −7 to 1, marker at −3
3. number line from −1 to 9, marker at 3
4. number line from −3 to 6, marker at 2
5. number line from −50 to 100, markers at 0, 50

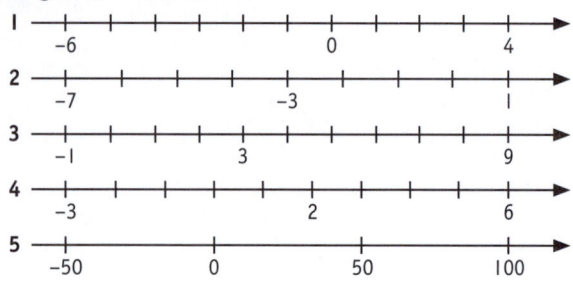

Quick Check
1. 0
2. −1
3. −1
4. 0
5. 13
6. 1
7. 3
8. −1
9. −1
10. −2

Investigating Decimal Addition
1. 2.4 + 4.2 = 6.6
2. 3.5 + 5.3 = 8.8
3. 6.3 + 3.6 = 9.9
4. 1.7 + 7.1 = 8.8
5. 5.6 + 6.5 = 12.1
6. The results are palindromes.
7. 12.4 + 41.2 + 24.1 = 77.7
8. 31.5 + 53.1 + 15.3 = 99.9
9. 24.3 + 32.4 + 43.2 = 99.9
10. 16.2 + 21.6 + 62.1 = 99.9
11. 51.6 + 65.1 + 16.5 = 133.2
12. The results are palindromes unless the three digits add to more than 9.

UNIT 25 STATISTICS & PROBABILITY
Muffin Sales
1. The missing amounts are all multiples of 3.
2. $18
3. 10 muffins
4. 22 muffins
5. It is a straight line.
6. The profit changes by the same amount each time – up by $3.

UNIT 25 MEASUREMENT & SPACE
Animal Mass
1. Black ant: 6 mg
2. Koala: 12 kg
3. Elephant: 4 t
4. Hummingbird: 20 g
5. Border collie: 18 kg

	The Creature	Eats per day	Eats in 10 days
6	Black ant	1·8 mg	18 mg
7	Koala	1·2 kg	12 kg
8	Elephant	66·7 kg	667 kg
9	Hummingbird	20 g	200 g
10	Border collie	900 g	9 kg

UNIT 25 NAPLAN*-STYLE QUESTIONS
1. −2
2. 6
3. 3·4 kg

UNIT 25 PROBLEM OF THE WEEK
Fun with Special Numbers
Challenge 1

	2	3	5	7	11	13	17	19	23	29
2	4	5	7	9	13	15	19	21	25	31
3		6	8	10	14	16	20	22	26	32
5			10	12	16	18	22	24	28	34
7				14	18	20	24	26	30	36
11					22	24	28	30	34	40
13						26	30	32	36	42
17							34	36	40	46
19								38	42	48
23									46	52
29										58

Two prime numbers add to make a square number 8 times.
Two prime numbers add to make a palindrome 3 times.

Challenge 2

	1	4	9	16	25	36	49	64	81
1	2	5	10	17	26	37	50	65	82
4		8	13	20	29	40	53	68	85
9			18	25	34	45	58	73	90
16				32	41	52	65	80	97
25					50	61	74	89	
36						72	85		
49							98		
64									
81									

Two square numbers add to make a prime number 12 times.
Two square numbers do not add to make a palindrome.

Challenge 3

	2	3	5	7	11	13	17	19	23	29
1	3	4	6	8	12	14	18	20	24	30
4	6	7	9	11	15	17	21	23	27	33
9	11	12	14	16	20	22	26	28	32	38
16	18	19	21	23	27	29	33	35	39	45
25	27	28	30	32	36	38	42	44	48	54
36	38	39	41	43	47	49	53	55	59	65
49	51	52	54	56	60	62	66	68	72	78
64	66	67	69	71	75	77	81	83	87	93
81	83	84	86	88	92	94	98	100	104	110

A square number can be made as the sum of a prime number and a square number 7 times.
A palindrome number can be made as the sum of a prime number and a square number 11 times.

UNIT 26 NUMBER & ALGEBRA
Fractions

Ingredients	3 muffins	9 muffins	12 muffins	15 muffins
Honey	$\frac{1}{8}$ cup	$\frac{3}{8}$ cup	$\frac{1}{2}$ cup	$\frac{5}{8}$ cup
Butter	$\frac{3}{16}$ cup	$\frac{9}{16}$ cup	$\frac{3}{4}$ cup	$\frac{15}{16}$ cup
Eggs	1	3	4	5
Apricot juice	$\frac{3}{8}$ tbs	$1\frac{1}{8}$ tbs	$1\frac{1}{2}$ tbs	$1\frac{7}{8}$ tbs
Mashed apricots	$\frac{1}{6}$ cup	$\frac{1}{2}$ cup	$\frac{2}{3}$ cup	$\frac{5}{6}$ cup
Sifted flour	1 cup	3 cups	4 cups	5 cups
Baking powder	$1\frac{1}{4}$ tsp	$3\frac{3}{4}$ tsp	5 tsp	$6\frac{1}{4}$ tsp

Quick Check

1 $\frac{1}{6}$ cup   5 $\frac{1}{8}$ kg   8 $\frac{2}{3}$ cup   12 $\frac{1}{2}$ kg
2 $\frac{5}{8}$ cup   6 $\frac{5}{12}$ cup   9 $2\frac{1}{2}$ cups   13 $\frac{2}{3}$ cup
3 $\frac{1}{3}$ cup   7 $\frac{1}{8}$ cup   10 $1\frac{1}{3}$ cups   14 $\frac{1}{2}$ cup
4 1 egg   11 4 eggs

Fractions on a Number Line

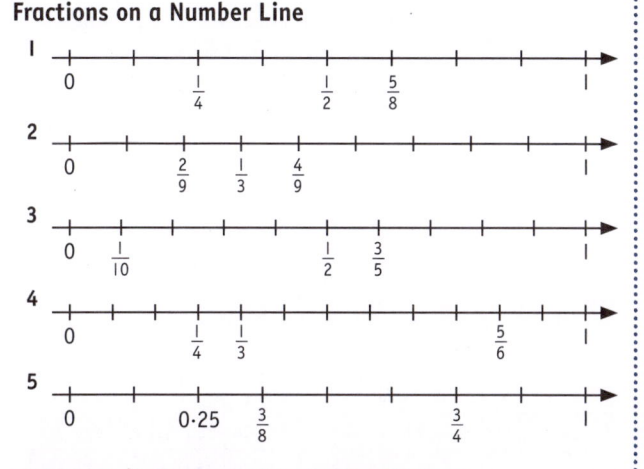

1 Number line from 0 to 1 with $\frac{1}{4}$, $\frac{1}{2}$, $\frac{5}{8}$
2 Number line from 0 to 1 with $\frac{2}{9}$, $\frac{1}{3}$, $\frac{4}{9}$
3 Number line from 0 to 1 with $\frac{1}{10}$, $\frac{1}{2}$, $\frac{3}{5}$
4 Number line from 0 to 1 with $\frac{1}{4}$, $\frac{1}{3}$, $\frac{5}{6}$
5 Number line from 0 to 1 with 0.25, $\frac{3}{8}$, $\frac{3}{4}$

UNIT 26 STATISTICS & PROBABILITY
The Bean Experiment

1 Day 7
2 2 cm
3 6 cm
4 Day 8 to Day 9
5 Open-ended, but about 12 cm given the answer to Q3.

UNIT 26 MEASUREMENT & SPACE
Congruent Faces

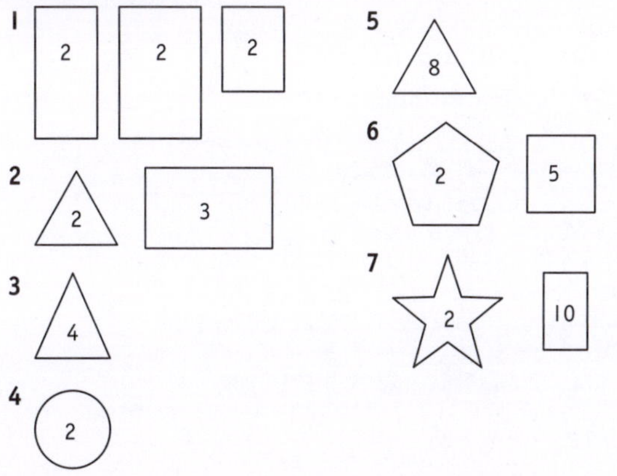

1 2, 2, 2
2 2, 3
3 4
4 2
5 8
6 2, 5
7 2, 10

UNIT 26 NAPLAN*-STYLE QUESTIONS

1 D   2 $\frac{3}{8}$ cup   3 First object

UNIT 26 PROBLEM OF THE WEEK
Fractions that Add to 1

Liam was $\frac{1}{28}$ away from 1.
Elsa made $\frac{1}{3} + \frac{2}{6} + \frac{3}{9} = \frac{3}{9} + \frac{3}{9} + \frac{3}{9} = 1$.
You made $\frac{1}{3} + \frac{1}{4} + \frac{2}{5} = \frac{20}{60} + \frac{15}{60} + \frac{24}{60} = \frac{59}{60}$ and were $\frac{1}{60}$ away from 1!
Elsa was the winner.

UNIT 27 NUMBER & ALGEBRA
Multiplying Decimals

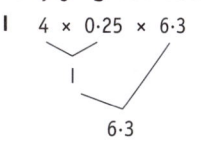

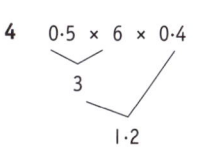

1 $4 \times 0.25 \times 6.3$ → 1 → 6.3
2 $0.2 \times 5 \times 8.3$ → 1 → 8.3
3 $50 \times 0.4 \times 15.3$ → 20 → 306
4 $0.5 \times 6 \times 0.4$ → 3 → 1.2
5 $50 \times 0.02 \times 6.8$ → 1 → 6.8

Quick Check

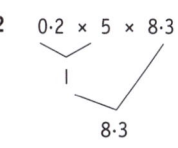

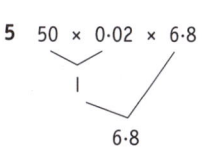

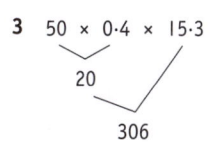

1 0.9   3 7.5   5 3.6   7 9.5   9 19.8
2 33   4 120   6 670   8 30   10 9.2

Decimal Multiplication Problems

1 22 cm   3 9.52 cm   5 1.8 m
2 1.78 m   4 34 m   6 $10

UNIT 27 STATISTICS & PROBABILITY
Making Comparisons

1 $170   3 Week 4   5 $410
2 $60   4 Week 5   6 $120

UNIT 27 MEASUREMENT & SPACE
Giving Directions and Using Coordinates

This is open-ended, but the paths should be something like:

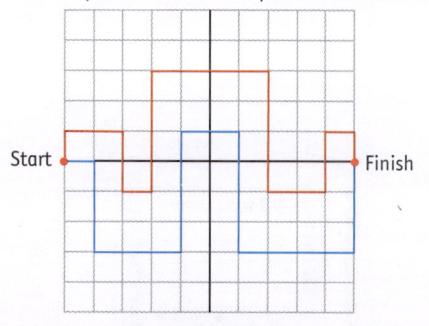

UNIT 27 NAPLAN*-STYLE QUESTIONS

1 376   3 Fourth diagram
2 $28

UNIT 27 PROBLEM OF THE WEEK
Dancing Robots

Open-ended

UNIT 28 NUMBER & ALGEBRA
Multiplying Decimals

2 $23 \times 3 + \frac{5}{10} \times 3 = 69 + 1.5 = 70.5$
3 $15 \times 4 + \frac{7}{10} \times 4 = 60 + 2.8 = 62.8$
4 $32 \times 3 + \frac{34}{100} \times 3 = 96 + 1.02 = 97.02$
5 $44 \times 2 + \frac{92}{100} \times 2 = 88 + 1.84 = 89.84$

6 $23 × 9 + \frac{7}{10} × 9 = 207 + 6·3 = 213·3$

7 $29 × 5 + \frac{64}{100} × 5 = 145 + 3·2 = 148·2$

Quick Check
1 2·1   3 3·2   5 4·2   7 1·46   9 0·54
2 4·8   4 0·09 6 0·18 8 2·2   10 25·9

Number Splitting for Division
1 256
   200 + 56
   ÷ 4
   50 + 14
   64
2 198
   180 + 18
   ÷ 3
   60 + 6
   66
3 378
   300 + 78
   ÷ 6
   50 + 13
   63
4 1239
   1200 + 39
   ÷ 3
   400 + 13
   413
5 1364
   1200 + 164
   ÷ 4
   300 + 41
   341
6 8127
   8100 + 27
   ÷ 9
   900 + 3
   903

UNIT 28 STATISTICS & PROBABILITY
New Sports Strip
1

Colours	Per cent	Number of students
Teal and white	20%	5
Royal blue and yellow	48%	12
Navy blue and red	32%	8

2 Open-ended

UNIT 28 MEASUREMENT & SPACE
Area and Decimals
1   2 × 2·4 = 4·8
    0·5 × 2·4 = 1·2
                6
2   2 × 5·5 = 11
    0·5 × 5·5 = 2·75
               13·75
3   4 × 4·5 = 18
    0·5 × 4·5 = 2·25
               20·25
4   3 × 3·5 = 10·5
    0·5 × 3·5 = 1·75
               12·25
5   2 × 3·6 = 7·2
    0·4 × 3·6 = 1·44
                8·64
6   2 × 4·3 = 8·6
    0·7 × 4·3 = 3·01
               11·61

UNIT 28 NAPLAN*-STYLE QUESTIONS
1 9·75 cm²   2 $2\frac{1}{2}$ 3 96%

UNIT 28 PROBLEM OF THE WEEK
Tiling the Patio
A coloured version of the patio will look like:

Grey tiles: 104
Terracotta tiles: 88
White tiles: 72

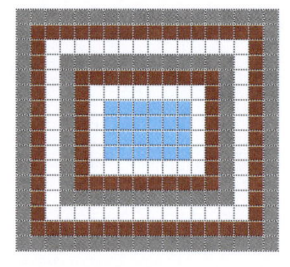

UNIT 29 NUMBER & ALGEBRA
Division and Fractions
1 1 remainder 2 = $1\frac{2}{8} = 1\frac{1}{4}$
2 2 remainder 2 = $2\frac{2}{5}$
3 3 remainder 3 = $3\frac{3}{4}$
4 5 remainder 2 = $5\frac{2}{3}$
5 5 remainder 1 = $5\frac{1}{4}$
6 6 remainder 3 = $6\frac{1}{2}$
7 6 remainder 5 = $6\frac{5}{7}$
8 6 remainder 4 = $6\frac{1}{2}$
9 3 remainder 2 = $3\frac{1}{4}$
10 25 remainder 2 = $25\frac{1}{2}$

Quick Check
1 $1\frac{1}{4}$ 3 $2\frac{1}{3}$ 5 $2\frac{5}{6}$ 7 5   9 $4\frac{3}{4}$
2 $1\frac{1}{5}$ 4 $1\frac{3}{5}$ 6 $5\frac{3}{4}$ 8 $2\frac{1}{4}$ 10 $9\frac{1}{3}$

Estimating with Percentages
1 16% of $85
   10% of $85 = $8·50
   5% of $85 = $4·25
   Discount Estimate = $12·75
2 24% of $90
   25% of $90 = $22·50
   Discount Estimate = $22·50
3 49% of $160
   50% of $160 = $80
   Discount Estimate = $80
4 18% of $180
   20% of $180 = $36
   Discount Estimate = $36
5 36% of $120
   25% of $120 = $30
   10% of $120 = $12
   Discount Estimate = $42
6 58% of $140
   50% of $140 = $70
   10% of $140 = $14
   Discount Estimate = $84

UNIT 29 STATISTICS & PROBABILITY
Printing the School Journal
1 10 pages
2 25 pages
3 25 + 20 = 45 seconds

UNIT 29 MEASUREMENT & SPACE
Metric Unit Conversions
1 156 millimetres = 15·6 centimetres = 0·156 metres
2 1556 metres = 1 kilometre and 556 metres or 1·556 kilometres
3 1456 grams = 1 kilogram and 456 grams or 1·456 kilograms
4 3365 millilitres = 3 litres and 365 millilitres or 3·365 litres
5 1·65 metres = 165 centimetres = 1650 millimetres
6 1·7 t = 1 t and 700 kg or 1700 kg
7 3372 m = 3 km and 372 m or 3·372 km
8 4450 mm = 445 cm = 4·45 m
9 7568 mL = 756·8 cL = 7·568 L
10 4·58 km = 4 km and 580 m or 4580 m

UNIT 29 NAPLAN*-STYLE QUESTIONS
1 2·25 m   2 $97·50   3 10 pages

UNIT 29 PROBLEM OF THE WEEK
Find My Number
Following the hint, the lists to work with are:

Clue 1	2	9	16	23	30	37	44	51	58	65	72	79	86	93
Clue 2	1	10	19	28	37	46	55	64	73	82	91	100	109	118
Clue 3	3	11	19	27	35	43	51	59	67	75	83	91	99	107
Clue 4	5	12	19	26	33	40	47	54	61	68	75	82	89	96
Clue 5	1	10	19	28	37	46	55	64	73	82	91	100	109	118
Clue 6	4	11	18	25	32	39	46	53	60	67	74	81	88	95

Clue 1: 23 is Alex's number.
Clue 2: 46 is Elsa's number.
Clue 3: 59 is Hai's number.
Clue 4: 75 is Tau's number.
Clue 5: 82 is Liam's number.
Clue 6: 95 is Ruby's number.

UNIT 30 NUMBER & ALGEBRA
Multistep Number Problems
1 $20 ÷ 8 = $2·50, $12 ÷ 8 = $1·50, $10 ÷ 8 = $1·25
   $2·50 + $1·50 + $1·25 = $5·25
2 $108 ÷ 4 = $27, $16·60 ÷ 4 = $4·15
   $27 + $4·15 = $31·15
3 $280 + $50 = $330
   $330 ÷ 6 = $55
4 $140 + $100 + $60 = $300, 25% of $300 = $75
   $300 − $75 = $225
5 6 × $24 = $144, $144 + $8·20 = $152·20,
   10% of $152·20 = $15·22, $152·20 + $15·22 = $167·42,
   $167·42 ÷ 4 = $41·86

Quick Check
1 $27   3 $12·50   5 $3·50   7 $30   9 $34
2 75c   4 $1·30   6 $14·25   8 $43·35 10 $32·76

162 TARGETING MATHS HOMEWORK: YEAR 6 © PASCAL PRESS ISBN: 9781925726596

Percentage Skill Builder

1. Estimate $9·70
   10% of $97 = $9·70
   1% of $97 = $0·97
   $9·70 + $0·97 = $10·67
2. Estimate $3·20
   20% of $16 = $3·20
   1% of $16 = $0·16
   $3·20 + $0·16 = $3·36
3. Estimate $6·25
   20% of $25 = $5
   4% of $25 = $1
   $5 + $1 = $6
4. Estimate $4·80
   10% of $48 = $4·80
   1% of $48 = $0·48
   $4·80 – $0·48 = $4·32
5. Estimate $80
   50% of $160 = $80
   1% of $160 = $1·60
   $80 + $1·60 = $81·60

UNIT 30 STATISTICS & PROBABILITY
Survey Results
- ■ pineapple chunk
- ■ cherry & hazelnut
- ■ choc chip & macadamia
- ■ banana & pistachio

UNIT 30 MEASUREMENT & SPACE
The Year 1 Timetable

1. Literacy: 8 h 45 min
2. Maths: 7 h 30 min
3. Science: 1 h 15 min
4. Art: 1 h 30 min
5. HASS: 1 h 30 min
6. Music: 45 min
7. Dance: 45 min
8. Health & PE: 2 h 15 min
9. Library: 45 min
10. 1 h

UNIT 30 NAPLAN*-STYLE QUESTIONS
1. 300 m
2. $24
3. 12:15 pm

UNIT 30 PROBLEM OF THE WEEK
The Busy Week
Open-ended

UNIT 31 NUMBER & ALGEBRA
Number Patterns

1. 0·375, 0·5, 0·625
   The rule is add 0·125.
2. 0·016, 0·02, 0·024
   The rule is add 0·004.
3. 0·017, 0·022, 0·027
   The rule is add 0·005.
4. 0·088, 0·099, 0·11
   The rule is add 0·011.
5. 1, 0·98, 0·96
   The rule is subtract 0·02.
6. 0·95, 0·8, 0·65
   The rule is subtract 1·5.
7. $\frac{1}{2}, \frac{2}{3}, \frac{5}{6}, 1$
   The rule is add $\frac{1}{6}$.
8. $\frac{3}{8}, \frac{1}{2}, \frac{5}{8}, \frac{3}{4}$
   The rule is add $\frac{1}{8}$.
9. $\frac{4}{5}, \frac{9}{10}, 1, 1\frac{1}{10}$
   The rule is add $\frac{1}{10}$.
10. $\frac{11}{12}, 1, 1\frac{1}{12}, 1\frac{1}{6}$
    The rule is add $\frac{1}{12}$.
11. $\frac{7}{12}, \frac{5}{12}, \frac{1}{4}, \frac{1}{12}$
    The rule is subtract $\frac{1}{6}$ (or $\frac{2}{12}$).
12. $2\frac{7}{8}, 2\frac{1}{2}, 2\frac{1}{8}$
    The rule is subtract $\frac{3}{8}$.

Quick Check

1. 0·011
2. 0·024
3. 0·975
4. 0·305
5. 0·4833
6. $\frac{1}{3}$
7. $\frac{3}{4}$
8. $\frac{11}{12}$
9. 2
10. $1\frac{1}{4}$

Estimation Strategies

	Amount	Estimate	Calculator Check
1	26% of $160	$40	$41·60
2	21% of $140	$28	$29·40
3	19 × 47	940	893
4	49 × 68	3400	3332
5	154 ÷ 7	20	22
6	192 ÷ 8	25	24

UNIT 31 STATISTICS & PROBABILITY
Percentage Chance

	Chance as a Percentage			
	Odd	Even	Prime	Square
Calculate: Remove 1 piece of paper	50%	50%	40%	10%
Calculate: Remove 1 piece of paper and replace it (10 times)	50%	50%	40%	10%

4. Because the results are subject to chance and are not certain.

UNIT 31 MEASUREMENT & SPACE
Angles

1. 120°, 60°
2. 80°, 100°
3. Any angle between 0° and 90° is correct. 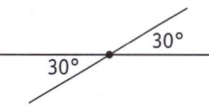
4. Any angle between 90° and 180° is correct. 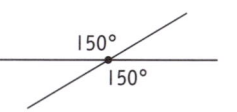
5. 150°, 150°; 60°, 60°, 60°, 180°; 30°, 30°
6. Any angles will do so long as the four angles add to 360°.

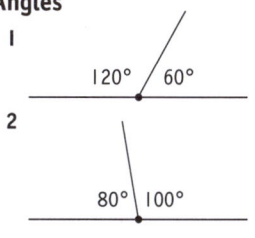

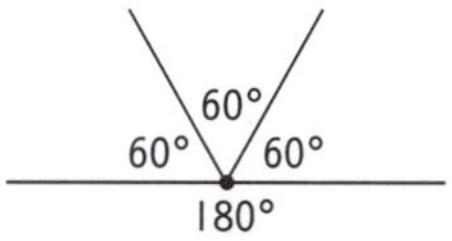

UNIT 31 NAPLAN*-STYLE QUESTIONS
1. $45
2. 20%
3. 90°

UNIT 31 PROBLEM OF THE WEEK
What Is my Number?

Challenge 1 Tau's clues are correct. 35 + 5 = 40 = 5 × 8
35 – 2 = 33 = 3 × 11

Challenge 2 Ruby's number is 41.

Challenge 3 Sara's number could be 61. It can be found by seeing that the lowest common multiple of 3, 4 and 5 is 60. If there is always a remainder of 1, then 61 has to be a possible solution. There are other possible solutions.

Challenge 4 Open-ended

UNIT 32 NUMBER & ALGEBRA
Function Machines

1. + 0·25
2. + 0·005
3. × 2
4. – 0·25
5. – 0·55
6. ÷ 3

Quick Check

1. Input 6·05, Output 8·9
2. Input 4·6, Output 8·1
3. Input 4·32, Output 6
4. Output 7·07, 8·99
5. Input 5, Output 4·35
6. Input 9·8, Output 3·65
7. Input 11·09, Output 7·95

Number Sentences

Alex: 15 + 6 + 3 × 4 – 2 = 31
Hai: 15 + 2 × 2 + 4 × 2 – 8 = 19
Liam: 15 – 3 – 4 + 5 × 3 = 23
Elsa: 15 + 6 – 5 + 3 × 4 = 28
Tau: 15 + 4 × 2 + 3 × 2 – 6 = 23

UNIT 32 STATISTICS & PROBABILITY
Reading Data

1. 6
2. Tuesday
3. 60
4. 6
5. Sara read $\frac{2}{5}$ of Tuesday's pages and Ruby read $\frac{3}{5}$ of Tuesday's pages.

UNIT 32 MEASUREMENT & SPACE
Area
1

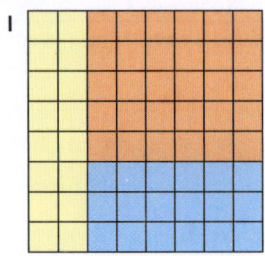

2 20 cm, 22 cm and 18 cm
3 18 cm², 16 cm², 30 cm²

UNIT 32 NAPLAN*-STYLE QUESTIONS
1 3 2 4·6 3 16 cm²

UNIT 32 PROBLEM OF THE WEEK
An Area Puzzle
First Challenge
1 15 cm² 2 5 cm 3 3 cm 4 12 cm²
Second Challenge
Open-ended

TERM 4 REVIEW

Review: Unit 25 and Unit 26
1 4 (between 0 and 6)
2 0 (between −3 and 5)
3 3
4 10½ minutes
5 49 g
6 ¼ cup
7 ⅙ cup
8 ¾ cup
9 ⅛ cup
10 1½ cups
11 2¾ cups
12 number line with 2/6, 1/2, 2/3
13 number line with 1/2, 5/8, 3/4
14 6 squares
15 2 crosses and 12 rectangles

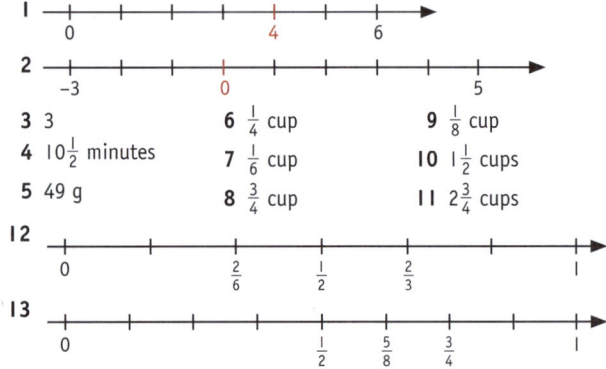

Review: Unit 27 and Unit 28
1 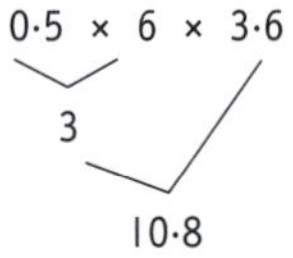 0·5 × 6 × 3·6 → 3, 10·8
2 0·2 × 6 × 3·5 → 1·2, 4·2 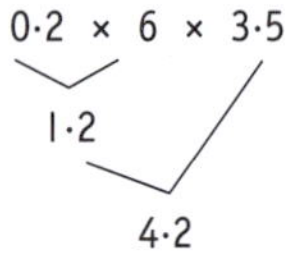
3 0·22 m
4 $300
5 $40
6 Week 2 and Week 5
7 3·2
8 0·21
9 4·2
10 0·45
11 287
280 + 7
÷ 7
40 + 1
41
12 1625
1500 + 125
÷ 5
300 + 25
325
13 8·75 cm²
14 11·25 cm²

Review: Unit 29 and 30
1 2⅖
2 2¼
3 2⅚
4 20% of $56 = $11·20
1% of $56 = $0·56
$11·20 + $0·56 = $11·76
5 25% of $78 = $19·50
1% of $78 = $0·78
$19·50 + $0·78 = $20·28
6 50% of $76 = $38
2% of $76 = $1·52
$38 + $1·52 = $39·52
7 70% of $48 = $33·60
3% of $48 = $1·44
$33·60 + $1·44 = $35·04
8 75 cm or 0·75 m
9 135·6 cL or 1·356 L
10 456·5 cm or 4·565 m
11 $21
12 $102
13 Blue cars: 12
14 Red cars: 6
15 Silver cars: 6
16 Yellow cars: 6
17 White cars: 18

Review: Unit 31 and Unit 32
1 0·13, 0·25, 0·37, 0·49, 0·61, 0·73.
The pattern rule is add 0·12.
2 0·96, 0·91, 0·86, 0·81, 0·76, 0·71.
The pattern rule is subtract 0·05.

	Amount	Estimate	Calculator Check
3	16% of $86	$13	$13·76
4	26% of $118	$29·50	$30·68

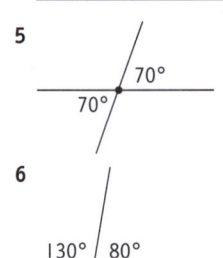

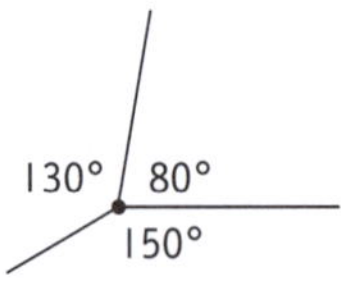

5 70°, 70°
6 130°, 80°, 150°
7 + 0·6
8 − 0·13
9 Elsa finished with 12 + 2 × 2 − 6 + 4 + 3 = 17 marbles.
10 Tau on Friday
Ruby on Sunday
11 Tau and Ruby both read 48 pages altogether.